Op  Geometry:
Geometry

Springer
New York
Berlin
Heidelberg
Barcelona
Hong Kong
London
Milan
Paris
Singapore
Tokyo

Open Geometry:
OpenGL® + Advanced Geometry

Georg Glaeser
Hellmuth Stachel

Springer

Georg Glaeser
University of Applied Arts, Vienna
Chair for Geometry
A-1010 Vienna
Austria

Hellmuth Stachel
Institute of Geometry
Vienna University of Technology
A-1040 Vienna
Austria

Library of Congress Cataloging-in-Publication Data
Glaeser, Georg.
    Open geometry : OpenGL + advanced geometry / Georg Glaeser,
Hellmuth Stachel.
        p.   cm.
    Includes bibliographical references and index.
    ISBN 0-387-98599-9 (pbk. : alk. paper)
    1. Computer graphics.   2. OpenGL.   3. Geometry—Data processing.
I. Stachel, Hellmuth.   II. Title.
T385.G576   1998
006.6'6—dc21   98-34428

Printed on acid-free paper.

Production managed by Steven Pisano; manufacturing supervised by Jeffrey Taub.
Typeset by Integre Technical Publishing Co., Inc., Albuquerque, NM.

9 8 7 6 5 4 3 2 1

Additional material to this book can be downloaded from http://extras.springer.com

ISBN 0-387-98599-9 Springer-Verlag New York Berlin Heidelberg   SPIN 10688020

Preface

This book is about graphics programming based on OPENGL. The programming language is C++. The programs will run under various operating systems, among them WINDOWS 9x, ALPHA-STATIONS (Digital workstations) and SILICON GRAPHICS workstations. Hardware is used if accessible. The book provides a graphics library. This library is based on OPENGL and expands the elementary routines. Thus, the reader is enabled to realize direct geometrical thinking without having to care much about implementation.

The enclosed modules provide the reader with solutions for:

- The most common intersection problems and measuring tasks of both planar and spatial geometry.

- The creation of arbitrary geometric objects, e.g., by means of different kinds of "sweeping."

- The creation of the most general solids by means of Boolean operations (intersection, union, and complements of solid polyhedra).

The book presents:

- A well documented, versatile, and robust geometry library. The reader can use it very easily and expand it in any way he/she likes.

- A programming course that provides a deeper insight into object-oriented thinking and programming. It contains an introduction to C++ (for beginners and intermediate programmers) that is influenced by the experience gained from thousands of programming hours (which may even be useful to experienced programmers).

- A profound introduction to special fields of geometry that also gives some relevant background information. For example, the theory of Boolean intersections of solid polyhedra is explained thoroughly, covering all relevant problems in detail. We also give an introduction into kinematics (the geometry of motion) and write about several special classes of surfaces like spiral surfaces or DUPIN-cyclides.

The authors emphasize the need for robust and efficient code. The results of programming are compatible with various advanced CAD systems such as 3D STUDIO MAX or AUTOCAD.

How to Read and Use this Book

This is not a book built up purely sequentially. This means that you do not have to read one chapter after the other in order to learn about OPEN GEOMETRY programming. If you are already a bit familiar with programming in a C++ environment, it is probably best to start with Chapter 2 to get into OPEN GEOMETRY as quickly as possible. Follow the instructions; create your first programs. Later on, you can still try to get a more profound knowledge about the rest. (And there is a lot to know about the beautiful and wide-ranging field of Geometry...)

The History of OPEN GEOMETRY

It was at the end of the 80s when the authors started with the idea of developing environments for geometrists in order to allow them to develop their ideas more efficiently. Working closely together, two different approaches were taken: Hellmuth Stachel concentrated on writing CAD systems.[1] Georg Glaeser developed a programming environment for Geometry programmers, first in Pascal (SUPERGRAPH, [7]), later on in C and C++ ([8]). Additionally, he wrote a book, *Fast Algorithms for 3D-Graphics in C* ([9]).

OPEN GEOMETRY is now a mixture of all the experiences made in these years. It includes the robust and thought-out algorithms of the CAD3D-system, combining it with the improved developed routines of SUPERGRAPH and the fast

---

[1]The first result was the CAD2D-system that was used in Austrian secondary schools, and later on the CAD3D-system (in cooperation with G. Glaeser and others), which won a prize for the best academic European educational software in the CAD sector.

algorithms in [9]. Therefore, in addition to all those thousands of hours of graphics programming, the powerful system OPENGL can be used as a perfect base for any graphics system.

It was not easy to combine all the different approaches. One of the main problems was the use of two—or actually three—different computer languages: Pascal, C, and C++. While C and C++ are compatible, there were a number of problems with Pascal. (The difficulties were twofold: First, C does not support nested functions—Stachel's code lives on nested functions. Second, the data types are incompatible.)

The other main problem was our goal to support as many systems as possible. The system in which OPEN GEOMETRY was created initially—and is still being extended—is WINDOWS NT. It is *the* system, in which OPEN GEOMETRY should run more or less without any major bugs.[2] WINDOWS 95 is also good, since it has the same user interface. The new WINDOWS 95 OPENGL drivers seem to be very robust, though hardware graphics acceleration and direct printing are not supported. The users of an ALPHA-STATION (Digital workstation) that fully supports WINDOWS NT will probably have the best unrestricted performance of OPEN GEOMETRY. In a UNIX environment system, OPEN GEOMETRY will run as well. At the present stage, however, we cannot provide a menu system.

The Future of OPEN GEOMETRY

Like almost any software, OPEN GEOMETRY is still in progress. We are now at a stage where a first release can be put on the market. But we will support our readers with innovations and extended libraries via the Internet. So please have a look at the Web page `http://www.hsak.ac.at/OpenGeometry/` every once in a while.

On the other hand, we would be glad to get responses and ideas from our readers. We are sure that people will contribute improvements and adaptations to other platforms that can then be made available via the Internet.

Acknowledgments

The completion of this book was not achieved by only two people: several people and institutions were involved to help get the work done.

We would like to thank:

- Michael Schrott from the Vienna University of Technology for his contribution of many nice demo programs and theory about mathematical surfaces.

---

[2]If any sophisticated software can ever be bug-free.

- Heinrich Pommer from the University of Technology, Vienna, for his suggenstions, ideas, and improvements.

- Helmut Klinger, who at 17 years of age is a promising programmer and contributed many hours of programming and good ideas.

- Thomas Grohser (M.A.R. Vienna) for his help in the early and the final stages.

- Jörg Peters (Department of Computer Science, Purdue University, West Lafayette) for his contributions in the test phase.

- Many of our students who contributed ideas and tested the system, among them Hannes Kaufmann.

- Veronika Sperl for her help with the English version.

- The Watcom Software Company in Waterloo, Ontario (Canada), especially to Kathy Kitsemetry. This company supported us with the Watcom C/C++11.0 compiler.

- Digital Equipment Austria, especially to Federica Hannel from the Marketing division. This company supported us temporarily with an ALPHA-STATION (Digital workstation).

- The creators of OPENGL: The OPENGL team at SILICON GRAPHICS has been led by Kurt Akeley, Bill Glazier, Kipp Hickman, Phil Karlton, Mark Segal, Kevin P. Smith, and Wei Yen.

- Dave Gillespie, who created the P2C-transpiler, thus enabling us to combine Pascal code and C code.[3]

Georg Glaeser
Hellmuth Stachel

---

[3] "P2C" © 1989, 1990, 1991 Free Software Foundation. To contact Dave Gillespie: daveg@synaptics.com

Contents

Graphics Programming

In this chapter, we discuss an apparently simple matter: you have a geometric concept and you want to work out a computer program to realize your ideas.

What is the best way to draw up a concept? How do you elaborate the ideas? What computer language is best? What has already been done so as not to reinvent the wheel?

1.1 Think Geometrically!

Example 1: The Incircle of a Triangle.

We start with a simple 2D program: we want to calculate the incircle of a triangle (Figure 1.1). The points below illustrate this:

1. Define the triangle ABC.

2. Draw the bisectrices through two points of the triangle (e.g., s_A and s_B through A and B).

3. Intersect the bisectrices in order to get the incenter: $s_A \cup s_B = I$.

4. Now determine at least one of the three points of tangency (T): intersect the normal to one side of the triangle (e.g., a) with this side.

5. The radius of the incircle is the distance of T from the incenter I.

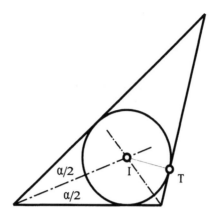

FIGURE 1.1. The incircle of a triangle (output of `BOOK/incircle.cpp`).

6. Draw a good diagram that shows both the result and the determination of the incenter.

Now have a look at the possible OPEN GEOMETRY code that fulfills the task. The methods of the classes *P2d*, *StrL2d*, *Circ2d*, etc., are explained in this book. The corresponding complete program on your disk is `BOOK/incircle.cpp`.

```
// We want to determine the incircle of a triangle

// First do the "pure geometry":
P2d A( −5, −5), B( 5, −5), C( 8, 7 ); // triangle ABC
StrL2d c( A, B ), b( C, A ), a( B, C ); // sides a, b, c
StrL2d sA( A, c.GetDir( ) − b.GetDir( ) ); // first bisectrix
StrL2d sB( B, a.GetDir( ) − c.GetDir( ) ); // second bisectrix
P2d InCenter = sA * sB; // intersection of the bisectrices
P2d T = a.NormalProjectionOfPoint( InCenter ); // point of tangency
Circ2d InCircle( Red, InCenter, InCenter.Distance( T ) ); // the incircle

// Now we show the result on the screen
sA.LineDotted( Red, 0, 10, 10, MEDIUM ); // show the bisectrices
sB.LineDotted( Red, 0, 6, 10, MEDIUM );
StraightLine2d( Black, A, B, THICK ); // outline the triangle
StraightLine2d( Black, B, C, THICK );
StraightLine2d( Black, C, A, THICK );
StraightLine2d( Gray, InCenter, T, THIN ); // show normal
InCircle.Draw( THICK ); // draw incircle
InCenter.Mark( Black, 0.2, 0.1 ); // mark center
T.Mark( Red, 0.2, 0.1 ); // mark point of tangency
InCenter.AttachString( Black, 0, −0.7, "I" ); // write names
```

```
T.AttachString( Black, 0.3, −0.5, "T" );
A.AttachString( Black, 2, 1.3, "$alpha$/2" ); // show half angles
A.AttachString( Black, 2.3, 0.3, "$alpha$/2" );
```

Example 2: The Common Normal of Two Straight Lines.

Next, we choose a 3D example: We want to determine the common normal of two straight lines that are not parallel. Geometrically, we do the following (Figure 1.2):

1. Define two nonparallel lines a and b.

2. Determine the direction $\vec{n}$ of the common normal. It is perpendicular to the direction vectors $\vec{a}$ and $\vec{b}$ of the given lines a and b: $\vec{n} = \vec{a} \times \vec{b}$.

3. Define a plane ψ that contains a and is parallel to $\vec{n}$ (normal vector $\vec{a} \times \vec{n}$).

4. Intersect ψ with b. The intersection point B is a point on the common normal n (n is given by B and $\vec{n}$).

5. Intersect n with a in order to get the corresponding foot $A \in a$ of the normal.

And here is, once again, a possible corresponding OPEN GEOMETRY C++ code (see also BOOK/common_normal.cpp):

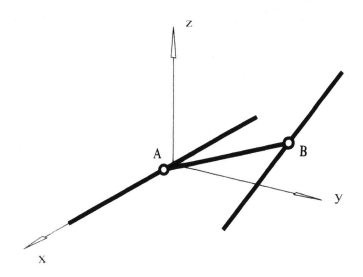

FIGURE 1.2. Common normal of two straight lines.

```
// common normal of two nonparallel straight lines a and b
StrL3d a( P3d( 0, 0, 0), V3d( 1, 0, 0 ) );
StrL3d b( P3d( 2, 4, 1), V3d( 3, 0, −1 ) );
V3d n;
P3d A, B;

// the geometrical solution

n = a.GetDir( ) ^ b.GetDir( ); // direction vector n⃗
Plane psi; // auxiliary plane
psi.Def( a.GetPoint( ), n ^ a.GetDir( ) );
B = psi * b; // foot on b
A = a.NormalProjectionOfPoint( B );

// By the way: Open Geometry offers the command CommonNormal( ),
// so that the above 5 command lines can be replaced by
a.CommonNormal( b, n, A, B );

// now show the result
ShowAxes( Gray, 6, 4, 3 );
a.Draw( Black, −5, 5, THICK );
b.Draw( Black, −5, 5, THICK );
Color col = PureRed;
StraightLine3d( col, A, B, THICK );
A.Mark( col, 0.2, 0.1 );
A.AttachString( col, −0.3, 0.3, "A" );
B.Mark( col, 0.2, 0.1 );
B.AttachString( col, 0.3, −0.3, "B" );
```

1.2 OpenGL

OpenGL means "Open Graphics Library." It is a software interface to graphics hardware. The library contains more than 100 distinct routines that allow production of interactive graphics (mainly 3D) applications.

The source code of the library is based on IRIS GL, developed for graphics workstations by SILICON GRAPHICS, INC. (SGI). In 1992, Microsoft and SGI decided to support this standard. It took four years to make the dream come true: OpenGL now runs bug-free on several platforms, among them WINDOWS 95, WINDOWS NT, ALPHA-STATIONS (Digital workstations) and, of course, on all SILICON GRAPHICS workstations.

The advantages of such a library are quite obvious:

- First, the commands cover a large part of the typically used graphics commands. This saves quite a lot of programming work; e.g., the simple OPENGL command *glEnable(GL_DEPTH_TEST)* allows the user to work with a very efficient hidden surface algorithm called "depth-buffering" or "z-buffering". From the moment you have called this routine, any further drawing is done considering depth values.

- With OPENGL, you can design graphics programs on any computer and display the graphics on any other computer. OPENGL is a hardware-independent interface, and therefore an excellent prerequisite for animated graphics via the Internet, e.g., VRML is based on OPENGL.

- More and more hardware manufacturers support OPENGL. Thus, 3D graphics can be done in real time, even on otherwise less powerful computers like PCs.

Of course, OPENGL also has some drawbacks:

- In order to achieve hardware-independency, OPENGL does not offer commands for performing windowing tasks or obtaining user input.

- OPENGL only supports the drawing of a small set of geometric primitives like points, lines, and polygons.

These drawbacks, however, are diminished—if not compensated for—by some OPENGL-related libraries that allow high-level drawing, among them the OPENGL Utility Library (GLU), the Auxiliary Library, and Open Inventor.

1.3 The Programming Language C++

Graphics programming can be done with many high-level computer languages. There are, however, several reasons why we chose C++:

- C++ is highly portable and efficient. Its predecessor, C, is a subset of C++.

- C++ compilers are available on any computer platform.

- OPENGL is written in C and C++, respectively. This makes it easy to include OPENGL code.

- C++ is very suitable for geometric thinking. It allows to overwrite operators; e.g., the union of two geometric primitives can be overwritten by the plus-sign. So, if p is a point and G is a straight line, and P is the plane that connects p and G, this can be written very clearly by $P = p + G$.

If you are an experienced C++ programmer, you may skip the following pages that are meant to give a very compressed overview about C++. If you are a C++ beginner, please refer additionally to books about C++.

1. Modules

   In general, the source code of a large program package is split up into several modules `file1.cpp`, `file2.cpp`, `file3.cpp`, etc. Normally, one of these files contains the main( )-function. This concept has been true for decades. But, when working in the WINDOWS environment, there is a difference:

   The function main( ) is hidden in the WINDOWS libraries. An ordinary WINDOWS application contains a function WinMain( ), which is now called by main( ) after some initializations. An MFC[1] application —such as OPEN GEOMETRY–does not have a clear starting point. It is driven by a single global instance of a class derived from the predefined base class CWinApp.[2]

   For the user of OPEN GEOMETRY, however, such sophisticated reflections are not necessary: OPEN GEOMETRY encourages to usually write a single module `TheUsersModule.cpp` that is then linked with other precompiled modules and libraries. To learn more about it, please look at Chapter 2, *Getting Started*. In any case, `TheUsersModule.cpp` does *not* contain the main( ) function!

2. Variables

   - Predefined Data Types

     In C (C++), there are only a few predefined data types.

     (a) Integer Variables

         - **int**

           Usually, the int variable is 4 bytes long. On some 16-bit plat-forms, however, it is considered to be a 2-byte variable. This type is guaranteed to be treated optimally by the compiler. Since its size is not standardized, it may be a tricky variable.

         - **short** (or **short int**)

           This type is 2 bytes long. It covers the values $[-65536, 65535]$ ($[-2^{15}, +2^{15} - 1]$). On 32-bit systems (and of course on 64-bit systems), this type may be processed a bit slower than a variable of type **int**. So, when it comes to a time-critical code and memory is not critical, use **int** or **long**, or—if you are working with OPENGL—*GLint*[3].

---

[1]Microsoft Foundation Classes.
[2]The function WinMain( ) is then called by one of the member functions of CWinApp.
[3]In this book, OPENGL keywords are written in *slanted letters*, OPEN GEOMETRY keywords are written in *italic letters*, and C keywords are written in **bold letters**.

GLint is usually identical to **long**—but, again, do not rely on that!

– **long** (or **long int**)

4-byte integer variable.

All the above mentioned types can be equipped with the keyword **unsigned**. If an integer variable has n bits, the unsigned variable then has the range $[0, 2^n - 1]$.

(b) Character Variables

In C (C++), character variables are nothing else but 1-byte integer variables (ranging from -128 to $+127$).

(c) Boolean Variables

Astonishingly, C (C++) does not provide a predefined Boolean type. Thus, the type has to be emulated by any kind of integer variable (and, indeed, we have seen lots of implementations). This can make the use of the type tricky and lead to hard-to-find errors!

In OPENGL, a type named *GLboolean* is provided (on PCs, it is indicated by **unsigned char**). In OPEN GEOMETRY, a *Boolean* variable is also **unsigned char**. It is not a good idea, however, to cut out the OPEN GEOMETRY Boolean definition. Some day *GLboolean* may be exchanged for a new platform.

(d) Floating-point Variables

– **float**

Four-byte floating-point variable, which is probably accurate enough for most graphics applications. On some machines (e.g., SGI-workstations), the math-processor accelerates **float** operations considerably [9].[4] On others, the **double** operations are favored (see also OPENGL-types).

OPENGL defines its own **float** type named *GLfloat*.

– **double**

Eight-byte floating-point variable, which is accurate enough for almost anything. Again, OPENGL defines its own **double** type named *GLdouble*. OPEN GEOMETRY consequently uses the type *Real*, which is currently identified with *GLdouble*. Nevertheless, this may be changed in the future. So please stick to *Real* if you program with OPEN GEOMETRY.

---

[4]The accuracy of **float** operations is not, however, the same as on other machines. This caused hard-to-find errors when developing our software.

– **long double**

Ten-byte floating-point variable for special purposes that are not of interest in our context.

- Predefined OPENGL Types

We have already mentioned several times that OPENGL defines its own types, essentially starting with capitalized *GL*, followed by the intended type. On PCs, there are the following conventions:

> **typedef unsigned int** *GLenum*;
> **typedef unsigned char** *GLboolean*;
> **typedef unsigned int** *GLbitfield*;
> **typedef signed char** *GLbyte*;
> **typedef short** *GLshort*;
> **typedef int** *GLint*;
> **typedef int** *GLsizei*;
> **typedef unsigned char** *GLubyte*;
> **typedef unsigned short** *GLushort*;
> **typedef unsigned int** *GLuint*;
> **typedef float** *GLfloat*;
> **typedef float** *GLclampf*;
> **typedef double** *GLdouble*;
> **typedef double** *GLclampd*;
> **typedef void** *GLvoid*;

- Self-Defined Types

The programming language C (and, of course, also C++) allows you to define new types by means of the syntax

typedef <predefined type> <new type> [< possibly dimensions >];

Here are three typical examples for type definitions:

> **typedef** *GLdouble Real*;
> **typedef** *Real Vector* [3]; // Index 0, 1, 2
> **typedef** *GLdouble Matrix* [3][3]; // Index [0][0] to [2][2]

Structures can be defined (in an old-fashioned way) as follows:

> **typedef struct**
> {
>   **double** x, y; // Or any other structure members.
>   // etc.
> } name_of_struct;

Here is an example for the declaration and initialization of a structure:

```
typedef struct
{
    double x, y;
} vector;
vector v = { 1.5, 2.5 };
```

3. Global Variables

The modules of a C++ program will usually share several global variables. In general, we tried to avoid global variables whenever possible. They make large programs hard to maintain and create the potential for conflicts between modules. On the other hand, such variables may speed up the code.

Global variables are declared in one of the modules, e.g., by

```
double Global_x, Global_y;
```

When you need the variables in another module, you write, e.g.,

```
extern double Global_x, Global_y;
Global_x = Global_y = 0;
```

The concept of OPEN GEOMETRY was to have one global class in common that contains all the information about global stuff. This class is constructed when an OPEN GEOMETRY application is started, and deleted when the application is finished. Therefore, several applications of OPEN GEOMETRY can run independently at the same time. (You can also run the same application parallel several times.)

4. Loops

C provides three kinds of looping or iteration.

- The **while** Statement

  is the simplest iteration. The syntax

  ```
  while ( logical expression )
  {
      // do something
  }
  ```

  probably does not need any further explanation. The same is true for

- The **do while** Statement

  which has the syntax

  ```
  do
  {
      // do something
  } while ( logical expression );
  ```

- The **for** Statement

  which is the most versatile tool, and it can replace the before-mentioned loops. A **for** loop has the syntax

  ```
  for (expression1; expression2; expression3 )
  {
      // one or more commands
  }
  ```

  The statement operates as follows. First, the initializing part *expression1* is evaluated (usually one or more variables are initialized). Then the conditional part *expression2* is evaluated. If *expression2* is false, the loop quits. Or else the commands in the loop are executed and *expression3* is evaluated; then *expression2* is tested again.

  Typical **for** statements are

  ```
  int i;
  for ( i = i_min; i <= i_max; i++ )
  {
      // do something
  }
  ```

or

  ```
  for ( float x = −2.0; x < 2.0; x += 0.25 )
  {
      // do something
  }
  ```

  A variable that is used only inside the loop can be declared and initialized in *expression1*. Such a declaration, however, is still valid outside the loop. Thus,

  ```
  for ( int i = i_min; i <= i_max; i++ )
  {
      // do something
  }
  for ( int i = i_min; i <= i_max; i++ ) // compiler error
  {
      // do something else
  }
  ```

  will produce a redefinition error.

  Due to the flexibility of the **for** statement, a tricky code like the following is possible:

  ```
  int i, j = 0;
  for ( i = 0; k < 100; j++ )
      // do something
  ```

  In this case, we have an infinite loop, probably due to a typing error.

  Another hard-to-find error is produced by the following code:

```
for ( i = 0; i < 100; i++ )
    // do something
    // do something else
```

The braces are missing. Therefore, it is better to put too many braces rather than too few. The compiler removes unnecessary braces anyway.

Any of the three kinds of iteration can be interrupted by a **break** statement. Also, by means of the **continue** statement, the residual statements of the loop can be jumped over.

This can sometimes make code easier to read, and also speed it up. On the other hand, programmers usually do not use these statements very often, since they can produce hard-to-find errors.

5. Functions

A function call (invocation) passes program control to the specified function. Being an expression, it can appear wherever an expression appears. Functions return values, unless they are declared as returning **void**.

- Prototyping

  In ANSI-C and in C++, functions must be declared before their first call.

  The syntax of a declaration is

  ```
  <type> name ( [<type> param1 [, <type> param2, ...] ] );
  ```

  The declaration can be implicit by including the code of the function:

  ```
  <type> name ( [<type> param1 [, <type> param2, ...] ] )
  {
      // Implementation of the function
  }
  ```

- Call by Value

  A parameter can be passed "by value" or "by reference." An example for a call by value is the following:

  ```
  typedef struct
  {
      Real x, y;
  } vector;
  double length( vector v )
  {
      return sqrt( v.x * v.x + v.y * v.y );
  }
  ```

$\vdots$

```
const vector v = { 5, 12 };
double len = length( v );
```

The parameter v is not changed. Even if it was changed in the function, the change would have no effect outside the function. To make obvious that the parameter will not be changed in the function, one should use the keyword **const**:

```
double length( const vector v )
{
    return sqrt( v.x * v.x + v.y * v.y );
}
```

Standard C passes arguments only by values. The contents of v are copied to the stack. This slows down the program a little bit. In fact, copying two **double** variables to the stack takes more time than a multiplication of two such variables ([9])!

A possible solution for speeding up the procedure is to pass a pointer to the structure:

```
double length( vector *v )
{
    return sqrt( v->x * v->x + v->y * v->y );
}
```

The call of the function now looks like this:

```
vector v = { 5, 12 };
double len = length( &v );
```

Note that the variable v must not be constant any more: it is not allowed to pass the address of a constant variable.

Luckily, C++ offers the following:

- Call by Reference

  Probably the best solution for the above-mentioned problem of passing structures is the following:

  ```
  double length( const vector &v )
  {
      return sqrt( v.x * v.x + v.y * v.y );
  }
  ```

Now we can pass constant variables as well without any loss of speed:

```
const vector v = { 5, 12 };
double len = length( v );
```

Calls by reference are not only performed faster, they also make code more legible and easier to write. As an example, we compare a C function and a C++ function that fulfill the task of multiplying the only parameter by two:

Solution 1 (call by value):

The function

```
void double_argument( int *argument )
{
    *argument *= 2;
}
```

has a hard-to-read implementation and an old-fashioned way of calling:

```
int x = 3;
double_argument( &x );
```

Solution 2 (call by reference):

The C++ implementation of the function has a readable code

```
void double_argument( int &argument )
{
    argument *= 2;
}
```

and a nontricky way of calling:

```
int x = 3;
double_argument( x );
```

There is only one blemish left. You might forget the & sign in the implementation of the function:

```
void double_argument( int argument )
{
    argument *= 2;
}
```

Now you have a call by value. The change of the argument remains undone outside the function. The compiler—at least the ones we tested out—does not give you a warning about that! The call

```
int x = 3;
double_argument( x );
```

is now useless: The value of x is still 3 after the function call.

- Inline Functions

  Function calls take up some time. When a variable is put on the stack, this means that it has to be copied to the stack. Putting a **double** variable on the stack takes more time than a multiplication of two such variables!

  C programmers usually use macros to avoid such a loss of time. Macros can be very efficient, but they also have disadvantages: they can be tricky and create hard-to-find errors. Also, debugging macros is much harder than debugging ordinary code.

  As an alternative, C++ offers the so-called **inline** functions. They allow you to speed up codes without the use of macros.

  Basically, **inline** functions do more or less the same as what a macro does. However, they work just like ordinary functions; but no time is lost for the function calls and the passing of the parameters.

  The code has to be available when the program is compiled. Thus, it has to be implemented into the source code before the first call of the function (or it has to be written into a header file that has to be included).

  Two drawbacks of **inline** functions have to be kept in mind:

  1. The executable file will be longer when **inline** functions are called upon frequently. Thus, it does not make sense to write **inline** functions with a code longer than only a few statements. (The acceleration is negligable.) When you write time-critical code, look out for segments that are visited frequently. It is mainly in these segments that **inline** functions make sense.

  2. There is no guarantee that the compiler really implements the functions inline. The keyword **inline** is seen as a "suggestion." Most compilers will give a warning, however, when a function could not be implemented inline.

     In particular, many compilers will not implement loops as **inline** functions.

  Summing up, we see that short functions without loops are suitable candidates for **inline** functions. Also, in some cases it might still be preferable to use a macro instead of an **inline** function.[5]

---

[5]In [9], examples are given where macros are executed considerably faster than **inline** functions ("Macromania").

The syntax is very clear: just write the keyword[6] **inline** in front of the function header.

- Macros

Macros are important preprocessor directives. For instance, you can define π by a macro

#define PI 3.1415926535898

and use this macro as follows:

double radius $= 5$;
double circumference $= 2 * $ PI $*$ radius;

Macros can be tricky, though, and if you are not very familiar with writing tricky macros, we do not encourage you to make extensive use of them. In general, inline functions are much safer.

There are a few very useful applications of preprocessor directives, however, that are used quite frequently; e.g., let the compiler take different code for different **define**s in order to create a system-dependent code:

#define PLATFORM_WINDOWS

#ifdef PLATFORM_WINDOWS
    // Do something WINDOWS-specific
#else
    // Do something else
#endif

Macros are also commonly used in header files: since it is a waste of time—and sometimes also creates compiler errors—header file should not be included more than once. Say you write a header-file name `my_header_file.h`. Then you should write the following preprocessor directives into this file in order to prevent the file from being included more than once. For example:

---

[6]Speaking of keywords: Just to be complete, we give a listing of keywords in C++: **asm, auto, break, case, catch, char, class, const, continue, default, delete, do, double, else, enum, extern, float, for, friend, goto, if, inline, int, long, new, operator, overload, private, protected, public, register, return, short, signed, sizeof, static, struct, switch, this, template, try, typedef, union, unsigned, void, volatile,** and **while.**

```
#ifndef __MY_HEADER_FILE_H__
  // Implementation
  // of your header file...
#define __MY_HEADER_FILE_H__
#endif // __MY_HEADER_FILE_H__
```

6. Structures Classes

- Data and Methods

  A structure (class) is a conglomerate of data and so-called methods (member functions), and is also a "public" class. Thus, the following declarations are equivalent:

  ```
  struct NameOfCStruct
  {
  // data
      int data1;
      Real data2;
  // member functions
      int funct1( );
      void funct2( );
  };
  class NameOfClass
  {
  public: // data
      int data1;
      Real data2;
  public: // member functions
      int funct1( );
      void funct2( );
  };
  ```

  As you can see, the only difference is that in a **struct**, all members are **public** by default, whereas they would be **private** as members of a **class**. We will soon explain what that means. At the moment, we will just talk about classes.

  We can declare instances of a class wherever we declare a variable. The syntax for access to the members looks as follows:

  ```
  NameOfClass InstOfClass;

  Real r = InstOfClass.data2;
  int i = InstOfClass.funct1( );
  ```

The implementation of the member functions can be inline or not. (The keyword **inline** is not explicitly necessary.) Candidates for inline implementations are frequently used member functions with few instructions.

```
class NameOfClass
{
public: // data
    int data1;
    Real data2;
public: // member functions
    inline int funct1( ) { return data1; }
    void funct2( );
};
void NameOfClass::funct2( )
{
    // noninline implementation
}
```

- Constructors

Members of classes can be initialized automatically by means of constructors. A **constructor** has the same name as the class itself. It can be a default constructor (no parameters) or take parameters. Several constructors are allowed. The implementation is the same as for ordinary member functions:

```
class NameOfClass
{
public: // constructors
    NameOfClass( ) { data1 = 0; data2 = −1; }
    inline NameOfClass( int value1, Real value2 );
public: // data
    int data1;
    Real data2;
public: // member functions
    inline int funct1( );
    void funct2( );
};
inline NameOfClass::NameOfClass( int value1, Real value2 )
{
    data1 = value1;
    data2 = value2;
}
```

In the above example, you can see how a constructor (like any member function) can be implemented **inline**, although the corresponding code is written outside the class declaration.

Constructors are especially useful when we deal with dynamic memory. In this case, they should always go together with destructors (see below).

- Virtual Functions

  Member functions can be **virtual**. This means that a pointer to the function (instead of a fixed address) is stored. This pointer is initialized automatically when the constructor of the instance is called. The only drawback of a virtual function is that the size of a class increases by the size of a pointer. The advantage is that virtual functions make programs much more flexible. In this book, we have several examples where virtual functions are essential.

- Destructors

  Destructors work similarly to constructors. They are called upon when an instance of a class is deleted. They only make sense in context with classes that contain dynamic memory. It is recommended to declare destructors as **virtual**.

  For a better understanding, please look at the following code:

  ```
  class DynamicClass
  {
  public: // constructor and destructor
      DynamicClass( int n ) { size = n; elem = new int [ size ]; }
      virtual ~DynamicClass( ) { delete [ ] elem; }
  public: // data
      int * elem;
      int size;
  };
  void some_function( )
  {
      DynamicClass x( 100 ); // allocates 100 integers (constructor!)
      for ( int i = 0; i < x.size; i++ )
          x.elem [i] = i;
      // Here the destructor is called automatically (memory freed!)
  }
  ```

  Note: A class may only have one destructor. A destructor never has parameters.

7. Operators

   C++ allows you to define operators between classes (binary operators) and operators on a class itself (unary operators), whereas examples for binary operators are the + operator or the > operator; examples for unary operators are the += operator or the ( ) operator. This unique feature of C++ is a really handy thing. We will discuss several implementations of operators. Here is just a short example for a class with the unary operator [ ] and the binary operator ==. Usually, binary operators are implemented as **friend** functions.

```
class DynamicClass
{
public: // constructor and destructor
    DynamicClass( int n ) { size = n; elem = new int [ size ]; }
    virtual ~DynamicClass( ) { delete [ ] elem; }
public: // data
    int * elem;
    int size;
public: // operators
    int & operator [ ] ( int i ) { return elem [i]; }
    friend int operator == ( DynamicClass &d1, DynamicClass &d2 );
};
void some_function( )
{
    DynamicClass x( 2 ), y( 2 ); // allocates 2 integers (constructor!)
    x[0] = y[0] = 10;
    x[1] = y[1] = x[0] − 3;
    if ( x == y )
        NULL; // do something (in this case nothing...)
    // Here the destructors of x and y are called!
}
int operator == ( DynamicClass &d1, DynamicClass &d2 )
{
    if ( d1.size != d2.size )
        return 0;
    for ( int i = 0; i < d1.size; i++ )
        if ( d1 [i] != d2 [i] )
            return 0;
    return 1;
}
```

8. Data Encapsulation

One of the fundamental rules of object-oriented programming is to protect data. This is essential for writing safe code. We will present examples for the need of data protection. Here we just show how to "encapsulate" the above-defined class:

```
class DynamicClass
{
public: // constructor and destructor
    DynamicClass( int n ) { size = n; elem = new int [ size ]; }
    virtual ~DynamicClass( ) { delete [ ] elem; }
private: // data
    int * elem;
    int size;
public: // member functions
    int GetValue( int i ) { return elem [i]; }
    void SetValue( int i, int val ) { elem [i] = val; }
    int GetSize( ) { return size; }
};
void some_function( )
{
    DynamicClass x( 50 );
    int i, sum;
    for ( i = 0; i < x.GetSize( ); i++ )
        x.SetValue( i, i * i );
    // Now calculate the sum of all elements
    for ( i = 0, sum = 0; i < x.GetSize( ); i++ )
        sum += x.GetValue( i );
}
```

At first glance, it seems to be a waste of time to declare data **private** and then make it accessible via member functions. But it is essential that it is not possible to change the size "from outside," epsecially for a dynamic class, as any change "by hand" would be fatal for the program. The only way to do so would be a call of a member function ChangeSize( ) or so. (Since dynamic classes are of great importance in geometric programming, we will soon talk about those classes in more detail when we talk about intelligent arrays.) However, the member functions themselves have access to all of the private data. Otherwise there would be no access at all!

9. Inheritance

Besides data encapsulation, inheritance is an important fundamental of object-oriented programming, as it helps to save large amounts of code. We will talk about inheritance throughout this book. But for the moment, a simple example should be enough.

Let Point be a base class and Circle be a "child" of this class. Circle inherits the members of Point. Access to **private** members of Point is only possible via **public** member functions of Point.

```
class Point
{
public:
    void Def( Real x0, Real y0 ) { x = x0; y = y0; }
    void Translate( Real dx, Real dy ) { x += dx; y += dy; }
private:
    Real x, y;


};
class Circle: public Point
{
public:
    void Def( Real x0, Real y0, Real r0 ) // overwrite Point::Def( )
    {
        Point::Def( x0, y0);
        radius = r0;
    }
private:
    Real radius;
};
void some_function( )
{
    Circle c; // no constructor
    c.Def( 3, 2, 7 ); // calls Circle::Def( )
    c.Translate( 1, 0 ); // calls Point::Translate( )
}
```

In this example, we can use the member function Translate( ) of Point in order to translate a circle.

Let us now see what happens when we equip the classes with constructors and destructors—although, in this simple case, this would not be necessary:

```
class Point
{
public:
    Point( ) { x = y = 0; }
    void Def( Real x0, Real y0 ) { x = x0; y = y0; }
    void Translate( Real dx, Real dy ) { x += dx; y += dy; }
    ~Point( ) { }; // dummy
private:
    Real x, y;

};
```

```
class Circle: public Point
{
public: // overwrite Def( )
   Circle( ) { radius = 0; }
   void Def( Real x0, Real y0, Real r0 )
   {
      Point::Def( x0, y0);
      radius = r0;
   }
   ~Circle( ) { }; // dummy
private:
   Real radius;
};
void some_function( )
{
   Circle c; // calls the constructor of Point and then
             //         the constructor of Circle
   c.Def( 3, 2, 7 ); // calls Circle::Def( )
   c.Translate( 1, 0 ); // calls Point::Translate( )
   // The compiler inserts the destructor of Circle and then
   // the destructor of Point (note the order!)
}
```

It is recommended to declare destructors as **virtual**. Theoretically, it is enough to declare the destructor of **Point** virtual. Therefore, all destructors of classes derived from **Point** are automatically **virtual**.

More examples are given in the following sections.

1.4 How to Develop Solid Code

In this section we will explain how to write solid code by means of data encapsulation.

Data encapsulation means that a class has variable members, but no instance of the class or child of the class is allowed to change these members.

For example, let us take a class called *Plane*. In a three-dimensional Cartesian coordinate system, a plane is well defined by its equation

$$n_x\, x + n_y\, y + n_z\, z = c.$$

For easier calculations, the normal vector

$$\vec{\mathbf{n}} = \begin{pmatrix} n_x \\ n_y \\ n_z \end{pmatrix} = (n_x,\, n_y,\, n_z)^T$$

shall always be normalized. Thus, it should not be allowed to change any of the values n_x, n_y n_z, c "by hand." A plane should only be given by

- Three space points.

- A point and the normal vector of the plane (which need not to be normalized).

- A point and a noncoinciding straight line.

- Two space points that are symmetric to the plane.

A plane can be intersected by a straight line or another plane. We might want to know the (oriented) distance of a space point from the plane or the normal projection of a point onto the plane, and so forth.

We now implement the class:

First we write a header file `plane.h` where we implement the interface of the class. Anyone who wants to use this class has to include this file. Although the user can see the private members normal and constant, there is no way to change them.[7]

```
#ifndef __PLANE_H__
class Plane
{
private:
    V3d normal;
    Real constant;
    P3d point;
public:
    void Def( const P3d &P, const P3d &Q, const P3d &R );
    void Def( const P3d &P, const V3d &n );
    void Def( const P3d &P, const StraightLine &g );
    void Def( const Rod3d &PQ );

    friend P3d operator * ( const Plane &e, const StrL3d &g ); // const;
    friend StrL3d operator * ( const Plane &e, const Plane &f ); // const;
    Real OrientedDistance( const P3d &P) const;
    Real Angle( const Plane &e ) const;
    P3d NormalProj( const P3d &P) const;

    void Translate( const V3d &v );
    void Rotate( const StrL3d &a, const Real w );
```

---

[7]In OPEN GEOMETRY the coordinate planes are predefined: *Plane XYplane, XZplane, YZplane.*

```
P3d GetPoint( ) const { return point; }
Boolean CarrierPlane( PO3d &o, Real tol = 0 ) const;
void SectionWithStraightLine( const StraightLine &g,
                P3d &S, Real &t ) const;

V3d n( ) const { return normal; }
Real c( ) const { return constant; }
};
#define __PLANE_H__
#endif // __PLANE_H__
```

The values of normal and constant can be used for any purpose by means of the public member functions n( ) and c( ).

There are some rules that should be followed when implementing a new class that make code easier to read and, what is more important, safer:

- When a member function of the class does not change the data of the class, use the **const** qualifier. This has two advantages:

  First, constant instances of the class (read-only, except during its one-time initialization) can only use constant member functions.

  Second, one can immediately recognize that the function is read-only and that the data is not changed, e.g., when our plane is rotated, the data of course changes. Thus, the member function Rotate( ) cannot be declared as constant.

  By the way, **friend** operators are nonmember functions and cannot be declared constant (compiler error "modifiers not allowed on nonmember functions" or similar), but you can still place a comment (like in our example).

- When a parameter of a member function is unchanged in the function, declare it as **const**. This is even more important, as the compiler guarantees that the variables will stay unchanged in the function. You can, but you need not, declare constant parameters that are passed by value, but a pass-by value automatically guarantees that the function does not change the variable (structure) being passed!

- Always "surround" the header file **xyz.h** with something like

  #ifndef __XYZ_H__

  ⋮

  #define __XYZ_H__

  ⋮

  #endif // __XYZ_H__

as this will both speed up the compilation and prevent "redefinition errors" in multimodule programs.

1.5 The Implementation of a Vector

One last word on data encapsulation is that there is no doubt that such an encapsulation is an extremely important step towards safe programming. In fact, it is one of the fundamentals of object-oriented design. Access functions ensure that your objects never contain invalid values. What is more, they let you change the implementation of the class very easily, as you just have to rewrite the class's member functions—the user's applications are not affected as long as the prototypes of the public member functions are not changed.

One only has to keep in mind that it *may* be a waste of energy in some cases, and that it may even slow down the code.

Such an example is the class *V23d* (a two- or three-dimensional vector). It has three data components x, y, z that need not be protected in the general case. Of course, just to obey the rules, one could write six member functions

```
Real GetX( );
Real GetY( );
Real GetZ( );
void SetX( Real x0 );
void SetY( Real y0 );
void SetZ( Real z0 );
```

which allow us to do all the necessary manipulations. In fact, all these functions are necessary if we deal with unit vectors! As long as we do not deal with unit vectors, however, it is somewhat troublesome to use the above functions.

So, let us start with the interface of the base class *V23d*.

```
class V23d
{
public:
    Real x, y, z;
public:
    V23d( );
    V23d( Real x0, Real y0, Real z0 = 0 );

    void operator ( ) ( Real x0, Real y0 ) { Def( x0, y0, 0 ); }
    void operator ( ) ( Real x0, Real y0, Real z0 ) { Def( x0, y0, z0 ); }
    void Def( Real x0, Real y0, Real z0 = 0 ) { x = x0; y = y0; z = z0; }
```

```
    Real Length( ) const;
    Real XYlength( ) const;
    Real SqrLength( ) const;
    void operator *= ( Real t );
    void operator /= ( Real t );
    V23d operator −( ) const;
    Boolean identical( const V23d &v, Real tol= 0 ) const;
    Boolean operator == ( const V23d &v ) const;
    Boolean operator != ( const V23d &v );
    void operator = ( const V23d &v );
    void operator = ( Vector v );
    void Print( char *str = "@", int dim = 3 ) const;
    void Normalize( V23d &norm ) const;
    void Normalize( );
    Real Distance( const P23d &P) const ;
    void InBetweenPoint( const P23d &e, Real t, P23d &p ) const;
};
```

From this class we will derive both a two-dimensional vector and a three-dimensional vector. Functions that these two types have in common are members of the base class.

First, a vector has to be defined somehow. This can be done by means of function Def( ). (The inline code can be seen in the interface of the class.) Based on this function, we can implement a second constructor besides the default constructor.

```
inline V23d::V23d( ) // default constructor
{
}
inline V23d::V23d( Real x0, Real y0, Real z0 )
{
    Def( x0, y0, z0 );
}
```

and a unary operator ( ):

```
// the following does not work with any compiler

void V23d::operator ( ) ( Real x0, Real y0, Real z0 = 0 )
{
    Def( x0, y0, z0 );
}
```

```
// If it does not work, it has to be replaced
// by two separate operators:

void V23d::operator ( ) ( Real x0, Real y0 )
{
    Def( x0, y0, 0 );
}
void V23d::operator ( ) ( Real x0, Real y0, Real z0 )
{
    Def( x0, y0, z0 );
}
```

Let $\vec{a} = (a_x, a_y, a_z)^T$ and $\vec{b} = (n_x, n_y, n_z)^T$ be two vectors. If they are meant to be two-dimensional, we let $a_z = b_z = 0$.

Then addition (subtraction) and scalar multiplication are defined by

$$\vec{a} \pm \vec{b} = \begin{pmatrix} a_x \pm b_x \\ a_y \pm b_y \\ a_z \pm b_z \end{pmatrix} \quad \text{and} \quad t\,\vec{a} = \begin{pmatrix} t\,a_x \\ t\,a_y \\ t\,a_z \end{pmatrix}.$$

A vector has a well-defined norm and length

$$|\vec{a}| = \left| \begin{pmatrix} a_x \\ a_y \\ a_z \end{pmatrix} \right| = \sqrt{a_x^2 + a_y^2 + a_z^2} = \sqrt{a\,a},$$

by means of which it can be normalized:

$$\vec{a}_0 = \frac{1}{|\vec{a}|}\,\vec{a} = \begin{pmatrix} a_x/|\vec{a}| \\ a_y/|\vec{a}| \\ a_z/|\vec{a}| \end{pmatrix}.$$

Furthermore, we have the dot product

$$\vec{a}\,\vec{b} = a_x\,b_x + a_y\,b_y + a_z\,b_z$$

and the cross product

$$\vec{a} \times \vec{b} = \begin{pmatrix} a_x \\ a_y \\ a_z \end{pmatrix} \times \begin{pmatrix} b_x \\ b_y \\ b_z \end{pmatrix} = \begin{pmatrix} a_y\,b_z - a_z\,b_y \\ a_z\,b_x - a_x\,b_z \\ a_x\,b_y - a_y\,b_x \end{pmatrix}.$$

Here is the implementation of the theory:

```
inline Real V23d::Norm( ) const
{
   return  x * x + y * y + z * z;
}
inline Real V23d::Length( ) const
{
   return  sqrt( Norm( ) );
}
inline Real V23d::XYlength( ) const
{
   return  sqrt( x * x + y * y );
}
inline V23d V23d::operator −( ) const
{
   return V23d( −x, −y, −z );
}
inline void V23d::operator *= ( Real t )
{
   x *= t; y *= t; z *= t;
}
inline void V23d::operator /= ( Real t )
{
   x /= t; y /= t; z /= t;
}
inline void V23d::operator = ( const V23d &v )
{
   Def( v.x, v.y, v.z );
}
inline Boolean V23d::operator == ( const V23d &v ) const
{
   return identical( v );
}
inline Boolean V23d::operator != ( const V23d &v )
{
   return identical( v ) ? false : true;
}
inline void V23d::Normalize( )
{
   Real len = Length( );
   if ( len == 0 )
      this−>Print("Troubles normalizing zero Vector");
   else {
      x /= len; y /= len; z /= len;
   }
}
```

```
inline void V23d::Normalize( V23d &norm ) const
{
   Real len = Length( );
   if ( len == 0 )
      this->Print("Troubles normalizing zero Vector");
   else
      norm.Def( x / len, y / len, z / len );
}
```

1.6 Classes That Contain Dynamic Memory

Allocating and Deleting Memory

In C++, memory should be allocated by means of the **new** operator, and it should be freed by the **delete** operator, as in the following example:

```
int *x;
x = new int;
*x = 100;
delete x;
```

In order to avoid the asterisk * with every call of the above variable x, one can use the following syntax:

```
int *x;
x = new int;
int &y = *x;
y = 100;
delete x;
```

Note that the value of y does not make sense after x was deleted.

Dynamic arrays (the size of which are calculated at time of running) are allocated as follows:

```
int *x;
int n = 100;
x = new int [n];
x[23] = 100;
delete [ ] x;
```

Note the order of the double brace [ ].

The allocating and deleting of memory are some of the most sensitive processes in computer programming. Thus, it is worthwhile writing macros for the allocation of dynamic arrays that are "safe." After the macros have been tested out thoroughly, they—and only they—should be used. Such macros could be like the following:

```
int *x = NULL;
int n = 100;
ALLOC_ARRAY( int, x, n, "x" );
x[23] = i;
// etc.
FREE_ARRAY( int, x, n, "x" );
```

Their implementation may have the code (see file `H/alloc_mem.h`)

```
#define ALLOC_ARRAY( typ, array, size, str )\
{\
   if ( ( size ) == 0 )\
   {\
      SafeExit( StrCat("0 bytes with new ", str ) );\
   }\
   else\
   {\
      if ( array != NULL ) Write( StrCat("set pointer to zero:", str ) );\
      array = new typ [( size )];\
   }\
}
#define FREE_ARRAY( typ, array, size, str )\
{\
   if ( array == NULL )\
   {\
      Write( StrCat("free NULL pointer:", str ) );\
   } else {\
      DeleteArrayInfo( array, str );\
      delete [ ] array;\
      array = NULL;\
   }\
}
```

"Intelligent" Arrays

As a very useful application, we now show how to develop C++ classes that handle arrays perfectly. The idea is that the array itself is hidden as a member of the class (structure). Inline operators allow you to read from and write to the elements of the array.

The goal is to write code like the following:

IntArray x(10000), y;

RandNum rnd(-100, 100); // initialize a random number in [-100, 100]

```
for ( int i = 0; i < x.size; i++ )
   x[i] = rnd( );
```

```
y = x; // The = operator has to be overwritten
y.Sort( );
Print( y.Average( ) );
   // by the way: in this case, the average value should converge to 0
```

// etc.

This is the corresponding structure (see file **H/intarray.h**). The constant DUMMY is used in several other implementations.

#ifndef __INT_ARRAY__

#define DUMMY -83561207 // An "impossible" number (Real or int).

```
struct IntArray
{
   int size;
   int *val;
   IntArray( ) { }
   IntArray( int n, int init_val = DUMMY )
   {
      Def( n, init_val );
   }
   void Def( int n, int init_val = DUMMY );
   int & operator [ ] ( int i ) const
   {
      if ( i > size )
         Write("idx wrong");
      return val[i];
   }
   void operator = ( const IntArray &other )
   {
      other.Copy( *this );
   }
   void Copy( IntArray &f ) const;
   void Sort( int i1 = 0, int i2 = -1, int sgn = 1 );
```

```
int Max( ) const;
int Min( ) const;
Real Average( ) const;

void Delete( )
{
    if ( val )
        FREE_ARRAY( int, val, size + 1, "cont");
}
virtual ~IntArray( )
{
    Delete( );
}
};

#define _INT_ARRAY_
#endif // _INT_ARRAY_
```

Here is the noninline implementation of the member functions:

```
void IntArray::Def( int n, int init_val )
{
    size = n; val = NULL;
    if ( size )
        ALLOC_ARRAY( int, val, size + 1, "cont");
    if ( init_val != DUMMY )
        for ( int i = 0; i <= size; i++ )
            val[i] = init_val;
}
void IntArray::Copy( IntArray &f ) const
{
    if (!size )
    {
        f.Delete( );
        return;
    }
    if ( size != f.size ) f.Def( size );
    memcpy( f.val, val, ( size + 1 ) * sizeof( int ) );
}
void IntArray::Sort( int i1, int i2, int sgn )
{
    if ( i2 < i1 )
        i2 = size - 1;
    QSort( i2 - i1 + 1, &val[i1], sgn );
}
```

```
int IntArray::Max( ) const
{
    int max = val[0];
    for ( int i = 1; i < size; i++ )
        if ( max < val[i] )
            max = val[i];
    return max;
}
int IntArray::Min( ) const
{
    int min = val[0];
    for ( int i = 1; i < size; i++ )
        if ( min > val[i] )
            min = val[i];
    return min;
}
Real IntArray::Average( ) const
{
    Real sum = val[0];
    for ( int i = 1; i < size; i++ )
        sum += val[i];
    return sum / size;
}
```

More-Dimensional Arrays

Sometimes we have to allocate higher-dimensional arrays dynamically. For example, let us assume that we want to allocate the two-dimensional array **int** $x[n][m]$. The array has $n\,m$ elements of the type **int**. The writing x[i][j] is turned into $*(x[i] + j)$ by the compiler. Thus, the computer needs information about the n pointers $x[i]$. Therefore, the allocation of the array has to be done in three steps:

1. Allocate the n pointers.

2. Allocate space for the entire array.

3. Initialize the rest of the pointers.

The array is freed in two steps:

1. Free the space for the entire array.

2. Free the space for the n pointers.

It is fairly complicated to rewrite such code for every new allocation, and there is always the danger of memory errors. This problem cannot be solved by a function, because we have to distinguish between different types of variables if the pointers are to be cast correctly. Once again, a C macro comes in handy. (Note the use of braces. This helps to avoid hard-to-find errors.)

Now we can use dynamically allocated, two-dimensional arrays just like static arrays:

```
int **x = NULL;
int n1 = 1000, n2 = 500;
ALLOC_2D_ARRAY( int, x, n1, n2, "x" );
for ( int i = 0; i < n1; i++ )
    for ( int j = 0; j < n2; j++ )
        x[i][j] = i + j;
FREE_2D_ARRAY( int, x, n1, n2, "x" );
```

The implementation of the macros can look as follows (see file H/alloc_mem.h):

```
#define ALLOC_2D_ARRAY( typ, array, size1, size2, str )\
{\
    ALLOC_ARRAY( typ *, array, size1, str );\
    array[0] = NULL;\
    ALLOC_ARRAY( typ, array[0], ( size1 ) * ( size2 ), str );\
    for ( int i = 1; i < size1; i++ )\
        array[i] = array[ i - 1] + size2;\
}
#define FREE_2D_ARRAY( typ, array, size1, size2, str )\
{\
    if ( array == NULL )\
        Write( StrCat("free NULL pointer *:", str ) );\
    else\
    {\
        FREE_ARRAY( typ, array[0], ( size1 ) * ( size2 ), str );\
        FREE_ARRAY( typ *, array, size1, str );\
    }\
}
```

2

Getting Started

In this chapter, we will show you elementary things like how to write a 2D application or a 3D application. We will also briefly mention how to get simple animation easily.

We assume that you have already installed the OPEN GEOMETRY system on your hard disk. Otherwise, please consult the installation guide in the appendix.

In the listings, you will see predefined types of objects, like *Circ2d* (a 2D circle), *Rect2d* (a 2D rectangle), *Sphere*, *Box*, and *RegPrism* (a regular prism). These objects then have methods like Def( ) (define), Draw( ) or Shade( ), Translate( ) or Rotate( ), etc. Do not worry too much about it, as we will carefully explain everything afterwards. We are quite sure that you will be able to understand the code intuitively, as this is one of the advantages of object-oriented programming.

2.1 A Simple 2D Program

In the directory 2D of the example directory X, you can find a file named mask2d.cpp (X/2D/mask2d.cpp[1]).

---

[1]Open Geometry is written both for the UNIX enironment and for the WINDOWS environment. In the WINDOWS 95 and WINDOWS NT evironment, the slashes (/) normally have to be written as backslashes (\). In a C++ program, however, you can always write

    #include "X/2D/mask2d.cpp"

instead of the tricky and system-dependent line

    #include "X\\2D\\mask2d.cpp"

which would not allow compatibility among the various platforms. So always use the first notation.

You can use this file to get started easily but first, please look at the code and you will see comments that explain how the program is built up.

Listing of program X/2D/mask2d.cpp (Figure 2.1):

```
#include "opengeom.h" // This is the magic include file

// Here you can declare your own global variables

void Scene::Init( )
{
    // Here you should initialize global variables
    // and prepare everything you will need for your
    // application.
}
void Scene::Draw( )
{
    ShowAxes( Red, 8 ); // Shows the axes in red color
    PrintString( Black, 5, 5, "Mask2d" ); // Write something on the screen
    TheWindow.ShowRaster( Gray, 1, 1, 0.5 );
        // This gives you some orientation. The raster size is one unit.
}
void Scene::Animate( )
{
    // Add your animation here (and only here!)
}
void Scene::CleanUp( )
{
    // Here you can 'clean up' your global variables
    // (if necessary).
}
void Projection::Def( )
{
    if ( FrameNum( ) == 1 ) // Initialization of the drawing window
    {
        xyCoordinates( -12.0, 12.0, -10.0, 10.0 );
    }
}
```

The user's application is controlled by the initialization part Scene::Init( ), the actual drawing part Scene::Draw( ), an animation part Scene::Animate( ), and the closing part Scene::CleanUp( ). Additionally, the projection (2D window or 3D camera) has to be defined by the user in Projection::Def( ).

For better understanding of what is happening, we will give additional information:

- There is one global instance of **class** Scene named TheScene (the users application) and an instance of the **class** Projection named TheCamera.[2] The executable program calls the member functions of these variables in the following order. At the very beginning, the frame number is set to 1. The user's global variables are then initialized by means of TheScene.Init( ). The projection is initialized by calling TheCamera.Def( ) a first time. This is the reason why we write

    if (FrameNum( ) == 1) . . .

    in the routine Projection::Def( ).

- Then the routine TheScene.Draw( ) is called the first time. Since we use double-buffering, the scene is drawn on an invisible backbuffer of the screen. When the drawing is done, the buffer is swapped to the visible frontbuffer.

    The user can now interact with the program: therefore, the window can be resized and the scene can be moved by means of the arrow keys, etc. Though the scene will be redrawn with such interactions, the frame number will still be 1.

- Essential changes of the scene are only made when the user forces a next frame, e.g., via menu. In this case—and only in this case—the frame number is increased by 1. Then the routines TheScene.Animate( ) and TheCamera.Def( ) are called in order to animate the application and/or to define a new camera.

    This means that the scene will not be animated just because the user changed the light source or because the window was resized, etc. In many sample programs this routine is left as a dummy function without any code.

- When the user quits the program, the function TheScene.CleanUp( ) is called. This has to be done, since the user might have allocated global memory that has to be available until the very end of the program. Such memory can be freed in the CleanUp( ) routine. In most sample programs, this routine is left as a dummy function without any code.

Here is a pseudocode for an OPEN GEOMETRY application: *italic writing* indicates that the routines are done by internal functions, and the underlined text emphasizes the call of the functions that are implemented by the user:

---

[2]The only way to change the properties of these variables is to call their member functions in the public member functions Scene::Init( ), Scene::Draw( ), Scene::Animate( ), and Projection::Def( ), respectively.

Pseudocode for all OPEN GEOMETRY applications:

Start application; open a window on the screen
Initialize internal globals
frame_number := 1
redraw := true

Scene::Init( )

Projection::Def( )

while not quit via menu or keyboard // main loop
{
   if (redraw)
   {   // display scene
     Clear screen (and z-buffer, if 3D Application)

     Scene::Draw( )

     Swap buffers (show drawing)
   }
   if (force next frame via menu, toolbar or keyboard)
   {   // auto animation
     frame_number := frame_number + 1

     Projection::Def( )

     Scene::Animate( )

     redraw := true
   }
   else if (changes via menu, toolbar or keyboard)
   {   // minor changes (camera, light, etc.)—no animation
     recalculate virtual camera, light, etc.
     redraw := true
   }
   else if (resize window via mouse or menu)
   {
     redraw := true
   }
   else // no changes at all
   {

```
            redraw := false
      }
} // end main loop
```

<u>Scene::Cleanup( )</u>

Free all internally used memory
End application; close window

Note that the coordinate system is not pixel-oriented. The user decides about the size of the drawing area (which has nothing to do with the window dimensions). The program will try to fit this area into the current screen as well as possible, and there will be no clipping when the area is exceeded.

In general, the drawn image should fit into an (x, y) area that has the size of about a manual sketch: $-10 \le x, y \le 10$ units.[3]

In order to compile the code **X/2D/mask2d.cpp**, you have to do the following, depending on the platform you are working on.

- You are working in a WINDOWS environment:

    1. Start your compiler (e.g., the Visual C++ Compiler Version 4.0 or higher or the WATCOM C++ Compiler Version 11.0 or higher).

    2. Load the workspace **OpenGeom**.

    3. Edit the file **try.cpp** in the OPEN GEOMETRY directory. It looks something like this:

        ```
        #include "stdafx.h" // Some include stuff. Leave it as it is.
        #include "og_main.h"
        ```

---

[3]This has two advantages:

First, before writing a 2D application, we will probably sketch the result. To get as close as possible to the idea, we can simply estimate the coordinates of given elements (in cm, inches or "drawing units"). When your drawing unit is an inch and you have a 20" monitor, the monitor displays the scene approximately $1 : 1$.

Second, many internal accuracy limits of the library functions are optimized for the drawing area $-10 \le x, y \le 10$, e.g., a point P is considered to coincide with a straight line s $(P \in s)$, when its distance is less than a certain accuracy limit $\varepsilon = 10^{-7}$. This turns out to be a good value for the recommended drawing area. In an area $1000 \le x, y \le 10000$, the limit ε would probably be too small, i.e., the program might not detect $P \in s$ due to a loss of accuracy during the calculations.

// Please choose one (and only one!) file from the following list
// and remove the comment sign at the beginning of this line.
// If there are other files that are not commented out, you have
// to comment them out (Otherwise, the compiler will try to
// compile several main files.)

//#include "X/2D/some_file.cpp"
#include "X/2D/mask2d.cpp" // This is the actual file
//#include "X/2D/another_file.cpp"
//#include "X/3D/file1.cpp"
//#include "X/3D/file2.cpp"
// etc. etc. (many more files...)

When you read the comments, you will know what to do.

4. Compile and run the program.

- You are working in a UNIX environment:

    1. Open at least two shells and change to the OPEN GEOMETRY directory.

    2. In the first shell, edit the file **try.cpp** and proceed as in Step 3 of the WINDOWS environment. Do not forget to save your changes in case you do not quit the editor.

    3. In the second shell, compile the program by means of the command line

        m

        (like <u>m</u>ake).

        After compiling, run the application by means of the command

        x

        (like e<u>x</u>ecute).

OPEN GEOMETRY should now open a window on the screen and show a coordinate system xy and the sample text **"Mask2d"** (Figure 2.1). If that works, you can start to expand this simple base.

For this purpose, rename the file X/2D/mask2d.cpp to another file name, like[4] X/2D/first2d.cpp. Then comment out the line

#include "X/2D/mask2d.cpp"

---

[4]For example, you can use the menu item **Safe As**.

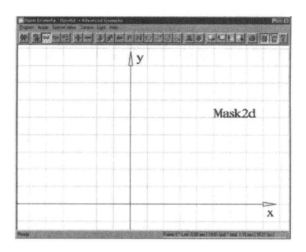

FIGURE 2.1. The output of `mask2d.cpp`.

and edit a new line

```
//#include "X/2D/mask2d.cpp"
#include "X/2D/first2d.cpp"
```

Edit X/2D/first2d.cpp. Make some changes like

```
#include "opengeom.h" // This is the magic include file
```

// Global variable
Circ2d circle; // 2D circle

```
void Scene::Init( )
{
    // Initialize global variables
    circle.Def( Green, 5, 0, 2, FILLED );
    // Mid point (5, 0), radius 2, not EMPTY
}
void Scene::Draw( )
{
    ShowAxes( Red, 8 ); // Shows the axes in red color
    circle.Draw( ); // Paint the green circle
    PrintString( Black, 5, −5, "A rotating circle..." );
}
void Scene::Animate( )
{
    circle.Rotate( Origin, 1 );
```

```
        // The circle will rotate around the origin by 1 degree
        // when you force the next image (but not when you just resize
        // the window or move the scene by means of the arrow keys, etc.)
}
void Scene::CleanUp( )
{
        // Nothing to 'clean up'
}
void Projection::Def( )
{
    if ( FrameNum( ) == 1 ) // Initialization of the drawing window
    {
        xyCoordinates( −12.0, 12.0, −10.0, 10.0 );
    }
}
```

Always be aware that it is this file that is currently being compiled. Thus, if a compile error occurs, the error has to be eliminated in this file.

Also, please be strict with yourself and write the animating code into the corresponding routine. Then the animation is only done when you explicitly force the next frame (for example, via menu or toolbar or by typing <Ctrl + N> or <Ctrl + F>. Whereas it is *not* done when you resize the image, translate the scene (by means of the arrow keys), or zoom the scene (by typing <Ctrl + Z> or <Ctrl + Shift + Z> or via menu).

In this book, we also use a header file **defaults2d.h** that contains the above-listed implementations of Scene::Animate( ), Scene::CleanUp( ), and Projection::Def( ). This is mainly in order to shorten the listings. The reader should not use this header file extensively, as it makes the program less flexible.

In the following chapter, we will say more about the writing of 2D code. Now we will briefly show how to write 3D code.

2.2 A Simple 3D Program

In OPEN GEOMETRY, 3D programs do not differ much from 2D programs. The major difference is that we have to define a "camera." Please have a look at the program X/3D/mask3d.cpp (Figure 2.2) that should be the base of your applications:

Listing of program X/3D/mask3d.cpp (Figure 2.2):

#include "opengeom.h" // This is the magic include file

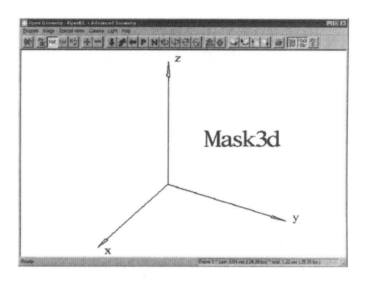

FIGURE 2.2. The output of `mask3d.cpp`.

```
// Declare your global variables here

void Scene::Init( )
{
    // Initialize your global variables here
    // Do any precalculations here
}
void Scene::Draw( )
{
    // Do the actual drawing here
    ShowAxes( Blue, 10 ); // Show the axes
    PrintString( Black, 3, 3, "Mask3d" ); // Print something
}
void Scene::Animate( )
{
    // Add your animation here
}
void Scene::CleanUp( )
{
    // This routine is called at the very end of the program.
    // Here you can free global memory that you have allocated
    // and not yet freed.
}
void Projection::Def( )
{
    if ( FrameNum( ) == 1 )
```

```
    {
        DefaultCamera( 28, 18, 12 );
        ParallelLight( 2, 1, 2 );
    }
}
```

Similiar to the 2D case, we also use a header file **defaults3d.h** that contains the above-listed implementations of Scene::Animate( ), Scene::CleanUp( ), and Projection::Def( )—again, mainly in order to shorten the listings. Do not use this header file extensively, as it makes the program less flexible.

The StandardCamera has the following properties:

- The projection center (the center of the lens) has the coordinates that are assigned by the parameters, in our case, (28, 18, 12).

- The target point ("look-at point") is—by default—the origin of the coordinate system.

- The camera is not "twisted." Therefore, the z-axis appears upright.

- The focal distance of the camera is about $50mm$. Thus, the standard camera creates images that are similar to ordinary photographs.

The scene is illuminated by parallel light in the direction (2, 1, 2). (As long as no 3D polygons are displayed, the light direction is of no importance.)

We now proceed similarly as in the 2D case and compile the program. First, we adapt the file **try.cpp** by commenting out the other included files (besides **og_main.h**, of course) and uncommenting **X/3D/mask3d.cpp**. Then, when we compile and execute the program, a resizeable window should be opened on the screen showing an xyz-coordinate system and the text **"Mask3d"**.

Now we want to write our first 3D program. First, we rename **X/3D/mask3d.cpp** to **X/3D/first3d.cpp** and then we adapt **try.cpp**

// #include "*X/3D/mask3d.cpp*"
#include X/3D/first3d.cpp"

and make some changes in **X/3D/first3d.cpp** (Figure 2.3):

Listing of program **X/3D/first3d.cpp** (Figure 2.3):

#include "opengeom.h"

Sphere TheMoon, TheEarth; // Global variables

The blue planet and its only moon...

FIGURE 2.3. The output of the first 3D program.

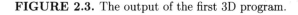

```
void Scene::Init( )
{
    TheEarth.Def( Blue, Origin, 1.2 );
    P3d Mid( 5, 0, 0 );
    TheMoon.Def( Gray, Mid, 0.3 );
    ScaleLetters(0.8, 0.9);
}
void Scene::Draw( )
{
    TheEarth.Shade( );
    TheMoon.Shade( );
    PrintString( Black, −4, 2,
                "The blue planet and its only moon..." );
}
void Scene::Animate( )
{
    TheMoon.Rotate( Zaxis, 3 );
}
void Scene::CleanUp( )
{
}
void Projection::Def( )
{
    if ( FrameNum( ) == 1 )
```

```
    {
        DefaultCamera( 28, 18, 12 );
        ChangeFocus( 180 ); // telephoto lens
        ParallelLight( 1, −1, 0.15 );
    }
}
```

In Projection.Def( ), we changed the focus f of our camera lens. The parameter f of ChangeFocus( ) indicates the focal distance in millimeters. Ordinary cameras usually have a focal distance of $35 \leq f \leq 70$, but telephoto lenses have a larger focal distance and wide-angle lenses a smaller one (but not smaller than 15 mm).[5]

One last word on the function Scene::CleanUp( ). We shall give a short listing where the code of this function is important. Otherwise, some memory will not be freed at the end of the program:

```
#include "opengeom.h"
int *X; // Ordinary GLOBAL pointer
IntArray Y; // This class is equipped with a destructor

void Scene::Init( )
{
    X = new int [1000]; // Assign pointer to first element of array
    Y.Def( 1000 );
    int *x0;
    x0 = new int [ 1000 ];
    // The variable x0 is only LOCAL. Thus, if you do not free the memory
    // explicitly, the compiler will automatically insert something like
    // delete [ ] x0;
}
void Scene::Draw( )
{
}
void Scene::Animate( )
{
}
void Scene::CleanUp( )
```

---

[5]If, for some reason, you try to let $f < 15$ mm, OPEN GEOMETRY will automatically move the camera position away from the scene and leave $f = 15$.

```
{
    delete [ ] X; // You have to free the array here!
    // Y is deleted automatically via destructor!
}
void Projection::Def( )
{
    if ( FrameNum( ) == 1 )
    {
        DefaultCamera( 10, 10, 10 );
    }
}
```

A global array of integer X is allocated in Scene::Init( ). If you do not free the array in Scene::CleanUp( ), then you cannot quit the program without loss of memory. When you run the program in the debug mode, there should be a debugger warning similar to "`detected memory leaks!`".[6]

When the pointer variable is local—like the pointer x0 in Scene::Init( )—it is only valid inside a function, and if you do not free it yourself, the compiler will insert it into the corresponding code.

Instances of "intelligent" dynamic classes—like the variable Y in the above program—will be freed automatically, even if they are global. The destructor is called upon when you quit the application.

2.3   Simple Animations

Now that you know a bit about programming with OPEN GEOMETRY, we want to show you how a scene should be animated. We introduce three short programs to show you what possibilities you have.

First, we take a very simple 3D program that draws something similar to a RUBIK'S cube. We consider three boxes that, together, have the shape of a cube (Figure 2.4). For the first 30 frames, we rotate the first box about the y-axis by 3° (Figure 2.4a), for the next 30 frames the second one, and for the next 30 frames, the third one. The boxes now again form a cubic shape, and we rotate the whole cube about the z-axis (3° for each frame, and that for 30 frames, Figure 2.4b). Now the boxes are rotated through 90°, and we have to rotate them around the x-axis (Figure 2.4c). We do that, one after the other, as we have done before, etc.

The corresponding code of the program looks like this:

---

[6]For this reason, you should run your applications (not only OPEN GEOMETRY programs) in the debugging mode every once in a while.

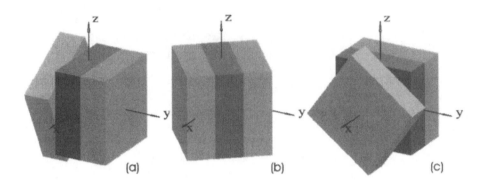

FIGURE 2.4. Animation of a pseudo-RUBIK's cube.

Listing of program BOOK/anim1.cpp (Figure 2.4):

```
#include "opengeom.h"
```

// Animate three boxes by means of rotations(similar to a RUBIK's cube)

Box box[3];

```
void Scene::Init( )
{
    for ( int i = 0; i < 3; i++ )  // define the 3 boxes
    {
        box[i].Def( Blue, 6, 2, 6 ); // dimensions
        box[i].Translate( −3, 2 * i − 3, −3 ); // center on the y-axis
    }
}
void Scene::Draw( )
{
    ShowAxes( Black, 5 );
    for ( int i = 0; i < 3; i++ )
        box[i].Shade( );
}
void Scene::Animate( )
{
    // This is the animation part:
    // The boxes are rotated about the y-axis, one after the other.
    // This takes 3 x 30 frames. Afterwards. all the three boxes are
    // rotated about the z-axis (another 30 frames).
    // The rotation process is repeated, this time with the x-axis, etc.
```

```
        int f = ( FrameNum( ) − 1 ) % 120;
        int cycle = ( FrameNum( ) − 1 ) / 120;
        StrL3d axis = ( cycle % 2 == 0 ? Yaxis : Xaxis );
        if ( f < 30 )
            box[0].Rotate( axis, 3 ); // Rotate first box
        else if ( f < 60 )
            box[1].Rotate( axis, 3 ); // Rotate second box
        else if ( f < 90 )
            box[2].Rotate( axis, 3 ); // Rotate third box
        else
            for ( int i = 0; i < 3; i++ ) // Rotate all the three boxes
                box[i].Rotate( Zaxis, 3 );
    }
    void Scene::CleanUp( )
    {
    }
    void Projection::Def( )
    {
        if ( FrameNum( ) == 1 )
        {
            DefaultCamera( 18, 10, 8 );
            ParallelLight( 2, 3, 4 );
        }
    }
```

With the appropriate graphics hardware, such an animation can easily be done in real time, i.e., 30 frames per second or more. Try to run this program and see if your configuration is a fast one.

Now we want to show you another example (Figure 2.5). This time, the objects of the scene stay constant. Only the camera is moved around or zoomed, or the direction of the light is changed.

Listing of program BOOK/anim2.cpp (Figure 2.5):

```
#include "opengeom.h"

RegPrism Cylinder[2];

void Scene::Init( )
{
```

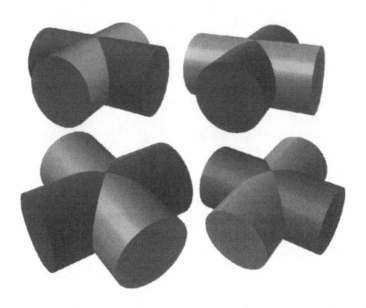

FIGURE 2.5. The output of the second animation.

```
    Real radius = 2, height = 8;
    int order = 90; // ==> cylinder is more or less smooth
    Cylinder[0].Def( Yellow, radius, height, order, SOLID, Xaxis );
    Cylinder[0].Translate( −height / 2, 0, 0 );
    Cylinder[1].Def( DarkBlue, radius, height, order, SOLID, Yaxis );
    Cylinder[1].Translate( 0, −height / 2, 0 );
}
void Scene::Draw( )
{
    Cylinder[0].Shade( );
    Cylinder[1].Shade( );
}
void Scene::Animate( )
{
    // The objects stay unchanged
}
void Scene::CleanUp( )
{
}

void Projection::Def( )
{
    if ( FrameNum( ) == 1 ) // Initialization of the camera
```

```
{
    DefaultCamera( 18, 10, 8 );
    ParallelLight( 2, 3, 4 );
    SetDepthRange( -5, 5 ); // this helps to improve z-buffering
}
int f = ( FrameNum( ) - 1 ) % 120;
if ( f < 60 )
    RotateHorizontally( 2 );
else if ( f < 70 )
    RotateVertically( 2 );
else if ( f < 80 )
    ZoomIn( 1.02 );
else if ( f < 90 )
    ZoomOut( 1.02 );
else if ( f < 100 )
    RotateVertically( -2 );
else
    LightDirection.Rotate( Zaxis, 5 );
}
```

Finally, we want to show you how to create realistic simulations of physical processes, e.g., the simulation of an object falling downwards under the influence of gravity (Figure 2.6).

A theoretical prerequisite for a realistic real-time animation is that your computer is able to create images that move at 30 frames per second. With the current state of technology, this is only possible for scenes that are not too complex. This does not, however, change the rules that you should obey. If the hardware is not fast enough for a real-time animation, you have to somehow take a snapshot of every frame and then replay the snapshots at 30 frames per second (we will explain, e.g., how we can create animated GIF files.)

Listing of program BOOK/`anim3.cpp` (Figure 2.6):

```
// This program shows how to write a time-dependent animation. Our
// goal is that the animation actually runs at 30 frames per second.
```

```
// A ball is falling to the ground and is reflected. It obeys the rules of
// gravitation: s = g/2 t^2 ⇒ t = √(2s/g) (where g is the constant of gravitation)
```

$$// \text{ gravitation: } s = \tfrac{g}{2}t^2 \Rightarrow t = \sqrt{\tfrac{2s}{g}} \text{ (where } g \text{ is the constant of gravitation)}$$

```
#include "opengeom.h"
```

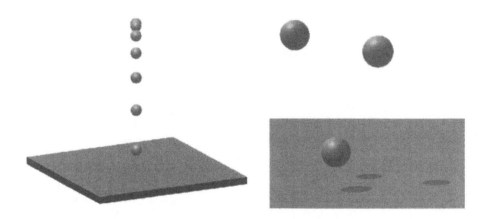

FIGURE 2.6. Objects under the influence of gravitation (see also demo program X/3D/bouncing.cpp).

Real TotalTime = 0; // "Relative time" from the start of the program
const *Real* g = 9.81; // The constant of gravitation

const *Real* s0 = 5; // The ball will fall down from a height of $s_0 = 5$ m

Sphere JumpingBall;
Box Base;

Real height(*Real* t) // height after t seconds.
{
    return s0 − (g/2) ∗ t ∗ t; // Formula: $s = s_0 - \frac{g}{2}t^2$
}

void Scene::Init( )
{
    const *Real* radius = 0.2;
    JumpingBall.Def(*LightOrange, Origin,* radius, 70);
    JumpingBall.Translate(0, 0, height(0));
    Base.Def(*Green,* 6, 6, 0.25);
    Base.Translate(−3, −3, −radius − 0.25);
        // Upper surface: z = −radius ==> center of ball has z = 0
}
void CalcSpherePosition( )
{
    const
        Real TimeForFallingToGround = sqrt(2 ∗ s0 / g), // $t = \sqrt{\frac{2s_0}{g}}$
        TimeForBouncingUpAndDown = 2 ∗ TimeForFallingToGround;
    Real t = TotalTime; // Current relative time

```
        while ( t > TimeForBouncingUpAndDown )
          t -= TimeForBouncingUpAndDown;
        // t is now the time difference from the last culmination
        if ( t > TimeForFallingToGround ) // ball is going up
          t = TimeForBouncingUpAndDown - t;
        JumpingBall.Translate( 0, 0, height( t ) - JumpingBall.GetCenter( ).z );
      }
      void Scene::Draw( )
      {
          CalcSpherePosition( );
          JumpingBall.Shade( );
          Base.Shade( );
      }
      void Scene::Animate( )
      {
          TotalTime += ( Real ) 1 / 30;
          // ==> with 30 frames per second the animation comes close to reality
      }
      void Scene::CleanUp( )
      {
      }
      void Projection::Def( )
      {
            if ( FrameNum( ) == 1 )
        {
                DefaultCamera( 5, 10, 3 );
                ParallelLight( 1, 1, 2 );
            ChangeTarget( 0, 0, 2 );
            }
      }
```

2.4 What to Do with Existing OPENGL Code

So far we have seen simple examples for writing OPEN GEOMETRY programs. We did not use any OPENGL function. Well, of course we did, but that happened secretly, when we used the library functions. In this section, we will show how you can still use any OPENGL code that you have developed earlier.

Please have a look at the following OPEN GEOMETRY2D program. First, we plot a rectangle by means of OPEN GEOMETRY, and then do the same by means of a typical OPENGL code.

Listing of BOOK/ogl2d.cpp

```
#include "opengeom.h"
#include "defaults2d.h"

void Scene::Init( )
{
}
void Scene::Draw( )
{
    Real x = 5,  y = 3, width = 10, height = 6, degrees = 30;

    // First a typical Open Geometry code
    // Plot an orange rectangle

    Rect2d rect( Orange, width, height, FILLED );
    // Scale, rotate and translate the rectangle
    rect.Scale( 0.9, 0.9 );
    P2d P( x, y );
    rect.Rotate( P, degrees );
    rect.Translate( −8, 0 );
    rect.Draw( THIN ); // Plot the rectangle

    // Now we switch to pure OPENGL code
    // Plot exactly the same rectangle

    glMatrixMode( GL_PROJECTION ); // change projection
    glPushMatrix( ); // save previous projection
    glOrtho( −1, 1, −1, 1, −1, 1 ); // actually not necessary
    glColor3d( 1, 0.5, 0 ); // orange

    // Scale, rotate and translate the rectangle
    // Note the order!
    glTranslated( −8, 0, 0 );
    // Rotation around (x, y) needs 3 lines in OpenGL
    glTranslated( x, y, 0 );
    glRotated( degrees, 0, 0, 1 );
    glTranslated( −x, −y, 0 );

    glScaled( 0.9, 0.9, 1 );
    glRectd( 0, 0, width, height ); // Plot the rectangle
    glPopMatrix( ); // undo changes of projection
}
```

You see, OPENGL is fully compatible with OPEN GEOMETRY. Thus, it should not be any problem to import previously written code into the new environment. Now a very simple 3D example (just for drawing lines):

Listing of BOOK/ogl3d.cpp

```
#include "opengeom.h"
#include "defaults3d.h"
#include <gl/glaux.h> // needed for the function auxSolidSphere( )

// Draw a rectangle and a sphere, once with OPEN GEOMETRY,
// the other time with OpenGL

void OpenGL_Light( )
{
    // This is just a sample function to work with lighting in OpenGL
    glShadeModel( GL_SMOOTH );
    glEnable( GL_LIGHTING );
    glEnable( GL_LIGHT0 );
    // Identify the given light direction with the OpenGL LIGHT0
    GLfloat Light0 [4];
    V3d pos = GetLightDir( );
    Light0 [0] = ( GLfloat ) pos.x;
    Light0 [1] = ( GLfloat ) pos.y;
    Light0 [2] = ( GLfloat ) pos.z;
    Light0 [3] = 0.0f; // The light source is a point of infinity!
    glLightfv( GL_LIGHT0, GL_POSITION, Light0 );

    // Define shininess and material
    GLfloat mat [] = { 1.0f, 1.0f, 1.0f, 1.0f };
    GLfloat shine [] = { 128.0f };
    glMaterialfv( GL_FRONT, GL_SPECULAR, mat );
    glMaterialfv( GL_FRONT, GL_SHININESS, shine );
    // etc., etc.
    // There are much more sophisticated things to follow.
}
void Scene::Init( )
{
}
void Scene::Draw( )
{
    ShowAxes( Green, 10 );
    Real x = 5, y = 3, width = 10, height = 6, degrees = 30;
    Boolean OpenGeometryCode = false;

    if ( OpenGeometryCode )
```

```
{
    Rect3d rect( Green, width, height, FILLED );
    rect.Translate( 0, 0, −4 );
    rect.Rotate( Zaxis, degrees );
    rect.Shade( );
    Sphere Ball;
    Ball.Def( Orange, Origin, 2 );
    Ball.Shade( );
}
else // OpenGL code
{
    OpenGL_Light( );
    auxSolidSphere( 2 ); // The ball
    // Now the rectangle
    glMatrixMode( GL_PROJECTION ); // change projection
    glPushMatrix( ); // save previous projection
    glTranslated( 0, 0, −2 );
    glRotated( degrees, 0, 0, 1 );
    glBegin( GL_POLYGON ); // start rectangle
    glVertex3d( 0, 0, 0 );
    glVertex3d( 0, height, 0 );
    glVertex3d( width, height, 0 );
    glVertex3d( width, 0, 0 );
    glEnd( ); // rectangle is done
    glPopMatrix( ); // save previous projection
    glMatrixMode( GL_PROJECTION ); // change projection
    glDisable( GL_LIGHTING ); // For further Open Geometry code.
}
}
```

When it comes to shading, things get a little more complicated. At the current stage, OPEN GEOMETRY does *not* work with OPENGL shading. The reason for this is that we had already developed our own shading algorithms before we switched to OPENGL. And we never managed to get as satisfying an output with the OPENGL shading functions as we did with our software. We especially had trouble with reflected light.

When you want to use OPENGL shading, you can do that with traditonal OPENGL code. But do not forget to disable lighting when OPEN GEOMETRY has to take over shading. Otherwise, you will just see hues of gray instead of nice color images.[7] Please have a look at the following sample:

---

[7]Both OPENGL shading and OPEN GEOMETRY shading are based on Gouraud shading. Palette-hues, however, are calculated differently.

Listing of BOOK/ogl3d2.cpp

```
#include "opengeom.h"
#include "defaults3d.h"
#include <gl/glaux.h> // needed for the function auxSolidSphere( )

// Draw a rectangle and a sphere, once with OPEN GEOMETRY,
// the other time with OPENGL

void OpenGL_Light( )
{
    // This is just a sample function to work with lighting in OPENGL
    glShadeModel( GL_SMOOTH );
    glEnable( GL_LIGHTING );
    glEnable( GL_LIGHT0 );
    // Identify the given light direction with the OPENGL LIGHT0
    GLfloat Light0 [4];
    V3d pos = GetLightDir( );
    Light0 [0] = ( GLfloat ) pos.x;
    Light0 [1] = ( GLfloat ) pos.y;
    Light0 [2] = ( GLfloat ) pos.z;
    Light0 [3] = 0.0f; // The light source is a point of infinity!
    glLightfv( GL_LIGHT0, GL_POSITION, Light0 );

    // Define shininess and material
    GLfloat mat [] = { 1.0f, 1.0f, 1.0f, 1.0f };
    GLfloat shine [] = { 128.0f };
    glMaterialfv( GL_FRONT, GL_SPECULAR, mat );
    glMaterialfv( GL_FRONT, GL_SHININESS, shine );
    // etc., etc.
    // There are much more sophisticated things to follow.
}
void Scene::Init( )
{
}
void Scene::Draw( )
{
    ShowAxes( Green, 10 );
    Real x = 5, y = 3, width = 10, height = 6, degrees = 30;
    Boolean OpenGeometryCode = false;

    if ( OpenGeometryCode )
    {
        Rect3d rect( Green, width, height, FILLED );
```

```
        rect.Translate( 0, 0, −4 );
        rect.Rotate( Zaxis, degrees );
        rect.Shade( );
        Sphere Ball;
        Ball.Def( Orange, Origin, 2 );
        Ball.Shade( );
    }
    else // OpenGL code
    {
        OpenGL_Light( );
        auxSolidSphere( 2 ); // The ball
        // Now the rectangle
        glMatrixMode( GL_PROJECTION ); // change projection
        glPushMatrix( ); // save previous projection
        glTranslated( 0, 0, −2 );
        glRotated( degrees, 0, 0, 1 );
        glBegin( GL_POLYGON ); // start rectangle
        glVertex3d( 0, 0, 0 );
        glVertex3d( 0, height, 0 );
        glVertex3d( width, height, 0 );
        glVertex3d( width, 0, 0 );
        glEnd( ); // rectangle is done
        glPopMatrix( ); // save previous projection
        glMatrixMode( GL_PROJECTION ); // change projection
        glDisable( GL_LIGHTING ); // For further Open Geometry code.
    }
}
```

As you can see, you will not have any difficulties including previously written OPENGL code. You can also mix pure OPEN GEOMETRY code with OPENGL code, as long as you disable OPENGL shading before it comes to OPEN GEOMETRY shading. You can also make intensive use of matrix transformations, which is a strength of OPENGL.

This is a good time to explain the difference of what we call "virtual coordinate transformation" and "real coordinate transformation" of an object, e.g., take a cube with its 8 vertices. In OPEN GEOMETRY, the coordinates of the vertices are stored in object space. When you apply an OPEN GEOMETRY translation, for example, this will change the coordinates of your cube. When you do your translation by means of OPENGL, this will only change the target point of the perspective. For the viewer, the following code will have the same result:

Listing of BOOK/transfrm.cpp

```cpp
#include "opengeom.h"
#include "defaults3d.h"

void Scene::Init( )

void Scene::Draw( )
{
   ShowAxes( Green, 8 );
   Box cube( Cyan, 6, 6, 6 ); // First corner is in ( 0, 0, 0 );
   // Say we want to center the cube around the origin:
   Boolean OpenGeom = ( FrameNum( ) % 2 == 1 ) ? true : false;
   if ( OpenGeom ) // Typical Open Geometry solution
   {
      cube.Translate( −3, −3, −3 );
      cube.Shade( );
   }
   else // Typical OpenGL solution
   {
      glPushMatrix( ); // save current matrix
      glTranslated( −3, −3, −3 );
      cube.Shade( );
      glPopMatrix( ); // restore matrix
   }
}
```

Maybe the OPENGL solution is a bit[8] faster (especially when the object consists of thousands of points). The advantage of the OPEN GEOMETRY solution is that it is more direct. Most of the time, we do not only want to simply display the object, but we also want to do calculations with it (e.g., calculate cast shadows). In this case, the direct method seems to be an advantage.[9]

Anyway, you have the choice of what to do, and if you really want to stick to the matrix-philosophy, stick to it.

---

[8]What is "a bit"? The transformation of 1,000 points requires 3,000 floating-point operations. That takes about a millisecond on an average PC, and much less on a workstation.

[9]A mixture of the two philosophies is to store a "personal matrix" for each object and globally keep the original coordinates. Whenever it comes to drawing or to calculations, the coordinates are temporarily changed. This weakens the argument that, after a larger number of transformations, the accuracy will get lost. Nevertheless, it needs hundreds of millions of transformations until the coordinates of the objects are seriously changed: keep in mind that we calculate with **double** precision!

3

Basic Objects

In this chapter, we will go a bit more into detail and explain the most common basic classes of OPEN GEOMETRY. Objects like vectors, points, straight lines, planes, and circles are implemented both in 2-space and in 3-space. In the next chapters we will extend these primitives to more complex geometric objects like curves, parametrized surfaces, polyhedra, etc.

First of all, however, we will explain some useful routines offered by OPEN GEOMETRY.

3.1 Some Useful Routines

In this section, we will list some useful routines that come with OPEN GEOMETRY. There are some main groups of these functions. These are pure mathematical functions and functions that deal with writing text on your screen.

Some Additional Mathematical Functions

In the following, we list a number of mathematical functions that are not part of the C library. Their names and parameters are more or less self-explanatory. Therefore, we just list the code of the header function `"mathfunc.h"`. The standard C library provides a number of mathematical functions that do not check errors, e.g., the `sqrt( )` function does not check whether the argument is negative or not. The program simply crashes when you attempt to calculate the square root of a negative number. Depending on the compiler you are using, the error is more or less hard to find. A security check takes only a tiny percentage rate of the calculation time of a square root. So, why not always make a security check?

Listing of H/mathfunc.h

```
#ifndef __MATH_FUNC__

inline Real Sqr( Real x ) // square of x
{
    return x * x;
}
inline int Signum( Real x ) // sign +1, 0 or −1
{
    return ( x < 0 ? −1 : ( x > 0 ? 1 : 0 ) );
}
// Security checks help to avoid hard-to-find errors
inline Real Sqrt( Real x ) // square root with security check
{
    if ( x < 0 )
        SafeExit( "illegal call of sqrt(x )(x <0 )" );
    return sqrt( x );
}
inline Real Tan( Real x ) // tangent function with security check
{
    Real s = sin( x ), c = cos( x );
    return c == 0 ? 1e30 * Signum( s ) : s / c; // avoid div. by zero
}
inline Real Log( Real x ) // logarithmic function with security check
{
    if ( x <= 0 ) // no logarithm of nonpositive numbers!
        SafeExit( "Illegal call of log(x )(x <=0)" );
    return  log( x );
}
inline int Round( Real x ) // closest integer
{
    return  ( int ) ( x + 0.5 );
}
inline Real Arc( Real degrees )  // arc length of an angle
{
    return degrees * ( PI / 180 );
}
inline Real Deg( Real arc )
    // angle in degree, corresponding to an arc length
```

```
{
    return arc * ( 180 / PI );
}
// Arc functions
inline Real ArcSin( Real x )
{
    const Real max = 1 - EPS, min = -( 1 - EPS );
    return ( x > max ? ( PI / 2 ) :
        ( x < min ? -( PI / 2 ): Re( atan( x / sqrt( 1 - x * x ) ) ) ) );
}
inline Real ArcCos( Real x )
{
    return ( PI / 2 ) - ArcSin( x );
}
inline Real ArcTan2( Real y, Real x )
    // returns a value in [-PI/2, 3PI/2 [
{
    if ( x > EPS )
        return atan( y / x );
    else if ( x < -EPS )
        return atan( y / x ) + PI;
    else if ( y > 0 )
        return ( PI / 2 );
    else return -( PI / 2 );
}
// min and max functions, both for integer and Real variables
inline Real maximum( Real a, Real b )
{
    return a < b ? b : a;
}
inline Real minimum( Real a, Real b )
{
    return a < b ? a : b;
}
inline int maximum( int a, int b )
{
    return a < b ? b : a;
}
inline int minimum( int a, int b )
{
    return a < b ? a : b;
}
void Tripod( V3d &a, V3d &b, V3d &n );
Real Integral( Real (*f)( Real ), Real t1, Real t2, int n = 100 );
int QuadrEquation( Real a, Real b, Real c, Real &x1, Real &x2 );
```

```
#define __MATH_FUNC__
#endif // __MATH_FUNC__
```

The routines Tripod( ) and Integral( ) need a short explanation (the function QuadrEquation( ) is explained in context with the procedure PrintString( )):

The procedure Tripod( ) takes a vector $\vec{n}$ and calculates an ortho-base $(\vec{h}, \vec{f}, \vec{n})$ with pairwise-orthogonal unit vectors, where h is horizontal. The function is equivalent to the command

    n.OrthoBase(h, f);

Note that $\vec{n}$ will be normalized!

The function Integral( ) calculates the integral $I = \int_{t_1}^{t_2} f(t)\, dt$ by means of Simpson's formula

$$I \approx \frac{dt}{3} \left[f(t_1) + 4 \sum_{k=0}^{n-1} f\big(a + (2k+1)dt\big) + 2 \sum_{k=1}^{n-1} f\big(a + 2k\, dt\big) + f(t_2) \right] \qquad (1)$$

$(dt = (t_2 - t_1)/n)$. The values t_1 and t_2 are the limits of the integral. The function f has to be defined via prototype *before* the calling of Integral( ). The number n tells the function how many intervals are to be taken (number of nodes in Simpson's formula). Default value is $n = 100$, which should be sufficient for most cases. (Choosing too high a value for n usually just increases the calculation time.)

Example:

// First the code of the function that is to be integrated.

```
Real f( Real t )
{
    return 1 / ( 1 + t * t );
}
```

```
// Now we can integrate the function
int number_of_nodes = 200;
Real t1 = 0, t2 = 1;
Real x = 4 * Integral( f, t1, t2, number_of_nodes );
    // In this case, we have x = π because of ∫₀¹ (1/√(1+t²)) dt = arctan 1 = π/4.
```

In this case, we have $x = \pi$ because of $\int_0^1 \frac{1}{\sqrt{1+t^2}} dt = \arctan 1 = \frac{\pi}{4}$.

Since the code of the function Integral( ) is short and might be useful, we give a listing:

    Real Integral(Real (*f)(Real), Real t1, Real t2, int n)

```
{
   if ( n % 2 ) n++;  // n should be even
   int sign = Signum( t2 − t1 );
   if ( sign == 0 )
      return 0;
   if ( sign < 0 )
   {
      Real temp;
      SwapElements( t1, t2, temp );
   }
   // Simpson's formula for the area below the curve ( = integral )
   Real area = f( t1 ) + f( t2 );
   Real dt = ( t2 − t1 ) / n;
   Real t = t1 + dt:
   int i, m = 4;
   for ( i = 1; i < n; i++ )
   {
      area += m * f( t );
      m = 6 − m; // m = 2 alternates with m = 4
      t += dt:
   }
   return sign * area * dt / 3;
}
```

Transparency (Opacity)

The following command allows you to draw transparent polygons or lines:

void SetOpacity(Real alpha);

> • OPEN GEOMETRY—Routine (prototype in `"useful.h"`)
>
> Enables OPENGL opacity (nontransparency or transparency, respectively).
>
> *Example:*
>
> SetOpacity(0.5);
>
> will draw the following graphic elements semitransparently. The parameter alpha must be in the interval $[0, 1]$. SetOpacity(1) means no transparency (default), SetOpacity(0) means fully transparent, i.e., invisible. (However, when the z-buffer is activated, this has an effect on a 3D drawing!)

OPENGL allows different kinds of transparencies. We therefore give a listing of the routine for those users who want to adapt it for their purposes.

```
void SetOpacity( Real alpha )
{
```

```
if ( alpha > 0.9999 )
{
    glDisable( GL_BLEND );
    Global.AlphaValue = (GLfloat) 1;
}
else
{
    if ( alpha < 0 || alpha > 1 )
        SafeExit("0 <=alpha <=1 requested");
    glEnable( GL_BLEND );
    glBlendFunc( GL_SRC_ALPHA, GL_ONE_MINUS_SRC_ALPHA );
    Global.AlphaValue = (GLfloat) alpha;
}
}
```

Creation of an "Aura"

void CreateAura(*ThinOrThick* style);

> • OPEN GEOMETRY—Routine (prototype in `"useful.h"`)

> Creates an aura around lines in 3-space. This may be very useful to support spatial imagination. After the (curved or straight) line has been drawn, the option is automatically turned off. The parameter is the linestyle in which the aura is drawn and it should be "thicker" than the line style of the line that is drawn. This is done by typing *MEDIUM*, *THICK*, or *VERY_THICK* (see `enums.h`), as shown in the following sample code:

> *Example:*

> ```
> P3d P( 1, 2, 0 ), Q ( 2, 0, 5 );
> CreateAura( THICK );
> StraightLine3d( PureGreen, P, Q, THIN );
> ```

> will first draw the line in background color and "thick." Thus, parts of the scene that are behind this aura are erased. Then the line is drawn as usual.

Another example is given in the listing that creates Figure 3.1 on page 86.

Commands for Writing on the Graphics Screen

void ShowString(**const char** *text);

> • OPEN GEOMETRY—Routine (prototype in `"useful.h"`)

> Displays a string (text) on the screen.

Example:

> ShowString("Exit by user");

will display

> Exit by user

void ShowInteger(const char *text, **int** value);
> - OPEN GEOMETRY—Routine (prototype in "useful.h")

Displays the value of an integer variable on the screen.

Example:

> **int** a = 3, b = 4, c = a * b;
> ShowInteger("value of c = " , c);

will result in

> value of c = 12

void ShowReal(const char *text, *Real* value);
> - OPEN GEOMETRY—Routine (prototype in "useful.h")

Displays the value of a real (**double** or **float**) variable on the screen
(max. five digits after the comma).

Example:

> *Real* a = 3, b = 4;
> ShowReal("hyp = " , sqrt(a * a + b * b));

will result in

> hyp = 5.00000

void PrintString(Color col, *Real* x, *Real* y, **char** *s, . . .);
> - OPEN GEOMETRY—Routine (prototype in "useful.h")

This is a very useful routine that allows you to display almost everything on the screen at the position (x, y). The low-quality output is
pixel-oriented; the high-quality output is vector-oriented. The so-called
ellipsis (. . .) works just like in C++:

Example 1:

> PrintString(*Black*, 0, 0, "t[%d] = %14.10f" , i, t);

will result in something like

> t[4] = -0.0000451523

(starting in the center of the screen).

Example 2:

> PrintString(Green, -10, -10, "$alpha$ = %.2f°" , a);

will result in something like

$\alpha = 30.07°$

(or $alpha$ = 30.07° with low-quality output),[1] starting in the lower left corner of the screen.[2]

Example 3:

PrintString(Black, -3, -5, "Salary = %10.2$Dollar$", the_salary);

will print something like

Salary = 2100.00$

more or less centered in the lower part of the screen.[3]

Example 4:

PrintString(Black, -3, -5, "\"quoted text\"");

In order to write a double quote ("), you have to protect the double quote by means of a backslash (\). This is due to the fact that C syntax does not allow double quotes inside strings.
The output is

"quoted text"

Example 5: This sample code additionally shows how the function QuadrEquation( ) works. It returns the number of real solutions for the equation $a x^2 + b x + c = 0$. When the solutions are complex conjugate, the variables x_1 and x_2 are the real and the imaginary part of the complex solutions $z_{12} = x_1 \pm i x_2$ (where i is the imaginary unit).

```
// How to solve a quadratic equation
Real x1, x2; // the solutions
int n; // number of solutions
n = QuadrEquation( 1, 2, 5, x1, x2 );
if ( n == 2 )
    PrintString( Black, -5, 0,
        "two real solutions:x1 =%.5f,x2 =%.5f", x1, x2 );
```

---

[1]The Greek letters are written as they are spelled, enclosed by $ signs: $beta$, $gamma$, $delta$, eta, $iota$, $kappa$, $epsilon$, mu, nu, pi, $zeta$, $theta$, chi, rho, $sigma$, tau, etc., will show as β, γ, δ, η, ι, κ, ε, μ, ν, π, ζ, θ, χ, ϱ, σ, τ, etc. Capital Greek letters begin with a capital Roman letter: $Omega$, Psi, $Lambda$, Xi, etc., and will produce the output Ω, Ψ, Λ, Ξ etc.

[2]PrintString always interprets the coordinates x and y as 2D coordinates. When we do 3D drawing, the output is written into a plane perpendicular to the main projection ray. As a result, the writing appears undistorted.

[3]The $ sign has to be spelled as $Dollar$, since it is interpreted as the beginning or the end of a character name.

```
        else if ( n == 1 )
            PrintString( Black, −5, 0,
                "double solution:x1 =x2 =%.5f", x1 );
        else
            PrintString( Black, −5, 0,
                "complex solutions:z =%.5f +-i *%.5f", x1, x2 );
```

void HiQuality(**Boolean** on_off);

> • OPEN GEOMETRY—Routine (prototype in `"useful.h"`)

Enables (disables) a high-quality output, e.g., vectorized letters. It also does line drawing in high quality (the difference is enormous when we draw thicker lines!), and it draws "smoother" circles. By default, high quality is disabled for reasons of speed (line drawing is done considerably more slowly). For printouts, or for when scaled letters are used, high-quality is automatically enabled.

Example:

> HiQuality( );

has the same effect as

> HiQuality(*true*);

void ScaleLetters(*Real* tx, *Real* ty = 0);

> • OPEN GEOMETRY—Routine (prototype in `"useful.h"`)

Letters can be scaled by this function.

Example 1:

> ScaleLetters(3);

has the same effect as

> ScaleLetters(3, 3);

and produces letters that are three times as large as standard letters.

Example 2:

> ScaleLetters(1.5, 1);

produces letters with 50% increased height and the same width as the standard letters.

void InclineLetters(*Real* degrees);

> • OPEN GEOMETRY—Routine (prototype in `"useful.h"`)

Letters will be inclined by this function.

Example:

> InclineLetters(75);

creates slanted letters.

InclineLetters automatically forces high-quality letters. Reflected letters can be achieved with negative inclination angles. Only angles between $-180°$ and $180°$ are allowed.

void RestoreLetters( );
> • OPEN GEOMETRY—Routine (prototype in `"useful.h"`)

Restores letters (original size, no inclination). This command is important when you change the letter size in the main routine

> Scene::Draw( )

(if not applied, this will most probably result in unexpected behavior of the program, when several frames are drawn).

void WriteNice(**Color** *col*, **char** *Text,
>   *Real* x, *Real* y, *Real* rot_deg,
>   *Real* opacity $= 1$, **Plane** &TextPlane = XYplane);

> • OPEN GEOMETRY—Routine (prototype in `"useful.h"`)

For 2D drawing, this routine is similar to the PrintString routine. Additionally, it allows you to rotate the text and to set an α-value for transparency ($0 \le \alpha \le 1$, default is $\alpha = 1$). When 3D drawing is done, the text is interpreted three dimensionally and put by default into the xy-plane.

Example 1:

> WriteNice(LightBlue, `"$Omega$"` , 0, 0, 30, 8);

When drawing two dimensionally, this command produces the Greek letter Ω, starting at the origin, rotated through $30°$, scaled by the factor 8.0 nontransparent.

When 3D mode is applied, the letter is put into the xy-plane and is rotated about the z-axis through $30°$.

Example 2:

> WriteNice(LightBlue, `"Hello world"` , 0, 0, 0, 4, 0.5, YZplane);

will write

> `Hello world`

into the yz-plane at position $(0, 0)$, no rotation, scale factor 4, α-value (opacity) 0.5.

Sorting

C provides sorting routines for the standard variable types. The call of the corresponding routine **qsort( )**, however, requires some experience, as one has to pass a pointer to a comparison function. OPEN GEOMETRY provides an easy-to-handle sorting routine for different types of variables.

void QSort(**int** size, **int** *array, **int** sgn = 1);
- OPEN GEOMETRY—Routine (prototype in `"useful.h"`)

  A one-dimensional field of integers (**array**) can be sorted by increasing and decreasing size. As a result, the contents of the array is changed.

  Example:

    int x[6] = { 5, 4, 3, 1, 10, -3 };
    QSort(6, x, -1);

  changes the array to

    { 10, 5, 4, 3, 1, -3 }.

void QSort(**int** size, *Real* *array, **int** sgn = 1);
- OPEN GEOMETRY—Routine (prototype in `"useful.h"`)

  Same as above with array of *Real* variables (**GLdouble**).

  Example:

    GLdouble x[6] = { 5.0, 4.0, 3.0, 1.0, 10.0, -3.0 };
    QSort(6, x);

  changes the array to

    { -3.0, 1.0, 3.0, 4.0, 5.0, 10.0 }.

  When you want to sort an array of **float** variables, this can be done with a "dirty trick," as long as the comparison

    sizeof(**int**) == **sizeof**(**float**)

  is true on your computer:

    float x[6] = { 5.0f, 4.0f, 3.0f, 1.0f, 10.0f, -3.0f };
    QSort(6, (**int** *) x);

  The same trick works for sorting pointers by size, as long as the comparison

    sizeof(**int**) == **sizeof**(**void** *)

  is true on your computer.[4]

---

[4]At the current state of technology, this is probably true on any platform. It may easily be, however, that this standard is changed in the future, e.g., in order to be able to handle more than 2^{32} bytes = $4GB$ RAM. So be careful with such tricks! You should at least include the following line somewhere in your program:

    if (**sizeof**(**int**) <> **sizeof**(**void** *))
        SafeExit(`"sorting of pointers will not work! "`);

A good optimizing compiler will remove the two lines from your code anyway, when the sorting works.

How to Exit the Program Safely

The following routine should be used to exit an OPEN GEOMETRY program.

void SafeExit(**char** ∗txt);

> • OPEN GEOMETRY—Routine (prototype in `"globals.h"`)
>
> When testing routines or any other code, it is often very useful to be able to make a safe exit with a user-defined message.
>
> *Example:*
>
> SafeExit(`"Divison by zero in my program"`);

Another Useful Function

char ∗StrCat(**const char** ∗s1, **const char** ∗s2);

> • OPEN GEOMETRY—Routine (prototype in `"globals.h"`)
>
> This OPEN GEOMETRY function does more or less the same job as the C function
>
> strcat(**char** ∗s1, **char** ∗s2)
>
> which appends s2 to s1 and terminates the resulting string with a null character. (The initial character of s2 overwrites the terminating null character of s1.) In contrast to the ordinary C function, StrCat checks overflow. Also, the behavior of StrCat is not undefined if the source and destination strings overlap. Always use StrCat instead of strcat in order to avoid hard-to-find errors (we had such errors several times, until we introduced our own function!). Typical examples, where the use of StrCat is important, are the functions SafeExit and ShowString.
>
> *Example:*
>
> ```
> char  name[ ] = "abd";
> if ( strcmp( name, "abc" ) )
>     ShowString( strcat("wrong name <", strcat(name, ">") ) );
> ```
>
> will cause a memory error. Use StrCat and it works.
>
> Here is a listing of the code of StrCat:
>
> ```
> char *StrCat( char *s1, char *s2 )
> {
>     static char Buffer [5] [512];
>     static int i = −1;
>     if ( strlen( s1 ) + strlen( s2 ) >= 512 )
>         TextBox( "warning:text in StrCat()too large");
>     i = ( i + 1 ) % 5;
> ```

```
        sprintf( Buffer[i], "%s%s", s1, s2 );
        return Buffer[i];
}
```

3.2 Vectors and Points

Vectors in 2-Space and 3-Space

The following **class** *V23d* is the base for 2D and 3D vectors, and also for 2D and 3D points:

class *V23d;*   → declaration in `"vector.h"`
> Base class for the following classes.

Constructors:

> *V23d*( ); // No initialization
> *V23d*(*Real* x0, *Real* y0, *Real* z0 = 0);
> > // With two parameters, initialization $(x0, y0, 0)$,
> > // else with $(x0, y0, z0)$

Operators:

> **void operator** ( ) (*Real* x0, *Real* y0);
> > // The components are set to $(x0, y0, 0)$
> **void operator** ( ) (*Real* x0, *Real* y0, *Real* z0);
> > // The components are set to $(x0, y0, z0)$
> **void operator** *= (*Real* t);
> > // Scaling with t
> **void operator** /= (*Real* t);
> > // Scaling with $1/t$
> *V23d* **operator** −( ) **const**;
> > // Scaling with -1
> **void operator** = (**const** *V23d* &v);
> > // Like ordinary = operator
> **void operator** = (*Vector* v);
> > // Assigns the values (v[0], v[1], v[2]) (v...array of **Real**s)
> *Boolean* **operator** == (**const** *V23d* &v) **const**;
> > // Checks if two vectors are identical (tiny tolerance)
> *Boolean* **operator** != (**const** *V23d* &v);
> > // Checks if two vectors are different (tiny tolerance)

Methods:

> **void** Print(**char** *text = "@", **int** dim = 3) **const**;
> // Displays the components as a message: 'text = (x, y, z)'.
> // When dim = 2 is chosen, the output is 'text = (x, y)'.
> **void** Normalize(*V23d* &norm) **const**;
> // Normalizes the vector and stores the new components in 'norm'
> **void** Normalize( );
> // Normalizes the vector ⇒ unit vector

class *V2d;*   → declaration in "vector.h"

> Describes a two-dimensional vector (x, y). Inherits the methods and operators of *V23d* (partly overwritten!).

Constructors:

> *V2d*( ); // No initialization
> *V2d*(*Real* x0, *Real* y0); // Initialization with $(x0, y0)$
> *V2d*(**const** *P2d* &P, **const** *P2d* &Q); // Init. with $\overrightarrow{PQ} = \vec{q} - \vec{p}$

Additional or overwriting operators:

> **friend** *V2d* **operator** + (**const** *V2d* &v, **const** *V2d* &w);
> // Vector addition $\vec{v} + \vec{w}$
> **friend** *V2d* **operator** − (**const** *V2d* &v, **const** *V2d* &w);
> // Vector subtraction $\vec{v} - \vec{w}$
> **void operator** += (**const** *V2d* &v);
> // Analogon to += operator of ordinary numbers
> **void operator** −= (**const** *V2d* &v);
> // Analogon to −= operator of ordinary numbers
> **friend** *Real* **operator** * (**const** *V2d* &v, **const** *V2d* &w);
> // Dot product $\vec{v}\,\vec{w}$
> **friend** *V2d* **operator** * (**const** *Real* t, **const** *V2d* &v);
> // Scale vector with real number: $t\,\vec{v}$

Additional or overwriting methods:

> *Real* PolarAngleInDeg( ) **const**;
> // Returns the polar angle φ of the vector $(-180° < \varphi \leq 180°)$
> *V2d* NormalVector( ) **const**;
> // Rotates the vector through $+90°$
> *Boolean* Collinear(**const** *V2d* &v, *Real* tol = 0) **const**;
> // Returns true if the vector is collinear with $\vec{v}$, else false.
> // If no tolerance is set, a tiny default tolerance is used.
> **void** Reflect(**const** *StrL2d* &g);
> // Reflects the vector at a straight line g.

void Rotate(*Real* angle_in_deg);
// Rotates the vector through angle (in degrees).

Sample code for better understanding:

V2d v(3, 0); // Init components via constructor
v.Def(2, 1); // Set (define) components via method Def( )
v(5, −5); // Set components via ( )−operator
v.Normalize( );
v.Print("v"); // output 'v(0.707, -0.707)'
ShowReal("Polar angle is ", v.PolarAngleInDeg( ));
    // See 'ShowReal( )'
    // output 'Polar angle is -45.00000'
V2d u; // Default constructor
u = v.NormalVector( );
ShowReal("dot product =", u * v); // 'dot product = 0.00000'

---

class *V3d*; → declaration in `"vector.h"`

Describes a three-dimensional vector (x, y, z). Inherits the methods and operators of *V23d* and *V2d* (partly overwritten!).

Constructors:

V3d( ); // No initialization
V3d(*Real* x0, *Real* y0, *Real* z0); // Initialization with $(x0, y0, z0)$
V3d(**const** *P3d* &P, **const** *P3d* &Q); // Init. with $\overrightarrow{PQ} = \vec{q} - \vec{p}$

Additional or overwriting operators:

friend *V3d* **operator** + (**const** *V3d* &v, **const** *V3d* &w);
    // Vector addition $\vec{v} + \vec{w}$
friend *V3d* **operator** − (**const** *V3d* &v, **const** *V3d* &w);
    // Vector subtraction $\vec{v} - \vec{w}$
void operator += (**const** *V3d* &v);
    // Analogon to += operator of ordinary numbers
void operator −= (**const** *V3d* &v);
    // Analogon to −= operator of ordinary numbers
friend *V3d* **operator** * (**const** *Real* t, **const** *V3d* &v);
    // Scaling by a real number
friend *Real* **operator** * (**const** *V3d* &v, **const** *V3d* &w);
    // Dot product $\vec{v}\vec{w}$
friend *V3d* **operator** ^ (**const** *V3d* &v, **const** *V3d* &w);
    // Vector product $\vec{v} \times \vec{w}$

Additional or overwriting methods:

Real XYLength( );
  // Returns the length of the vector in (x, y)−projection: $\sqrt{x^2 + y^2}$
Real Slope( ) **const**;
  // Returns the elevation angle φ of the vector in degrees
  // $(-90° < \varphi \le 90°)$
void Cartesian(*Real* dist, *Real* azim_in_deg, *Real* elev_in_deg);
  // Calculates the Cartesian coordinates of a vector, where the
  // spherical coordinates (length, azimuth, and elevation in degrees)
  // are given.
void Spherical(*Real* &length,
                    Real &azim_in_deg, *Real* &elev_in_deg) **const**;
  // Calculates the spherical coordinates of a vector (length, azimuth,
  // and elevation in degrees) from its Cartesian coordinates x, y, z.
void MatrixMult(*RotMatrix* &A, *V3d* &result);
  // Multiplication by a rotation matrix (see RotMatrix)
void AssignTo(*Vector* v);
  // Copy vector to an array **double** [3]
void Rotate(**const** *V3d* &a, *Real* angle_in_deg);
  // Rotate about a vector
void Reflect(**const** *Plane* &e);
  // Reflect at a plane
Boolean Collinear(**const** *V3d* &v, *Real* tol = 1e−4) **const**;
  // Check if vector is collinear with another vector v.
  // Default tolerance is 1e−4
void OrthoBase(*V3d* &unit_vec1, *V3d* &unit_vec2);
  // Normalize vector and calculate two unit vectors so that the
  // three vectors form an ortho−base and unit_vec1 are horizontal.
  // Note that the vector is changed!

Sample code for better understanding:

```
V3d v( 3, 0, 1 ); // Init components via constructor
v.Def( 2, 1, 5 ); // Set (define) components via method Def( )
v( 5, -5, 5 * sqrt(2) ); // Set components via ( )−operator
v.Normalize( );
v.Print( "v" ); // output 'v( 0.5, -0.5, 0.707 )'
Real len, azim, elev;
v.Spherical( len, azim, elev );
ShowReal( "azim =", azim ); // 'azim = -45.00000'
ShowReal( "elev =", v.Slope( ) ); // 'elev = 45.00000'
v = Xdir; // ( 1, 0, 0 )
```

$$V3d \; \mathsf{y} \; = \; Ydir; \; // \; (0, \, 1, \, 0 \;)$$
$$V3d \; \mathsf{z} \; = \; \mathsf{v} \; {}^{\wedge} \; \mathsf{y}; \; // \; \vec{z} = \vec{v} \times \vec{y} = (0, 0, 1)^T = Zdir$$
$$Real \; \mathsf{dot\_product} \; = \; \mathsf{y} \; * \; \mathsf{z}; \; // \; 0$$

In OPEN GEOMETRY, the direction vectors of the coordinate axes are predefined: *Xdir*, *Ydir*, and *Zdir*. In 2-space you should use the *V2d* instances *Xdir2d*, *Ydir2d*.

Points in 2-Space and 3-Space

class *P23d*; → declaration in `"points.h"`

Describes a 2D or 3D point. Inherits the methods and operators of *V23d*, *V2d*, *V3d*.

Constructors:

P23d( ); // Default constructor; no initialization
P23d(*V23d* &v); // Initialization with a vector (V23d, V2d, V3d)

Additional operators:

// No operators

Additional methods:

void Mark(*Color* col, *Real* r1, *Real* r2 = 0, **int** Dim = 2) **const**;
// Mark a point with two filled concentric circles.
// Outer circle: radius r1, color = col.
// Inner circle: radius r2, col = background color.
// By default, the point is interpreted two dimensionally.
// See also P3d::Mark( )
Real Distance(**const** *P23d* &P) **const** ;
// Returns the distance from another point P
P23d InBetweenPoint(**const** *P23d* &other, *Real* t) **const**;
// Returns a point between the current point and another point.
// t = 0: the point itself, t = 1: the other point
// t = 0.5: the mid point, t = −1: the reflected point, etc.

In OPEN GEOMETRY, the origin of the coordinate system is predefined as *P23d Origin.*

class *P2d*; → declaration in `"points.h"`

Describes a 2D point $(x, \, y)$. Inherits the methods and operators of *P23d* and thus, also those of *V23d*, *V2d*, *V3d*.

Constructors:

// See V2d constructors

Additional operators:

inline friend *P2d* **operator** + (**const** *P2d* &v, **const** *V2d* &w);
inline friend *P2d* **operator** − (**const** *P2d* &v, **const** *V2d* &w);
    // Allows to add or subtract vectors to a point
inline friend *P2d* **operator** ∗ (**const** *Real* t, **const** *P2d* &v);
    // Scaling of a point. Overwrites vector scaling
inline friend *V2d* **operator** + (**const** *P2d* &v, **const** *P2d* &w)
inline friend *V2d* **operator** − (**const** *P2d* &v, **const** *P2d* &w)
    // Add or subtract points like vectors
P2d & **operator** = (**const** *P2d* &P);
P2d & **operator** = (**const** *P23d* &P);
P2d & **operator** = (**const** *V2d* &v);
    // Make these types compatible

Additional methods:

void Def(*Real* x0, *Real* y0);
    // Set coordinates to (x0, y0)
void Translate(*Real* dx, *Real* dy);
    // Translate point by means of the vector (dx, dy)
void Translate(**const** *V2d* &v);
    // Translate point by means of the vector v
void Rotate(**const** *P2d*& center, *Real* angle_in_deg);
    // Rotate point about a center through an angle given in degrees
void Scale(*Real* kx, *Real* ky);
    // Scale point in two directions (affine transformation)
void Write(*Color* col, *Real* x0, *Real* y0, **char** ∗ text, **int** size);
    // This will write the coodinates of the point in color col
    // at the position (x0, y0) in a legible manner:
    // 'text(x, y)' (3 digits after the comma).
    // Default char size is 1 unit
void AttachString(*Color* col, *Real* dx, *Real* dy, **char** ∗ text);
    // Writes an output in color col at the position (x + dx, y + dy).
    // You can write almost everything by means of C syntax
P2d Center(*P23d* &P);
    // Returns the center (midpoint) between the point and point P
Real PolarAngleInDeg( ) **const**;
    // See V2d;
void Reflect(**const** *StrL2d* &g);
    // Reflect the point at a straight line g

<u>class</u> *P3d;* → declaration in `"points.h"`

Describes a 3D point (x, y, z). Inherits the methods and operators of *P2d* and thus also of *V23d, V2d, V3d, P23d, P2d*.

Constructors:

P3d( ); // Default constructor; no initialization
P3d(*Real* x0, *Real* y0, *Real* z0); // Initialization with (x0, y0, z0)
P3d(*V3d* &v); // Initialization with a 3D vector

Overwriting operators:

inline friend *P3d* **operator** + (**const** *P3d* &v, **const** *V3d* &w);
inline friend *P3d* **operator** + (**const** *P3d* &v, **const** *P3d* &w);
inline friend *P3d* **operator** + (**const** *P3d* &v, **const** *V2d* &w);
inline friend *P3d* **operator** − (**const** *P3d* &v, **const** *V3d* &w);
inline friend *P3d* **operator** − (**const** *P3d* &v, **const** *P3d* &w)
inline friend *P3d* **operator** ∗ (**const** *Real* t, **const** *P3d* &v);
// Compatibility to the related classes
P3d & **operator** = (**const** *P3d* &P);
P3d & **operator** = (**const** *P2d* &P);
P3d **operator** = (**const** *V3d* &v);

Additional—partly overwriting—methods:

void Def(*Real* x0, *Real* y0, *Real* z0);
void Def2d(*Real* x0, *Real* y0);
void Def(*Vector* v);
// Three kinds of assigning values to the coordinates
P23d Image( ) **const**;
// Returns the intersection point of the projection
// ray with 'the image plane', i.e., a plane orthogonal
// to the main projection ray (and coinciding with the
// target point of the projection).
void Mark(*Color* col, *Real* r1, *Real* r2 = 0, **int** Dim = 3) **const**;
// Marks a point in space by means of two circles:
// Outer circle: Radius r1, color col
// Inner circle: Radius r2 (default = 0), color = background color
// The circles are interpreted three dimensionally!
void MarkPixel(*Color* col) **const**;
// Plots a pixel at the image of the point (see Image( ))
void AttachString(*Color* col, *Real* dx, *Real* dy, **char** ∗ text) **const**;
// Attaches a string to the point (at the 'Image' plus a
// 2D vector (dx, dy) in the 'image plane').
void Rotate(**const** *StrL3d* &axis, *Real* angle_in_deg);
// Rotates the point about an oriented straight line (the axis)
// through the given angle in degrees

void Rotate( );
 // Applies a predefined 3D rotation (see Rotation3d)
 // in order to speed up the code.
void Screw(**const** *StrL3d* &axis, *Real* angle_in_deg, *Real* parameter);
 // Applies a helical motion, given by the axis and parameter
void Screw(**const** *HelicalMotion* &S);
 // Applies a "screw motion" (helical motion) (see HelicalMotion).
void Translate(*Real* dx, *Real* dy, *Real* dz);
 // Translate point by means of the vector (dx, dy, dz)
void Translate(**const** *V3d* &v);
 // Translate point by means of the vector v
void Scale(*Real* kx, *Real* ky, *Real* kz)
 // Applies extended scaling (affine transformation)
void Reflect(**const** *Plane* &e);
 // Reflects the point at the plane.
Real DistFromPlane(**const** *Plane* &e) **const**;
 // Returns the oriented distance from the plane.
Boolean IsInPlane(**const** *Plane* &e, *Real* tol = 1e−4) **const**;
 // Checks if the point coincides with the plane
 // (default tolerance 1e−4)
Real Dist2(*P3d* &P) **const**;
 // Returns the square of the distance to a point.
 // Sometimes, this helps to speed up code, since no sqrt is needed.
Real Dist_in_xy_projection(*P3d* &P) **const**;
 // Returns the distance to another space point in a top view.
P3d Center(*P3d* &P) **const**;
 // Midpoint between the point and another point P
Boolean Collinear(**const** *P3d* &P, **const** *P3d* &Q,
 // *Real* tol = 1e−4) **const**;
 // Checks if the point coincides with the straight line PQ
 // (default tolerance 1e−4).
void Inversion(**const** *Sphere* &sphere);
 // Inverts the point at a given sphere (see Sphere)

3.3 Straight Lines

class *StrL2d;* → declaration in `"strl2d.h"`

Describes an oriented straight line in 2-space. Base class.

Constructors:

StrL2d( ); // Dummy constructor. No initialization.
StrL2d(**const** *P23d* &P, **const** *V23d* &r);
 // The line is given by a point and a direction vector.

// The direction vector will be normalized in any case.
// See also method Def( ).
StrL2d(**const** *P2d* &P, **const** *P2d* &Q);
// The line is given by two points.

Operators:

friend *P2d* **operator** $*$ (**const** *StrL2d* &g1, **const** *StrL2d* &g2);
// Intersection point of two straight lines g_1 and g_2.
// When the lines are parallel, a "point of infinity" is taken,
// when the lines are identical, the result is an arbitrary point
// on the line. See also method **SectionWithStraightLine( )**
Boolean **operator** $==$ (**const** *StrL2d* &other) **const**;
// Are two lines identical from the mathematical point of view?

Methods:

// First some methods to define the straight line.

void Def(**const** *P23d* &P, **const** *V23d* &r);
// Define line by means of a point and a direction vector:
// $\vec{x} = \vec{P} + \lambda \vec{r}$
// The vector need not be normalized (it will be normalized to a
// direction vector $\vec{r}_0$).
// Internally, the line has the equation $\vec{x} = \vec{P} + t\,\vec{r}_0$.
// 3D points and 3D vectors are interpreted two dimensionally.
void Def(**const** *P2d* &P, **const** *P2d* &Q);
// Define line by means of two points. Internally, the line has
// the equation $\vec{x} = \vec{P} + t\,\vec{r}_0$ with $\vec{r} = \vec{Q} - \vec{P}$.

// Now some 'mathematical' methods.

V2d GetDir( ) **const**;
// Returns the normalized direction vector $\vec{r}_0$.
P2d GetPoint( ) **const**;
// Returns the point that was used for the definition of the line.
V2d GetNormalVector( ) **const**;
// Returns the normalized normal vector $\vec{n} \perp \vec{r}_0$.
Real GetConst( ) **const**;
// Returns the constant c of the straight line $n_x\,x + n_y\,y = c$.
void SetDir(**const** *V2d* &newdir);
// Change direction vector (newdir need not be normalized)
void SectionWithStraightLine(**const** *StrL2d* &g, *P23d* &P,
            Real &t, *Boolean* &parallel) **const**;
// Similar to the $*$ operator. The result, however, is more detailed:

// The parameter t to the point (with respect to the current
// line) is passed by reference, and the flag parallel is set.
Real OrientedDistance(*P23d* &P);
  // Returns the oriented distance of a point. When the origin of the
  // coordinate system is not on the same side of the straight line,
  // the distance will be negative.
P2d InBetweenPoint(*Real* t) **const**;
  // Returns the point $\vec{x} = \vec{P} + t\,\vec{r}_0$.
Real GetParameter(**const** *P2d* &P) **const**;
  // Returns the parameter t in the vector equation $\vec{x} = \vec{P} + t\,\vec{r}_0$.
StrL2d GetNormal(**const** *P2d* &P) **const**;
  // Returns a straight line perpendicular to the current one,
  // coinciding with P.
StrL2d GetParallel(*Real* dist) **const**;
  // Returns a str. line parallel to the current one with distance dist.
P2d NormalProjectionOfPoint(**const** *P2d* &P) **const**;
  // Returns the normal projection of the point P onto the line.
Boolean IsParallel(**const** *StrL2d* &other, *Real* tol = 1e−8) **const**;
  // Checks if the lines are parallel. The angle between the direction
  // vectors must not differ more than a certain tolerance.
Boolean ContainsPoint(**const** *P2d* &P, *Real* tol = 1e−4) **const**;
  // Checks if a point coincides with the line, i.e., if its distance is
  // smaller than a given tolerance.

// Some methods for the application of transformations.

void Translate(**const** *V2d* &v);
  // Translate the line by means of a 2D vector
void Rotate(**const** *P2d* &center, *Real* angle_in_deg);
  // Rotate line about a center through a given angle (in degrees).
void Reflect(**const** *StrL2d* &g);
  // Reflect the line at a given line g.

// Finally some drawing methods:

void Draw(*Color* col, *Real* t1, *Real* t2, *ThinOrThick* thick) **const**;
  // Draws the line in color col from the point that corresponds
  // to the parameter t_1 to the point that corresponds to the
  // parameter t_2. You have to specify the width of the line:
  // THIN, MEDIUM, THICK, VERY_THICK.
void LineDotted(*Color* col, *Real* t1, *Real* t2, **int** n,
     ThinOrThick thick) **const**;
  // Similar to the ordinary drawing.
  // Draws the line as dash-dot, with n intervals.

void Dotted(*Color* col, *Real* t1, *Real* t2, **int** n, *Real* rad) **const**;
// Similar to the ordinary drawing; draws the line dotted
// (n 'dots', i.e, small circles with radius **rad**).

Sample code for better understanding:

P2d P(5, 0), Q(0, 5);
StrL2d a(P, Q);
// In order to draw the line PQ, you can use
// the routine StraightLine2d( ):
StraightLine2d(*Black*, P, Q, *THIN*);
// The following statement has exactly the same effect:
a.Draw(*Black*, 0 , P.Distance(Q), *THIN*);
StrL2d b = a;
// Now rotate the line b through 50 degrees
P2d Center(0, 0);
b.Rotate(Center, 50);
b.Dotted(*Black*, 0 , P.Distance(Q), 20, 0.1);
P2d S = a * b; // The intersection point
S.Mark(*Gray*, 0.2, 0.1);

For convenience, OPEN GEOMETRY supports a type *Rod2d*, which is actually a "polygon with two vertices" (see *Poly2d*).

class *Rod2d;* → declaration in `"strl2d.h"`
Describes a "rod." Derived from *Poly2d*.

Definitions:

void Def(*Color* col, *Real* x1, *Real* y1, *Real* x2, *Real* y2);
void Def(*Color* col, **const** *P2d* &P, **const** *P2d* &Q);

Additional methods (see also Poly2d):

void Draw(*ThinOrThick* thick);
void Dotted(**int** n, *Real* rad); // Radius of tiny circles
void LineDotted(**int** n, *ThinOrThick* thick);

Sample code for better understanding:

Rod2d rod;
rod.Def(*Magenta*, −5, 0, 0, 5);

```
rod.Draw( THICK );
rod.Rotate( Origin, 45 );
rod.Dotted( 20, 0.05 );
```

class *StrL3d;* → declaration in `"strl3d.h"`

Describes a straight line in 3-space. Base class.

Constructors:

```
// See also constructors for StrL2d
StrL3d( ); // Default constructor
StrL3d( const P3d &P, const V3d &r ); // Point + direction
StrL3d( const P3d &P, const P3d &Q ); // 2 points
```

Operators:

friend *P3d* **operator** ∗ (**const** *StrL3d* &g, **const** *StrL3d* &h);
friend *P3d* **operator** ∗ (**const** *Plane* &plane, **const** *StrL3d* &s);

Methods:

// First some methods to define the straight line.
void Def(**const** *P3d* &P, **const** *V3d* &r);
// Define line by means of a point and a direction vector:
// $\vec{x} = \vec{P} + \lambda \vec{r}$
// The vector need not be normalized (it will be normalized to a
// direction vector $\vec{r}_0$ automatically).
// Internally, the line has the equation $\vec{x} = \vec{P} + t\,\vec{r}_0$.
void Def(**const** *P3d* &P, **const** *P3d* &Q);
// Define line by means of two points. Internally, the line has
// the equation $\vec{x} = \vec{P} + t\vec{r}_0$ with $\vec{r} = \vec{Q} - \vec{P}$.

// Now some "mathematical" methods.

V3d GetDir( ) **const**;
// Returns the normalized direction vector $\vec{r}_0$.
P3d GetPoint( ) **const**;
// Returns the point that was used for the definition of the line.
void SetDir(**const** *V3d* &newdir);
// Change direction vector (**newdir** need not be normalized)
Real Distance(*P3d* &P) **const**;
// Returns the distance of a point ($>= 0$)
P3d InBetweenPoint(*Real* t) **const**;
// Returns the point $\vec{x} = \vec{P} + t\,\vec{r}_0$.

Real GetParameter(*P3d* &P) **const** ;
// Returns the parameter t in the vector equation $\vec{x} = \vec{P} + t\,\vec{r}_0$.
P3d NormalProjectionOfPoint(**const** *P3d* &P^) **const**;
// Returns the normal projection of the point dist onto the line.
Boolean IsParallel(**const** *StrL3d* &other, *Real* tol = 1e−8) **const**;
// Checks if the lines are parallel. The angle between the direction
// vectors must not differ by more than a certain tolerance.
void CommonNormal(**const** *StrL3d* &g, *V3d* &dir,
        P3d &F, *P3d* &Fg) **const**;
// Determines the common normal of the line and the str. line g.
// F and Fg are the feet of this line, dir is the
// direction of the common normal.

// Some methods for the application of transformations.

void Translate(*V3d* &v);
// Translate the line by means of a 3D vector
void Rotate(*StrL3d* &a, *Real* angle_in_deg);
// Rotate the line about a 3D axis through a given angle (in deg).
void Screw(*HelicalMotion* &S);
// Apply a helical motion.
void Reflect(**const** *Plane* &e);
// Reflect at a plane

// Drawing routines

void Draw(*Color* f, *Real* t1, *Real* t2, *ThinOrThick* thick,
        Real offset = *STD_OFFSET*) **const**;
// Draws the line in color col from the point that corresponds
// to the parameter t_1 to the point that corresponds to the
// parameter t_2. You have to specify the width of the line:
// THIN, MEDIUM, THICK, VERY_THICK.
// When the line is to be drawn on a polygon, one should
// use an offset (otherwise the z-buffer will have some
// side-effects), which we will describe later on.
void LineDotted(*Color* col, *Real* t1, *Real* t2, **int** n,
        ThinOrThick thick, *Real* offset = *STD_OFFSET*) **const**;
// Similar to the ordinary drawing.
// Draws the line line-dotted, with n intervals.
void Dotted(*Color* col, *Real* t1, *Real* t2, **int** n, *Real* rad) **const**;
// Similar to the ordinary drawing; draws the line dotted
// (n 'dots', i.e, small circles (pseudospheres) with radius rad).

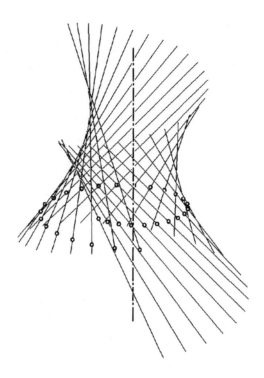

FIGURE 3.1. The output of the sample program for straight lines in 3-space.

Listing of program BOOK/straight_lines3d.cpp (Figure 3.1):

```
// Draw the straight lines on a general-ruled helical surface
// and mark their intersection points on the xy-plane.
P3d P( 2, 0, 0 );
V3d dir( 0, 1, -1 );
StrL3d s( P, dir );
const int max = 30;
Real angle = 360.0 / max;
Real delta_z = angle / 70;
HelicalMotion H( Zaxis, angle, delta_z );
for ( int i = 0; i < max; i++ )
{
    CreateAura( MEDIUM );
    s.Draw( Black, -4, 7, THIN );
    P3d S = XYplane * s; // Intersection with xy-plane.
    S.Mark( Black, 0.08, 0.04 );
    s.Screw( H );
}
```

CreateAura(*VERY_THICK*);
Zaxis.LineDotted(*Black*, −5.0, 7.0, 20, *MEDIUM*);

In OPEN GEOMETRY, three axes are predefined: *Xaxis*, *Yaxis*, and *Zaxis*. These are identical with the Cartesian coordinate axes.

For convenience, OPEN GEOMETRY also supports a class *Rod3d* (derived from *Poly3d*). Its definitions and methods are quite similar to those of class *Rod2d*.

3.4 Planes

In Chapter 1, we discussed the development of the class *Plane*. We also gave a listing of the implementation for this class. Here we just quickly repeat the major methods:

class *Plane*; → declaration in `"plane.h"`
        Plane in 3-space. Base class.

Constructors:

    Plane( ); // Default constructor.
    Plane(**const** *P3d* &P, **const** *P3d* &Q, **const** *P3d* &R);
      // Three noncollinear points determine a plane.
    Plane(**const** *P3d* &P, **const** *V3d* &n);
      // Point plus normal vector.
    Plane(**const** *P3d* &P, **const** StraightLine &g);
      // Point plus noncoinciding straight line.
    Plane(**const** *Rod3d* &PQ);
      // The plane is defined as symmetry plane of a rod.

Equivalent definitions:

    void Def( ); // Default constructor.
    void Def(**const** *P3d* &P, **const** *P3d* &Q, **const** *P3d* &R);
    void Def(**const** *P3d* &P, **const** *V3d* &n);
    void Def(**const** *P3d* &P, **const** StraightLine &g);
    void Def(**const** *Rod3d* &PQ);

Operators and methods:

    friend *P3d* **operator** ∗ (**const** *Plane* &e, **const** *StrL3d* &g);
      // const: Intersection of plane and straight line.
    friend *StrL3d* **operator** ∗ (**const** *Plane* &e, **const** *Plane* &f);
      // const: Intersection line of two planes.

V3d n( ) **const** { **return** normal; }
// Returns the normalized normal vector.
Real c( ) **const** { **return** constant; }
// Returns the constant.
P3d GetPoint( ) **const** { **return** point; }
// Returns a point of the plane.
void Translate(**const** *V3d* &v);
// Translates the plane.
void Rotate(**const** *StrL3d* &a, **const** *Real* w);
// Rotates the plane.
void SectionWithStraightLine(**const** StraightLine &g,
    P3d &S, *Real* &t) **const**;
// Similar to the ∗ operator, but more detailed.
Real OrientedDistance(**const** *P3d* &P) **const**;
// Returns the oriented distance of a point from the plane.
Real Angle(**const** *Plane* &e) **const**;
// Returns the angle between two planes (in arc length!).
Real AngleInDeg(**const** *Plane* &e) **const**
// Returns the angle between two planes (degrees!).
P3d NormalProj(**const** *P3d* &P) **const**;
// Returns the normal projection of a point onto the plane.

3.5 Geometrical "Objects"

The word "object" is a very comprehensive word, not only in daily life, but also in terms of programming. Since we deal mainly with geometry, an object in a narrower sense may be a "conglomerate of points." For some reason it turned out to be useful to introduce an abstract base class *O23d*, and to derive two classes *O2d* and *O3d* from this class. Geometrical objects contain dynamic memory. Thus, they are supplied both with constructors and destructors.

All three classes are abstract in the sense that the user will usually not declare instances of such a class but rather declare instances of classes that are derived from these classes. The following table shows the most important dependencies in the OPEN GEOMETRY hierarchy:

Base classes in 2-space or 3-space:
  V23d ... vectors
    P23d ... points
  O23d ... conglomerate of points

Major base classes in 2-space:

    V2d ... vectors; actually derived from *V23d*

    P2d ... points; actually derived from *V2d*

    StrL2d ... straight lines (infinite)

    Conic ... conic sections

    O2d ... conglomerate of points in 2-space

        Circ2d ... ordinary circles

        L2d ... curved lines

            ParamCurve2d ... lines given via equations

            PathCurve2d ... path curves during a movement

        Poly2d ... polygons

            Rod2d ... bar between two points

            Rect2d ... rectangles

            RegPoly2d ... regular polygons

            ComplexPoly2d ... complex polygons (nonconvex, loops)

Major base classes in 3-space:

    V3d ... vectors; actually derived from *V23d*

    P3d ... points; actually derived from *V3d*

    StrL3d ... straight lines (infinite)

    Plane ... infinite planes

    Conic3d ... planar conic sections in space

    O3d ... conglomerate of points in 2-space*:*

        L3d ... curved lines

            PathCurve3d ... given via equations

            ParamCurve3d ... path curve during movement

            Spline3d ... cubic splines

        Poly3d ... polygons

            Rod3d ... straight line (finite)

            Rect3d ... rectangles

            RegPoly3d ... regular polygons

                Circ3d ... circles in 3-space

            ComplexPoly3d ... nonconvex polygons, polygons with loops

    Box ... parallelepipedum

    RegFrustum ... regular frustums

        RegPrism ... regular prisms

        RegPyramid ... regular pyramids

    ParamSurface ... parameterized surfaces

        SurfOfRevol ... surfaces of revolution

    Polyhedron ... polyhedra, consisting of convex faces

    Solid ... complex closed polyhedra consisting of complex faces

The class *O23d* stores some very elementary data like the number of points, a dynamic array of (two- or three-dimensional) points, and color information. For detailed information, please look at the header file `o23d.h`.

<u>class *O23d*;</u> → declaration in "o23d.h"

Describes a conglomerate of points in 3-space. Base class.

Defining (allocating) and deleting objects:

void Def(*Color* col, **int** numOfPoints) ;
void Delete( ) ;

Operators:

void operator = (*O23d* &other) ; // Copy one object to another
P3d &**operator** [ ] (**int** i) ; // Access to the points

Methods common to all objects:

int Size( ) ;
  // Returns the number of points.
void ChangeColor(*Color* new_color) ;
  // Allows to change the color of the object.
P23d GetBaryCenter( ) **const**;
  // Bary center...average coordinates of all points.
  // Works in 2-space and 3-space.
void GetBoundingBox(*Box* &bbox) **const**;
  // Bounding box with axis-parallel sides.
  // In 2-space, the box is flat.

The copy operator works as expected: it copies color information, the size of the conglomerate, and the coordinates of the points. The points can be set by means of the [ ] operator:

Sample code for better understanding:

```
O23d A, B;
A.Def( Green, 3 ); // Three points
A[1] = P3d( 1, 0, 0 ); // Index starts with 1
A[2] = P3d( 0, 1, 0 );
A[3] = P3d( 0, 0, 1 );
B = A; // Copies all the points
A.Delete( ); // Destroys A
```

The above code works both for 2D and 3D objects. Please note two important things that are true for all OPEN GEOMETRY objects with dynamic memory:

- The index of the points starts with 1. The reason for this is somehow "historical." (The predecessor of OPEN GEOMETRY was entirely written in Pascal.) C-programmers usually start with index 0.

- No matter if you deal with 2D objects or with 3D objects, the points will be stored in an array of 3D points.

The classes *O2d* and *O3d* inherit data and methods of *O23d*:

<u>**class** *O2d*;</u> → declaration in `"o2d.h"`

> Describes a conglomerate of points in 2-space (the points, however, are stored as 3D points). Derived from *O23d*.

> *Some methods for translating, rotating, scaling, and reflecting 2D objects:*

> > **void** Translate(*Real* dx, *Real* dy);
> > **void** Translate(*V2d* &v);
> > **void** Scale(*Real* kx, *Real* ky);
> > **void** Rotate(*P23d* &center, *Real* angle_in_deg);
> > **void** Reflect(**const** *StrL2d* &strLine);
> > **void** AssignVertices(*Coord2dArray* koord);
> > // Assign coordinate-array to the points of the object.

The class *O3d* not only inherits data and member functions from *O23d*, but also from an abstract base class named *Prop3d* that contains some data about physical properties. (We will explain the methods of this class later on.)

<u>**class** *O3d*;</u> → declaration in `"o3d.h"`

> Describes a conglomerate of points in 3-space. Derived from *O23d* and *Prop3d*.

> *Additional method for defining the points via an array:*

> > **void** Def(*Color* f, **int** n, *Coord3dArray* P);

> *Some methods for translating, rotating, scaling, and reflecting 3D objects:*

> > **void** Translate(*Real* dx, *Real* dy, *Real* dz);
> > **void** Translate(**const** *V3d* &v);
> > **void** Scale(*Real* kx, *Real* ky = 0, *Real* kz = 0);
> > **void** Rotate(**const** *StrL3d* &a, *Real* w);
> > **void** Screw(*HelicalMotion* &S);
> > **void** Reflect(**const** *Plane* &plane);
> > **void** FitIntoSphere(*Real* radius);

// A sometimes useful routine when you import data
// from other systems like 3D Studio or CAD3D
void AssignVertices(*Coord3dArray* koord);
// Somtimes useful in order to assign coordinates to the points.

Sample code for better understanding:

Coord3dArray three_points = { { 1, 0, 0 }, { 0, 1, 0 }, { 0, 0, 1 } };
O3d A;
A.Def(*Orange*, 3, three_points);
A.Scale(0.8, 1.2);
A.Rotate(*Xaxis*, 30);

3.6 Circles

Circles are fundamentally geometric objects, and one might expect that OPENGL supports this kind of object, at least in 2-space. This is not the case, however, as a circle is—in terms of OPENGL philosophy—nothing else but a closed polygon with an accordingly high (but noninfinite) number of vertices. The more vertices that are taken, the smoother the circle will appear. On the other hand, it does not make sense to take too many vertices, since OPENGL displays the result on the raster screen.

A 2D circle is a good example for showing the reader how the OPEN GEOMETRY library grew, step by step:

A possible but comparatively slow code to display a 2D-circle is the following:

```
GLint n = 80; // A 'circle' with 80 points
GLdouble radius = 3;
GLdouble angle = 0, delta_angle = 2 * PI / ( n − 1 );
GLdouble x_mid = 1, y_mid = 0.5; // Center of the circle
glColor3d( 0, 0, 0 ); // Black
glBegin( GL_LINE_STRIP ); // Begin a polygon
for ( GLint i = 0; i < n; i++, angle += delta_angle )
    glVertex2d( x_mid + radius*cos( angle ), y_mid + radius*sin( angle ) );
glEnd( ); // Display the polygon
```

Trigonometric functions slow down code, but with the use of tables, the executable can be sped up a little, even though the code is much longer.

```
GLint n = 80; // A 'circle' with 80 points
GLdouble radius = 3;
GLdouble angle = 0, delta_angle = 2 * PI / ( n − 1 );
GLdouble x_mid = 1, y_mid = 0.5; // Center of the circle
glColor3d( 0, 0, 0 ); // Black
glBegin( GL_LINE_STRIP ); // Begin a polygon
GLint i, imax = n / 8 − 1;
// Create a table for sin and cos.
GLdouble rSin [10], rCos [10];
for ( i = 0; i <= imax; i++, angle += delta_angle )
{
    rSin [i] = radius * sin( angle );
    rCos [i] = radius * cos( angle );
}
glPushMatrix( );
glTranslated( x_mid, y_mid, 0 ); // This saves some additions
// Now draw the circle in eight steps, using the symmetries of a circle.
for ( i = 0; i <= imax; i++ )
    glVertex2d( rCos [i], rSin [i] );
for ( i = imax; i >= 0; i−− )
    glVertex2d( rSin [i], rCos [i] );
for ( i = 0; i <= imax; i++ )
    glVertex2d( −rSin [i], rCos [i] );
for ( i = imax; i >= 0; i−− )
    glVertex2d( −rCos [i], rSin [i] );
// Lower part of the Circle
for ( i = 0; i <= imax; i++ )
    glVertex2d( −rCos [i], −rSin [i] );
for ( i = imax; i >= 0; i−− )
    glVertex2d( −rSin [i], −rCos [i] );
for ( i = 0; i <= imax; i++ )
    glVertex2d( rSin [i], −rCos [i] );
for ( i = imax; i >= 0; i−− )
    glVertex2d( rCos [i], −rSin [i] );
glEnd( ); // Display the polygon
glPopMatrix( );
```

And now the final OPEN GEOMETRY code that does the same job, but in this case a little faster and—what is more—with more flexibility. OPEN GEOMETRY will use less points on smaller circles and much more than 80 points for large circles. Also, when the scene is printed, the program will take this into account and increase the number of points temporarily.[5]

```
P2d center( 1, 0.5 );
Circ2d circ( Black, center, 3, EMPTY );
circ.Draw( );
```

class *Circ2d;* → declaration in "circ2d.h"
> Circle in 2-space. Derived from *O2d.*

Constructors:
> *Circ2d*( ); // Default constructor
> *Circ2d*(*Color* col, **const** *P2d* &Mid, *Real* radius,
> > *FilledOrNot* filled = *EMPTY*); // Classic definition.
> *Circ2d*(*Color* col, **const** *P2d* &A, **const** *P2d* &B, **const** *P2d* &C,
> > *FilledOrNot* filled = *EMPTY*); // Definition by three points

Equivalent and additional definitions:
> **void** Def(*Color* col, **const** *P2d* &M, *Real* r,
> > *FilledOrNot* filled = *EMPTY*);
> **void** Def(*Color* col, *Real* xm, *Real* ym, *Real* r,
> > *FilledOrNot* filled = *EMPTY*);
> > // Similar to the above definition.
> **void** Def(*Color* f, **const** *P2d* &A, **const** *P2d* &B, **const** *P2d* &C,
> > *FilledOrNot* filled = *EMPTY*); // 3 points

Additional methods, e.g., intersection with straight lines and other circles:
> *P2d* Mid( ) **const**; // Returns the center.
> **int** SectionWithStraightLine(**const** *StrL2d* &g,
> > *P23d* &S1, *P23d* &S2) **const**;
> > // Returns the number of intersection points S1, S2 (0, 1, or 2).

---

[5]By the way, the user can take advantage of the trigonometric tables that OPEN GEOMETRY automatically creates when the executable is started: the values of $\sin \alpha$, $\cos \alpha$, and $\tan \alpha$ ($\alpha = 0, 1, 2, \ldots 359$) are stored in a variable named *SinCosTan* as follows:

```
int alpha;
Real cos_alpha, sin_alpha, tan_alpha;
alpha = 130; // 0 <= alpha < 360
cos_alpha = SinCosTan.c [alpha];
sin_alpha = SinCosTan.s [alpha];
tan_alpha = SinCosTan.t [alpha];
```

int SectionWithCircle(**const** *Circ2d* &k,
    P23d &S1, *P23d* &S2) **const**;
    // Returns the number of intersection points S1, S2 (0, 1, or 2).
void Draw(*ThinOrThick* thick = *THIN*) **const**;

Sample code for better understanding:

P2d A(0, 0), B(5, 0), C(6, 8);
Circ2d c1(*Green*, A, B, C, *EMPTY*); // Circle through A, B, C
RandNum random(2, 5); // Create random numbers in [2, 5].
// Every call of random( ) creates a new random number.
P2d Mid2(random( ), random( ));
Real radius2 = random( );
Circ2d c2(*Blue*, Mid2, radius2, *EMPTY*);
P2d S[2]; // A maximum of two intersection points
int n = c1.SectionWithCircle(c2, S[0], S[1]);
// Show circles and possible intersection points
c1.Draw( );
c2.Draw( );
for (**int** i = 0; i < n; i++)
    S[i].Mark(*Red*, 0.2, 0.1);

---

class *Circ3d*;   → declaration in "circ3d.h"
    Circle in 3-space. Derived from *O3d*, *Poly3d*, *RegPoly3d*.

Constructors:

Circ3d( ); // Default constructor
Circ3d(*Color* col, **const** *P3d* &Center, **const** *V3d* &Normal, *Real* rad,
    int numOfPoints, *FilledOrNot* filled = *EMPTY*);
    // Classical definition via center, axis-direction, radius.
Circ3d(*Color* f, **const** *P3d* &PointOnCircle, **const** *StrL3d* &axis,
    int numOfPoints, *FilledOrNot* filled = *EMPTY*);
    // Given is a point on the circle and the axis.
Circ3d(*Color* col, **const** *P3d* &A, **const** *P3d* &B, **const** *P3d* &C,
    int numOfPoints, *FilledOrNot* filled = *EMPTY*);
    // Circle is given by three points.

Equivalent definitions:

Def(*Color* col, **const** *P3d* &Center, **const** *V3d* &Normal, *Real* radius,
    int numOfPoints, *FilledOrNot* filled = *EMPTY*);
    // Classical definition via center, axis-direction, radius.

Def(*Color* f, **const** *P3d* &PointOnCircle, **const** *StrL3d* &axis,
　　int numOfPoints, *FilledOrNot* filled = *EMPTY*);
　　// Given is a point on the circle and the axis.
Def(*Color* col, **const** *P3d* &A, **const** *P3d* &B, **const** *P3d* &C,
　　int numOfPoints, *FilledOrNot* filled = *EMPTY*);
　　// Circle is given by three points.

Additional methods, e.g., intersection with straight lines and other circles:

int SectionWithPlane(**const** *Plane* &p, *P3d* &S1, *P3d* &S2);
　　// Returns the number of intersection points.
P3d P(*Real* angle_in_rad);
　　// Returns point on the parametrized circles (param. angle_in_rad).

Listing (Figure 3.2):

```
int days_from_the_beginning_of_spring = 70;
   // Count each month with 30 days ==> June 11
Real sigma =
    90 − 23.45 * sin( Arc( days_from_the_beginning_of_spring ) );
// Simulation of the sun-path.
// Calculate sunrise and sunset.
Real lattitude = 48; // Vienna/Austria or border U.S.A./Canada
Real radius = 5;
V3d pole_direction;
pole_direction.Cartesian( 1, 0, lattitude );
V3d c = radius * cos( Arc( sigma ) ) * pole_direction;
P3d Center = c;
```

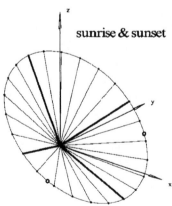

FIGURE 3.2. Sample program for *Circ3d*: sunrise and sunset.

```
Circ3d sunpath( Orange, Center, pole_direction, radius, 100 );
ShowAxes( Black, 7 );
sunpath.Draw( THIN );
for ( int hours = 0; hours <= 24; hours++ )
{
    P3d sun = sunpath.P( Arc( 15.0 * hours ) );
    StraightLine3d( Orange, Origin, sun, hours % 6 ? THIN : THICK);
    sun.Mark( Orange, 0.05 );
}
P3d SunRise, SunSet;
int n = sunpath.SectionWithPlane( XYplane, SunRise, SunSet );
SunRise.Mark( Black, 0.1, 0.05 );
SunSet.Mark( Black, 0.1, 0.05 );
PrintString( Black, 1, 6, "sunrise &sunset");
```

Circ3d is not only derived from *Obj3d*, but also from *Poly3d*, and *RegPoly3d*, and it inherits the methods of the latter classes as well (see next chapter).

4

Curved Lines and Polygons

In this chapter, we describe how to work with polylines and polygons. A polyline is a set of points that is connected by straight edges in a given order. Polygons are closed polylines. Polygons can be convex or non-convex (in the latter case they can also consist of several "loops"). They can be filled with constant color, shaded according to certain illumination models, "textured" etc. Finally, we will also introduce conics (conic intersections).

4.1 Polylines, Path Curves, Parameterized Curves

In this section we will explain how to define and draw polylines in 2-space and 3-space. Such lines can be given by a discrete number of points. They can also be path curves during a given motion (animation), and they can simply be given by parameterized equations.

The class $L2d$ (a 2D line) is derived from $O2d$. It is, roughly speaking, a polyline in 2-space.

<u>**class** $L2d$;</u> $\rightarrow$ declaration in `"lines2d.h"`

Lines (closed or not closed polygons) in 2-space. Derived from $O2d$.

Constructor:

$L2d(\ )$; // Default constructor

Additional methods:

>   void Draw(*ThinOrThick* thick, *Real* max_dist = −1);
>   // For max_dist > 0 a line segment is only drawn,
>   // when the two adjacent points have a smaller distance.
>   // This is useful for the drawing of curves with points at
>   // infinity (like hyperbolas).
>   *V2d* Tangent(**int** i); // Approximates the tangent in the i-th point.
>   void Close( ); // The curve will be drawn closed.

Sample code for better understanding:

```
L2d polygon;
Coord2dArray P =
        {{ −1, 0 }, { 0, −1.41 }, { 2, 0 }, { 0, 2.82 }, { −4, 0 }};
polygon.Def( Gray, 5, P );
polygon.Draw( THICK );
```

From *L2d* we derived the classes *ParamCurve2d* and *PathCurve2d*. (The class *CubicSpline2d* will be described separately.)

class *ParamCurve2d;*   → declaration in `"lines2d.h"`

>   An **abstract class** for a smooth 2D curve, defined by a parametric representation. Derived from *O2d* and *L2d*. In order to define a specific curve, the user has to derive an additional class from this class!

Additional methods:

>   void Def (*Color* f, **int** n, *Real* umin, *Real* umax);
>   // umin and umax are the parameter limits for the curve.
>   // The program will calculate n points on the curve, corresponding
>   // to evenly distributed parameter values in between.
>   **virtual** *P2d* CurvePoint(*Real* u) = 0; // Dummy
>   **virtual** *V2d* TangentVector(*Real* u);
>   // Returns the "exact" tangent vector at parameter u.
>   **virtual** *StrL2d* Tangent(*Real* u);
>   // Returns the 'exact' tangent at parameter u.
>   **virtual void** GetOsculatingCircle(*Real* u, *Color* col, *Circ2d* &osc_circ);
>   // Defines osculating circle at parameter u.
>   **virtual** *Real* ArcLength(*Real* u1, *Real* u2, **int** accuracy = 300);
>   // Returns the arc length $int_{u_1}^{u_2} \sqrt{\dot{x}^2 + \dot{y}^2} \, du$.
>   // By default, the curve is interpolated by a 300-sided polygon.

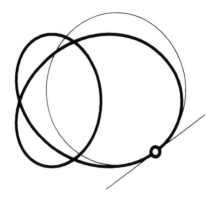

FIGURE 4.1. A parameterized 2D curve with tangent and osculating circle.

Listing of program BOOK/paramcurve2d.cpp (Figure 4.1):

```
#include "opengeom.h"
#include "defaults2d.h"

// ParamCurve2d is an abstract class. The user cannot instantiate
// this class due to the purely virtual member function CurvePoint( ).
// Therefore, we have to derive our own class from ParamCurve2d:

class MyCurve: public ParamCurve2d
{
public:
   virtual P2d CurvePoint( Real u )
   {
       // Here the user can insert the parametric representation
       // of a 2D-curve. In our case, the result is a trochoid
       // of higher degree.
       Real x = 3 * cos( 2 * u ) - 2 * cos ( u );
       Real y = 3 * sin( 2 * u );
       return P2d( x, y );
   }
};

MyCurve curve;
void Scene::Init( )
{
   curve.Def( Blue, 200, 0, 2 * PI );
   ShowReal("arc length =", curve.ArcLength( 0, 2 * PI ) );
}
void Scene::Draw( )
```

```
{
    curve.Draw( THICK );
    Real u = 2.7;
    curve.Tangent( u ).Draw( Black, −3, 3, THIN );
    Circ2d osc_circle;
    curve.GetOsculatingCircle( u, Black, osc_circle );
    osc_circle.Draw( THIN );
    curve.CurvePoint( u ).Mark( Black, 0.2, 0.1 );
}
```

class *PathCurve2d*;   → declaration in `"lines2d.h"`

A 2D curve of unknown size (maximum size $MAX\_POLY\_SIZE = 3000$).
Derived from *O2d* and *L2d*. Used for the determination of path curves
during movements.

Constructor:

PathCurve2d(*Color* c = *Gray*, **int** max_points = MAX_POLY_SIZE,
               Real critical_distance = 0);
// Allows max_points on the path curve.
// Declares the path to be 'closed' when the first point and the
// last point have a distance less than critical_distance.

Additional method:

void AddPoint(**const** *P2d* &P);
// Add point P to the curve.

Sample code for better understanding:

```
PathCurve2d path( Orange, 500, 0.5 );
// This means: Add a maximum of 500 points to the curve.
// If the first point and a newly added point have a distance
// of less than 0.5, the curve is considered to be "closed," and
// no more points are added.
RandNum rand( −5, 5 ); // Create random numbers in [−5, 5]
for  ( int i = 0; i < 500; i++ )
{
    P2d NewRandomPoint( rand( ), rand( ) ); // Random coords.
    path.AddPoint ( NewRandomPoint );
}
path.Draw( THIN );
```

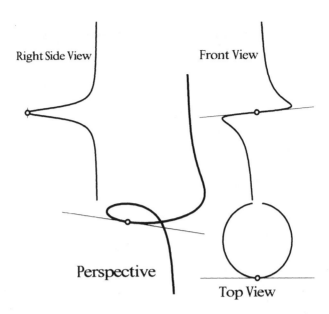

FIGURE 4.2. A cubic circle.

The classes *L3d* (a 3D line) and the classes *ParamCurve3d* and *PathCurve3d* that are derived from it are very similar to the corresponding classes in 2-space. Therefore, they are not explicitly listed. For more details, look at *lines3d.h.*

Figures 4.2 and 4.3 show examples for 3D curves. Their equations can be seen in the corresponding listings (see also: X/MORE3D/CubicCircle.cpp).

Listing of program X/3D/paramcurve3d.cpp (Figure 4.2):

```
#include "opengeom.h"
#include "defaults3d.h"


// ParamCurve3d is an abstract class. The user cannot instantiate
// this class due to the pure virtual member function CurvePoint( ).
// Therefore, we have to derive our own class from ParamCurve3d:

class MyCurve: public ParamCurve3d
{
public:
    P3d CurvePoint( Real u )
    {
        // Here the user can insert the parametric representation
        // of a 3D curve. In our case, the result is a "cubic circle,"
        // i.e., a space curve of degree 3 through the conjugate
```

```
                    // complex absolute points at infinity. (Analogous to ordinary
                    // circles).
                    const Real r = 3, h = r / 6; // Radius and "height"
                    return P3d( r * cos( u ), r * sin( u ), h * Tan( u / 2 ) );
            }
};

MyCurve CubicCircle;

void Scene::Init( )
{
    int number_of_points = 101;
    Real param1 = −3, param2 = −param1;
    CubicCircle.Def( Black, number_of_points, param1, param2 );
}

void Scene::Draw( )
{
    CubicCircle.Draw( THICK );
    Real u0 = 0;
    CubicCircle.Tangent( u0 ).Draw( Black, −5, 5, THIN );
    CubicCircle.CurvePoint( u0 ).Mark( Red, 0.2, 0.1 );
}
```

FIGURE 4.3. A rotoid curve. Watch the aura around the curve, the midcircle, and the z-axis.

Listing of program X/3D/paramcurve3d2.cpp (Figure 4.3):

```cpp
#include "opengeom.h"
#include "defaults3d.h"

const Real a = 5, b = 3;

class MyCurve: public ParamCurve3d
{
public:
    P3d CurvePoint( Real u )
    {
        const Real n = -6;
        Real r = a + b * cos ( n * u );
        return P3d( r * cos( u ), r * sin( u ), b * sin( n * u ) );
    }
};

MyCurve Curve;
Circ3d Circ;

void Scene::Init( )
{
    int number_of_points = 301;
    Real param1 = -PI, param2 = -param1;
    Curve.Def( Black, number_of_points, param1, param2 );
    Circ.Def( PureRed, Origin, Zdir, a, 150, EMPTY );
}

void Scene::Draw( )
{
    CreateAura( VERY_THICK );
    Zaxis.Draw( DarkGray, -8, 8, THICK );
    CreateAura( VERY_THICK );
    Curve.Draw( THICK );
    CreateAura( VERY_THICK );
    Circ.Draw( THICK );
}
```

4.2 Spline Curves

Sometimes it can be useful to use so-called spline curves instead of parameterized curves. We will now distinguish betweenapproximating splines and interpolating splines: In general, approximating splines do not contain "knot points." They

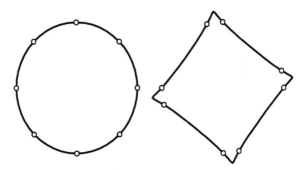

FIGURE 4.4. The shape of cubic splines heavily depends on whether the knots are distributed uniformly (left image) or not (right image).

are mostly determined by tangents. Famous approximating splines are the so-called Bézier curves ([4]).

Among the interpolating splines, we chose the cubic splines and implemented the classes *CubicSpline2d* and *CubicSpline3d*. These splines contain the given knot points, and build up out of a series of cubic parabolas (spans) in between the knots. In the knots, two neighboring spans have the same curvature (thus, a cubic spline is a C^2 curve, i.e., its curvature varies continuously). Cubic splines are usually easy to define. You only has to keep two things in mind:

- For best results, cubic splines require uniformly distributed knots. In Figure 4.4, we chose two sets of eight points on a circle. In the image to the left, the points are distributed uniformly; in the image to the right, they are not. The difference in the result is remarkable.

- Without additional information, the behavior at the end points of a cubic spline is more or less unpredictable (Figure 4.5).

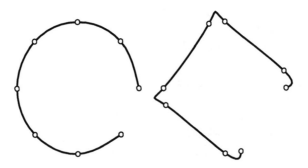

FIGURE 4.5. Usually, the tangents at the end points of a spline are hard to predict.

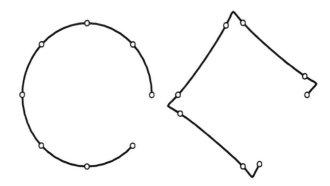

FIGURE 4.6. By means of additional "invisible knots," the tangents at the end points can be controlled.

This can be overcome by a little trick:

By means of the function InvisibleKnots( ), we add "invisible knots" to the curve: two at the beginning, and two at the end. The tangents at the ends of the spline are now determined (Figure 4.6). If the first and the last knot are identical, then OPEN GEOMETRY adds such points automatically (Figure 4.4).

<u>**class** *CubicSpline2d;*   → declaration in `"splines.h"`</u>

Derived from *L3d* and is an abstract class called *Spline3d* that is of no further interest to the user.

Constructor:

CubicSpline2d( ); // Default constructor

Definitions:

void Def(*Color* col, **int** in_between_points, *L2d* &knots);
// Calculates points in between.

Additional methods:

void InvisibleKnots(**const** *P23d* &Left 1, **const** *P23d* &Left 2,
                        const *P23d* &Right 1, **const** *P23d* &Right 2);
// This function has to be called *before* the definition!

Listing of program BOOK/spl2d6.cpp (Figure 4.6):

```
#include "opengeom.h"
#include "defaults2d.h"

CubicSpline2d Spline1, Spline2;
   // Splines are given by "base points."
```

```
const int N = 8;
L2d Base1( Gray, N ), Base2( Gray, N );

void Scene::Init( )
{
    // The first spline is given by uniformly distributed
    // points. A point P is rotated N times about the origin
    // through 45 degrees.
    // For N = 9, the first and the last point are identical.
    P2d P0( 5, 0 ), P = P0;
    for ( int i = 1; i <= N; i++ )
    {
        Base1 [i] = P;
        P.Rotate( Origin2d, 45 );
    }
    Base1.Translate( −6, 0 );
    Spline1.InvisibleKnots( Base1 [N−1], Base1 [N], Base1 [1], Base1 [2] );
    Spline1.Def( Black, 5, Base1 );
    // The second spline is given by nonuniformly distributed
    // points: a point P is rotated N times about the origin
    // through the alternate angles of 15 and 75 degrees.
    // For N = 9, the first and the last point are identical.
    for ( i = 1, P = P0; i <= N; i++ )
    {
        Base2 [i] = P;
        P.Rotate( Origin2d, i % 2 ? 15: 75 );
    }
    Base2.Translate( 6, 0 );
    Spline2.InvisibleKnots( Base2 [N−1], Base2 [N], Base2 [1], Base2 [2] );
    Spline2.Def( Black, 5, Base2 );
}
void Scene::Draw( )
{
    Spline1.Draw( MEDIUM );
    Base1.MarkPoints( Black, 0.15, 0.1 );
    Spline2.Draw( MEDIUM );
    Base2.MarkPoints( Black, 0.15, 0.1 );
}
```

The final number of points on the spline is $n + f \cdot (n-1)$, where n is the number of knots and f is the number of points in between the knots. It is directly available by means of the function Size( ) that is a member of all objects.

The 3D analogon of *CubicSpline2d* is *CubicSpline3d*. There are no major differences in the implementation. Simply exchange all occurrences of *2d* by *3d*.

4.3 Closed Polygons

OPEN GEOMETRY also provides a class for closed polylines. These polygons can be filled and shaded, and can also be equipped with textures.

class *Poly2d*; $\rightarrow$ declaration in `"poly2d.h"`
    Closed polygons in 2-space. Derived from *O2d*.

Constructors:

> *Poly2d*( );
> *Poly2d*(*Color* col, **int** numOfPoints, *FilledOrNot* filled = *EMPTY*);
> *Poly2d*(*Color* col, **int** numOfPoints, *Coord2dArray* points,
>   *FilledOrNot* filled = *EMPTY*);

Additional methods:

> **void** Def(*Color* col, **int** numOfPoints, *FilledOrNot* filled = *EMPTY*);
> **void** Def(*Color* col, **int** numOfPoints, *Coord2dArray* points,
>   *FilledOrNot* filled = *EMPTY*);
> **void** Draw(*ThinOrThick* thick);
>   // Draws the outline
> **void** Shade( );
>   // Plots the filled polygon. In 2-space, 'pure colors'
>   // are taken, since shading does not make sense.
> **void** ShadeWithTexture(*TextureMap* &Map,
>   *Real* ScaleX = 1, *Real* ScaleY = 1,
>   *Real* RotAngleInDeg = 0,
>   *Real* TranslateX = 0, *Real* TranslateY = 0,
>   *Boolean* repeat = true);

Sample code for better understanding:

> *Coord2dArray* points = { { −4, −4 }, { 4, −4 }, { 0, 4 } };
> *Poly2d* poly(*Green*, 3, points, *EMPTY*);
> poly.Translate(−1, −1);
> SetOpacity(0.5);
> poly.Shade( );
> poly.ChangeColor(*Black*);
> poly.Draw(*THICK*);

The class *Poly3d* (defined in `poly3d.h`) works analogously to *Poly2d* and need not be explained explicitly. Shading in 3-space works a little different from "shading" in 2-space: in 3-space, the color of the polygon is influenced by its inclination to the light rays. Thus, if you shade a blue polygon, the hue of blue will depend on the position of the polygon. This hue is chosen from a blue palette that is created when the program is started.

In 2-space, the polygon will always be painted in pure blue. (In fact, OPEN GEOMETRY has a predefined color named PureBlue.) If you want a 3D polygon to be always painted in the same color (independent of its position), use "pure colors" (e.g., PureBlue).[1]

When you need additional colors to the predefined ones, you can create new palettes easily and use them just like the predefined ones:

```
// Create the palette in the initialization part Scene::Init( ).
Color MyOwnBlue = NewColor( 1 );
CreateNewPalette( MyOwnBlue, 100, 0.1, 0.2, 0.4,  0.95, 0.95, 1 );

// Now use the new color like the other colors.
Coord2dArray points = { { −4, −4 }, { 4, −4 }, { 0, 4 } };
Poly2d poly( MyOwnBlue, 3, points );
poly.Shade( );
```

CreateNewPalette( ) has to be called in the initialization part of the program, i.e., in Scene::Init( ). The function takes eight parameters: the first one is the name. Actually, this is an enumerated integer (see `enums.h`). It has to be initialized by means of the OPEN GEOMETRY macro *NewColor( )*. The second parameter is the palette size n: the program will create a palette with n hues. The residual six parameters are the RGB triples (r, g, b) with $0 \leq r, g, b \leq 1$ as the darkest hue and the brightest hue of the palette, respectively. Thus, if you want to create a new "pure color," let n = 2 and pass two identical triples.

For convenience, OPEN GEOMETRY supports "Rectangles":

class *Rect2d;*   → declaration in `"poly2d.h"`

        Closed rectangle in 2-space. Derived from *O2d* and *Poly2d*.

    Constructors:

        Rect2d( ); // Default constructor.
        Rect2d(Color col, *Real* length, *Real* width,
               FilledOrNot filled = *EMPTY*);
        // Parallel to the axes, first point = origin.

---

[1]The other predefined pure colors are *PureWhite, PureGray, PurePink, PureMagenta, PureCyan, PureYellow, PureGreen, PureRed, PureOrange, PureBrown.*

Defining method:

> **void** Def(*Color* col, *Real* length, *Real* width,
>   *FilledOrNot* filled = *EMPTY*) ;
> // See corresponding constructor.

Another important child of *Poly2d* is a regular polygon:

<u>**class** *RegPoly2d*;</u>   → declaration in "poly2d.h"

> Closed regular polygon in 2-space. Derived from *O2d* and *Poly2d*.

Defining methods and additional methods:

> **void** Def(*Color* col, **const** *P2d* &FirstElem, **const** *P2d* &mid,
>   **int** n, *FilledOrNot* filled = *EMPTY*) ;
> // Center and a vertex are given.
> **void** Def(*Color* col, **const** *P2d* &mid, *Real* rad,
>   **int** n, *FilledOrNot* filled = *EMPTY*) ;
> // Center and radius are given.
> // First vertex lies on x-parallel through the center.
> **void** Def(*Color* col, **const** *P2d* &vertex1, **const** *P2d* &vertex2,
>   **int** n, **int** orientation = 1, *FilledOrNot* filled = *EMPTY*) ;
> // Two adjacent vertices and the orientation (+1 or −1) are given.
> *P2d* GetCenter( ) **const**; // Returns the center.
> *Real* GetRadius( ) **const**; // Returns the radius.

Listing of program BOOK/pentagon.cpp (Figure 4.7):

```
#include "opengeom.h"
#include "defaults2d.h"
// A regular pentagon is given by two vertices.
// Draw the polygon and its circumcircle.
```

FIGURE 4.7. A regular polygon with its circumcircle.

```
RegPoly2d Poly;
Circ2d Circumcircle;
void Scene::Init( )
{
    P2d A( -3, 0 ), B( 3, 0 );
    Poly.Def( Yellow, A, B, 5, 1, FILLED );
    Circumcircle.Def( Black, Poly.GetCenter( ), Poly.GetRadius( ) );
}
void Scene::Draw( )
{
    Poly.Shade( );
    Circumcircle.Draw( THICK );
}
```

Analogously to the two-dimensional case, OPEN GEOMETRY supports rectangles and regular polygons in space (classes *Rect3d* and *RegPoly3d*, derived from *Poly3d*). A regular 3D-*n*-gon can be given by a vertex and the axis, or by the center, the axis-direction, and the radius.

4.4 Texture Mapping

One of the most innovative inventions of computer graphics was the introduction of textures. OPEN GEOMETRY fully supports OPENGL standard for texture mapping. The textures that are mapped onto a polygon are bitmaps. Due to an OPENGL convention, the size of the bitmap should be a power of two (e.g., 512×256). Quadratic images are fine for many applications as they can still be scaled by means of the scaling parameters in the function ShadeWithTexture( ).

Listing of program BOOK/textures2d.cpp (Figure 4.8):

```
#include "opengeom.h"
#include "defaults2d.h"
Poly2d Poly;
TextureMap Pic( "BMP/snail.bmp" );

void Scene::Init( )
{
    Coord2dArray points = { { -4, -4 }, { 4, -4 }, { 4, 4 }, { -4, 4 } };
    // When you use 'NoColor', the color of the texture will
    // not be affected. When you use another color, the image
```

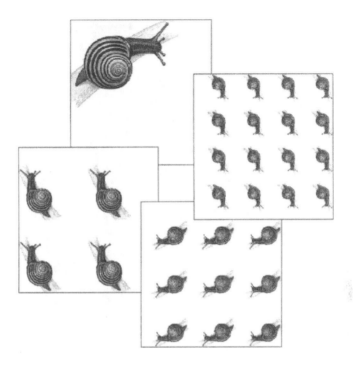

FIGURE 4.8. Texture mapping with 2D polygons.

```
    // will additionally be shaded in this color; e.g., if you
    // choose color Green, the texture will appear greenish.
    Poly.Def( NoColor, 4, points, EMPTY );
    Poly.Translate( 5, 2 ):
}
void Scene::Draw( )
{
    for ( int i = 1; i <= 4; i++ )
    {
        Poly.Rotate( Origin2d, 90 );
        Poly.ShadeWithTexture( Pic, i, i, −90 );
        Poly.Outline( Black, THIN );
    }
```

The next example shows how to map textures on 3D polygons. The bitmaps are
scaled and rotated.

FIGURE 4.9. Texture mapping with 3D polygons.

Listing of program X/3D/nice.cpp (Figure 4.9):

```
#include "opengeom.h"
#include "defaults3d.h"

TextureMap TMap[3];
Poly3d R[3];

void Scene::Init( )
{
    Coord3dArray P0 = { {−4, −4, 8}, {−4, 4, 8}, {4, 4, 8}, {4, −4, 8} };
    R[0].Def( PureWhite, 4, P0, FILLED );
    Coord3dArray P1 = { {4, 4, −8}, {−4, 4, −8}, {−4, 4, 8}, {4, 4, 8} };
    R[1].Def( PureWhite, 4, P1, FILLED );
    R[1].Copy( R[2] );
    R[2].Rotate( Zaxis, −90 );
    TMap[0].LoadFromBitmapFile( "BMP/elegance.bmp" );
    TMap[1].LoadFromBitmapFile( "BMP/bird_anim.bmp" );
    TMap[2].LoadFromBitmapFile( "BMP/speed.bmp" );
}
```

```
void Scene::Draw( )
{
    Real rot_angle [3] = { 0, 90, 0 };
    Real scale_factor [3] = { −1, 1, 1 };
    for ( int i = 0; i < 3; i++ )
        R [i].ShadeWithTexture( TMap [i], 1, scale_factor [i], rot_angle [i] );
}
```

A final example shows how textures can be painted on colorless 3D-polygons in order to create realistic images with trees. The listing of the header file `tree.h` can be found on the enclosed CD. The methods of the classes *Box* and *RegPrism* are explained in the following chapter.

Listing of program `X/3D/trees.cpp` (Figure 4.10):

```
#include "opengeom.h"
#include "defaults3d.h"
#include "tree.h"
```

FIGURE 4.10. Texture mapping with 3D polygons: trees in a geometrical scene. The textures are mapped on "invisible" polygons.

```
Tree Tree1, Tree2;
Box Base;
RegPrism Column;

void Scene::Init( )
{
   Tree1.Def( 8, "BMP/tree1.bmp" );
   Tree1.Rotate( Zaxis, 240 );
   Tree1.Translate( 2, 7, 0 );
   Tree2.Def( 10, "BMP/tree2.bmp" );
   Tree2.Scale( 0.6, 0.7, 0.8 );
   Base.Def( Brown, 20, 20, 1 );
   Base.Translate( −10, −10, −1 );
   Column.Def( Gray, 0.5, 5, 30, SOLID );
   Column.Translate( 5, 5, 0 );
}
void draw_scene_without_trees( )
{
   SetOpacity( 1.0 );
   Base.Shade( );
   for ( int i = 0; i < 6; i++ )
   {
      Column.Shade( );
      Column.Rotate( Zaxis, 60 );
   }
}
void draw_trees( )
{
   Tree1.Draw( );
   Tree2.Draw( );
}
void Scene::Draw( )
{
   draw_scene_without_trees( );
   draw_trees( );
}
```

4.5 Complex Polygons, Tesselation

Nonconvex polygons can be very complicated. OPENGL is able to "tesselate"
such polygons. This means that the polygon is triangulated or cut into so-called
"triangle strips," respectively. This feature is very valuable, as the code behind

the tesselation is really robust, and it would take a lot of work to rewrite it. The price for the tesselation, however, is an enormous loss of speed. This is not so bad as long as we plot only a few complex polygons. When it comes to hundreds or thousands of such polygons, the animation of a scene will slow down considerably.

The class *ComplexPoly2d* (a 2D line) is derived from *Poly2d*. It is, roughly speaking, a set of polylines in 2-space that form the complex polygon (we call them loops). These loops must be closed convex or nonconvex polygons without holes.

An ordinary nonconvex polygon without holes can be interpreted as a complex polygon with one loop.

class *ComplexPoly2d*; → declaration in `"complex_poly.h"`

     Closed nonconvex polygons (loops) in 2-space. Derived from *Poly2d*.

Constructor:

    ComplexPoly2d( ); // default constructor

Definitions:

    void Def(*Color* col, **int** NLoops, *Poly2d* *loop);
        // NLoops is the number of loops,
        // loop is an array of polygons, i.e., a pointer to the first polygon.
    void Def(**const** ComplexPoly2d &cp); // Copy the complex poly cp

Additional methods:

    void Fill( ); // Fill in given color.
    void Shade( ); // Equivalent to Fill( ).
    void Outline(*Color* col, *ThinOrThick* style); // Just draw the outline.

Listing of program `X/2D/complex_poly2d.cpp` (Figure 4.11):

```
ShowAxes( Blue, 5, 5, 2 );


// The complex polygon shall consist of four loops (polygons).
const int nLoops = 4;
Poly2d p [nLoops];
int n = 40;
p[0].Def( Gray, n, FILLED );
Real delta = 2 * PI / n, fi = 0;
for ( int i = 1; i <= n; i++, fi += delta )
      p[0][i]( 2 * cos( fi ) − 2, 3 * sin( fi ) );
p[1] = p[0]; p[1].Scale( 0.9, 0.6 ); p[1].Translate( −0.2, 0 );
```

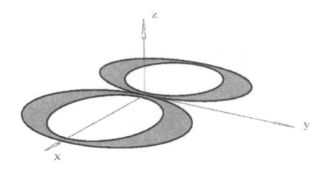

FIGURE 4.11. The output of the sample complex polygon.

```
p[2] = p[0]; p[2].Reflect( Yaxis2d ); p[2].Scale( 1.2 );
p[3] = p[1]; p[3].Reflect( Yaxis2d ); p[3].Scale( 1.2 );

// Now combine the four loops to one complex polygon.
ComplexPoly2d complex_poly;
complex_poly.Def( Gray, nLoops, p );
complex_poly.Fill( );
complex_poly.Outline( Black, MEDIUM );
```

Figure 4.11 shows a complex polygon that consists of four loops, each of which is an ellipse. The result is "the number 8." Figure 4.12 shows a result, where the loops intersect and shading does not work!

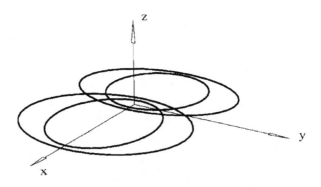

FIGURE 4.12. The loops of the complex polygon must not intersect. Otherwise, the shading algorithm does not work. When you design a complex polygon, always use the method Outline( ) additionally. It outlines the loops and shows intersections.

Although defined in 2-space, the complex polygon of Figure 4.11 was drawn in 3-space, since the camera definition was three dimensional. (All z-values were automatically initialized with 0.)

Usually, when we work in 3-space, we should use the class *ComplexPoly3d* (derived from *Poly3d*) which is defined quite analogously to a two-dimensional class. The method Fill( ) should be replaced by Shade( ). Anything else works the same way.

For better understanding, we give two more examples for defining complex polygons. The first example (Figure 4.13) shows the section of the Otto-engine (a piston moves inside a cylinder). The scene consists of two complex polygons (the "cylinder" consists of two disjoint loops, the "piston" consists of two adjacent symmetrical loops), the coordinates of which are given in a natural manner, being measured from a sketch.

Since both polygons are symmetrical with regard to the x-axis, we define one loop and reflect this loop at the x-axis. The corresponding code looks like this:

Listing of program BOOK/cp2d5.cpp (Figure 4.13):

```cpp
#include "opengeom.h"
#include "defaults2d.h" // In order to shorten the listing!

ComplexPoly2d Piston, Cylinder;
void define_cylinder( )
{
    const int nLoops = 2;
```

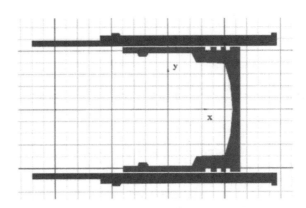

FIGURE 4.13. Two complex polygons, given by an array of coordinates (Otto-engine).

```
        Poly2d p [nLoops];
        Coord2dArray
           coords =  { { 9.7, 5.4 }, { 9.7, 6.5 },{ 9.2, 6.5 },{ 9.2, 6.3 },
                       { −4.2, 6.3 },{ −4.3, 6.5 }, { −5.0, 6.5 }, { −5.0, 6.3 },
                       { −6, 6.3 }, { −6, 5.9 }, { −12, 5.9 }, { −12, 5.4 } };
        p [0].Def( Gray, 12, FILLED );
        p [0].AssignVertices( coords );
        p [0].Copy( p [1] );
        p [0].Reflect( Xaxis2d );
        Cylinder.Def( Black, nLoops, p );
}
void define_piston( )
{
        const int nLoops = 2;
        Poly2d p [nLoops];
        Coord2dArray
           coords =  { { 5.7, 0 }, { 5.5, −2.2 }, { 5.0, −3.9 }, { 2.5, −4.0 },
                       { 2.1, −4.8 }, { 0, −4.8 }, { −1.7, −4.8 }, { −1.9, −4.5 },
                       { −2.6, −4.5 }, { −2.7, −4.8 }, { −4, −4.8 }, { −4, −5.3 },
                       { 3.3, −5.3 }, { 3.3, −5.0 }, { 3.8, −5.0 }, { 3.8, −5.3 },
                       { 4.3, −5.3 }, { 4.3, −5.0 }, { 4.7, −5.0 }, { 4.7, −5.3 },
                       { 5.1, −5.3 }, { 5.1, −5.0 }, { 5.5, −5.0 }, { 5.5, −5.3 },
                       { 6.4, −5.3 }, { 6.4, 0 } };
        p [0].Def( Gray, 26, FILLED );
        p [0].AssignVertices( coords );
        p [0].Copy( p [1] );
        p [0].Reflect( Xaxis2d );
        Piston.Def( PureRed, nLoops, p );
}
void Scene::Init( )
{
        define_cylinder( );
        define_piston( );
}
void Scene::Draw( )
{
        ShowAxes2d( Black, 3.2 );
        TheWindow.ShowRaster( Gray, 1, 1, 0.6 );
        TheWindow.ShowRaster( Black, 5, 5, 0.8 );
        Cylinder.Fill( );
        Piston.Fill( );
}
```

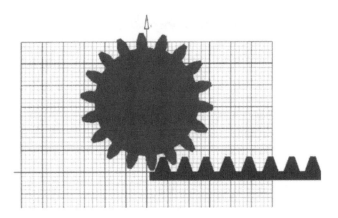

FIGURE 4.14. A gear wheel and a gear rack (two nonconvex polygons).

The second example shows a gear wheel and a gear rack (Figure 4.14).

Both objects are complex polygons with one nonconvex loop, consisting of a larger number of vertices. It would be boring to determine all the coordinates of the vertices from a drawing, as the wheel consists of eighteen congruent parts, each of which is given by eleven points. And the rack has eight congruent parts, each with five vertices. Please have a look at the following listing.

Listing of program BOOK/cp2d6.cpp (Figure 4.14):

```
#include "opengeom.h"
#include "defaults2d.h"

ComplexPoly2d Wheel, Rack;

void define_Wheel( )
{
    const int nLoops = 1;
    Poly2d p [nLoops];
    const int jmax = 18;
    // 18 teeth of the wheel, each of which is given by 11 vertices.
    Real coords [11 * jmax] [2] =
        { { −1.8, 3.9 }, { −0.4, 3.7 },{ −0.2, 3.4 },{ −0.2, 2.7 },
          { 0, 1.9 },{ 0.85, 0.3 }, { 1.8, 0.35 }, { 2.2, 1.5 },
          { 2.5, 2.7 }, { 2.4, 3.7 }, { 2.5, 4 } };
    P2d Center( 0, 16.2);
    Rotation2d.Def( Center, 20 );
    for ( int i = 0; i < 11; i++ )
    {
        P2d P(coords [i] [0], coords [i] [1]);
```

```
        for ( int j = 1; j < jmax; j++ )
        {
            P.Rotate( );
            coords [i + 11 * j] [0] = P.x;  coords [i + 11 * j] [1] = P.y;
        }
    }
    p [0].Def( Gray, 11 * jmax, FILLED );
    p [0].AssignVertices( coords );
    Wheel.Def( Red, nLoops, p );
}
void define_Rack( )
{
    const int nLoops = 1;
    Poly2d p [nLoops];
    const int jmax = 8;
    // 8 teeth of the rack, each of which is given by 5 vertices.
    Real coords [5 * jmax + 2] [2] =
        { { 0.7, 0 }, { 1.9, 0 }, { 3.25, 3.5 }, { 4.5, 3.5 }, { 5.8, 0 } };
    for ( int i = 0; i < 5; i++ )
    {
        P2d P (coords [i] [0], coords [i] [1]);
        for ( int j = 1; j < jmax; j++ )
        {
            P.Translate( 5.15, 0 );
            coords [i + 5 * j] [0] = P.x;  coords [i + 5 * j] [1] = P.y;
        }
    }
    // Now add the lower rectangle.
    int k = 5 * jmax;
    coords [k] [0] = coords [k - 1] [0];
    coords [k] [1] = coords [k - 1] [1] - 2;
    k++;
    coords [k] [0] = coords [0] [0];
    coords [k] [1] = coords [0] [1] - 2;

    p [0].Def( Gray, 5 * jmax + 2, FILLED );
    p [0].AssignVertices( coords );
    Rack.Def( Black, nLoops, p );
}

void Scene::Init( )
{
    define_Wheel( );
    define_Rack( );
```

```
}
void Scene::Draw( )
{
    ShowAxes2d( Black, 33 );
    TheWindow.ShowRaster( Gray, 1, 1, 0.6 );
    TheWindow.ShowRaster( Black, 5, 5, 0.8 );
    Rack.Fill( );
    Wheel.Fill( );
}
```

4.6 Conics

Conics are planar intersections of quadratic cones or quadrics. They can also occur when the intersection of two quadrics degenerates into a pair of two planar curves. Figure 4.15 shows an example of such a situation. The corresponding can be found on the enclosed CD (X/3D/cone_x_cone.cpp).

In the above example, we calculated a sufficient number of points on the conics so as to be able to display them. As it is well known from projective geometry, a conic is determined by five points. Therefore, it would have been possible to just calculate five intersection points and then make use of the OPEN GEOMETRY class *Conic*:

class *Conic*;   → declaration in "conic.h"

      Describes a conic in 2-space, or in 3-space in the xy-plane. Base class.

    Constructors:

      Conic( ); // Default constructor.

FIGURE 4.15. Two conics as degenerated intersection of two quadratic cones.

Definition:

> **void** Def(*Color* col, **int** numPoints, **const** *P2d* P [5]);
> // numPoints is the number of points on the approximating
> // polygon. Calculations with the conic are not done with these
> // approximations but with the exact mathematical equation!

Methods and operators:

> *TypeOfConic* **type**( );
> // returns the type: *ELLIPSE, HYPERBOLA,*
> // *PARABOLA* or *IRREGULAR.*
> *P2d* GetCenter( ); // returns the center
> *P2d* GetA( ); // A, B are the points on the major axis.
> *P2d* GetB( );
> *P2d* GetC( ); // C, D are the points on the minor axis.
> *P2d* GetD( );
> *Real* DistMA( ); // Half length of the major axis.
> *Real* DistMC( ); // Half length of the minor axis.
> *StrL2d* MajorAxis( );
> *StrL2d* MinorAxis( );
> *StrL2d* Asymptote1( );
> *StrL2d* Asymptote2( );
> **void** GetCoefficients(*Real* c [6]);
> // The equation of the conic is then
> // $c[0]x^2 + c[1]xy + c[2]y^2 + c[3]x + c[4]y + c[5] = 0.$
> **int** SectionWithStraightLine(**const** *StrL2d* s, *P2d* &S1, *P2d* &S2);
> // Returns the number of intersection points (≤ 2)
> // and calculates the corresponding points S1 and S2.
> **void** Draw(*ThinOrThick* thick, *Real* max_radius = DUMMY)
> // Draws the conic (one or two branches). When a radius is speci-
> // fied, only the part inside a circle around the center is drawn
> // (this is useful when drawing hyperbolas).
> **int** Size( ); // Returns the number of points on each branch.

Listing of program X/2D/conic.cpp (Figure 4.16):

```
#include "opengeom.h"

P2d P [5]; // The 5 points on the conic
StrL2d s( Origin, V2d( 2, 1 ) );
void SetPoints( )
{
    RandNum rnd( −5, 5 ); // Creates random numbers from −5 to 5
    P [0]( −3, Round( rnd( ) ) );
```

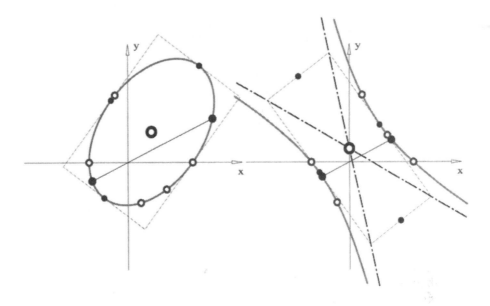

FIGURE 4.16. Conics given by five points. We look for points on the axes, intersection points with a straight line, etc.

```
   P[1]( -1, 2 - Round( rnd( ) ) );
   P[2]( 1, Round( rnd( ) ) );
   P[3]( 3, Round( rnd( ) ) );
   P[4]( 5, 0);
}
void Scene::Init( )
{
   HiQuality( );
   SetPoints( );
}
void Scene::Draw( )
{
   ShowAxes( Red, 8 );
   Conic conic;
   conic.Def( Orange, 300, P );
   if ( conic.Exists( ) )
   {
      conic.Draw( THICK, 10 );
      P2d A = conic.GetA( ), B = conic.GetB( );
      P2d C = conic.GetC( ), D = conic.GetD( );
      P2d M = conic.GetCenter( );
      if ( conic.type( ) != IRREGULAR )
```

```
    {
        Poly2d rect( Gray, 4 );
        V2d a = A − M, c = C − M;
        rect [1] = M + a + c;
        rect [2] = M − a + c;
        rect [3] = M − a − c;
        rect [4] = M + a − c;
        rect.Draw( THIN );
    }
    if ( conic.type( ) == HYPERBOLA )
    {
        Real t = 10;
        conic.Asymptote1( ).LineDotted( Black, −t, t, 20, MEDIUM );
        conic.Asymptote2( ).LineDotted( Black, −t, t, 20, MEDIUM );
    }
    // Intersect the conic with this line.
    P2d S [2];
    int n = conic.SectionWithStraightLine( s, S [0], S [1] );
    // Display the intersection points.
    for ( int i = 0; i < n; i++ )
        S [i].Mark( Blue, 0.2 );
    StraightLine2d( Blue, S [0], S [1], THIN );
    const Real r = 0.15;
    if ( conic.type( ) != IRREGULAR )
    {
        A.Mark( Black, r );
        B.Mark( Black, r );
        C.Mark( Black, r );
        D.Mark( Black, r );
    }
    M.Mark( Black, 2 * r, r );
    }
    // Mark the given points.
    for ( int i = 0; i < 5; i++ )
        P [i].Mark( Green, 0.2, 0.1 );
}
void Scene::Animate( )
{
    SetPoints( );
}
void Scene::CleanUp( )
{
}
void Projection::Def( )
```

```
{
    if ( FrameNum( ) == 1 ) // Initialization of the drawing window
    {
        xyCoordinates( −15.0, 15.0, −15.0, 15.0 );
    }
}
```

If the conic is given by its implicit equation:

$$Ax^2 + Bxy + Cy^2 + Dx + Ey + F = 0, \tag{1}$$

the sign of the expression

$$\Delta = B^2 - 4AC \tag{2}$$

is a criterion for the type of the conic ($\Delta > 0 \ldots$ hyperbola, $\Delta = 0 \ldots$ parabola, $\Delta < 0 \ldots$ ellipse).

When three of the five given points are collinear, the conic is irregular, i.e., it degenerates into two lines (which can coincide).

Conics can also be given by four points and a tangent in one point, or three points and the tangents in two of them, etc. These cases will be implemented in a future version of OPEN GEOMETRY. For the time being, you can help yourself by substituting the tangent by an additional point on the tangent that is very close to the point of tangency. (But don't go too close; a distance of 10^{-3} is sufficient for most cases. Otherwise, the algorithms might get instable.)

A conic in 3-space (which is still planar, of course) can be treated by means of the class *Conic3d* (definition in `conic.h` as well). Its implementation looks very much the same as the implementation of the two-dimensional case. Just replace all occurrences of *P2d* and *StrL2d* by *P3d* and *StrL3d*. The first three points are taken for the determination of the conic's plane; the others are "adjusted" if they are not perfectly complanar. The conic's plane is available via GetPlane( ). The intersection with an arbitrary plane is done by means of the method SectionWithPlane( ):

> *Plane* GetPlane( ); // Returns the carrier plane.
> **int** SectionWithPlane(**const** *Plane* s, *P3d* &S1, *P3d* &S2);
>   // Intersects the conic with the plane s. Returns the number
>   // of intersection points (0, 1, or 2) and calculates these points.

This method returns the number of intersection points. In the three-dimensional case, OPEN GEOMETRY works with a projection of the conic and solves the problem in 2-space. (The direction of the projection is always one of the three main directions x, y, and z.)

5

Primitive Elements in Space

In the previous chapter, we introduced basic geometrical elements like points, lines, polygons, conics, etc. In this chapter we will describe how simple polyhedra like "boxes" (parallelepipedums), prisms, cylinders, pyramids, cones, and frustums, etc., are implemented in OPEN GEOMETRY. We also describe our "virtual camera."

5.1 Boxes

class *Box;* → declaration in `"pyrprism.h"`

>   Describes an ordinary "box" in 3-space. Inherits the methods and operators of *O23d* and *O3d*.

Constructors:

>   *Box*( ); // Default constructor
>   *Box*(*Color* col, *Real* x, *Real* y, *Real* z);
>   // x, y, and z are the dimensions.
>   // One corner is the origin of the coordinate system.

Additional methods:

>   **void** Def(*Color* col, *Real* x, *Real* y, *Real* z);
>   // See constructor.
>   **void** Draw(*Boolean* remove_hidden_lines,
>   *ThinOrThick* thick, *Real* offset = *STD_OFFSET*) /* const */;

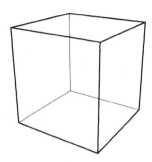

FIGURE 5.1. Visible and invisible edges of a box.

// Draw the edges (wireframe). The offset can be
// changed, if you want to paint the edges onto a shaded cube.
void WireFrame(*Boolean* remove_hidden_lines,
        ThinOrThick thick, *Real* offset = *STD_OFFSET*) /* const */;
    // Same as Draw( ).
void Shade(*Boolean* reflect = true) /* const */;
    // Shade reflecting or matte.
void ShadeBackfaces(*Boolean* reflect = true) /* const */;
    // Shade only the backfaces (reflecting or matte).
    // This is useful for transparent boxes (Figure 5.2).
void Transform(*Polyhedron* &P) **const**;
    // Convert the box into a polyhedron.
void GetSides(*Real* &x, *Real* &y, *Real* &z);
    // Calculates side lengths.

Listing (Figure 5.1):

```
// Draw a cube with thin invisible edges
Box cube( Black, 4, 4, 4 );
// Center the cube at the origin
cube.Translate( −2, −2, −2 );
cube.WireFrame( false, THIN ); // Draw all edges thin
cube.WireFrame( true, THICK ); // Redraw all visible edges thick
```

Transparent Boxes

Since boxes are easy to create in OPEN GEOMETRY, we take this opportunity
to show how the transparency feature can be used in order to get good images.
Figure 5.2 shows a transparent cube in a transparent box (e.g., an "exhibit").

FIGURE 5.2. Transparent boxes.

Of course, the realism of the image is not perfect, as there is no refraction calculated. (We have an example with refraction in this book: the swimming pool.)

Please have a look at the corresponding code:

Listing of program `book/exhibit.cpp` (Figure 5.2):

```
#include "opengeom.h"
#include "defaults3d.h"
  // default camera, dummies for animation and cleanup.
Box Desk, GlassBox, Exhibit;
void define_centered_cube( Box &cube, Color c, Real side )
  // cube centered at the origin (auxiliary routine)
{
    cube.Def( c, side, side, side );
    Real s = −side / 2;
    cube.Translate( s, s, s );
}
void Scene::Init( )
{
    // First define the desk.
    Desk.Def( Brown, 10, 10, 1 );
    Desk.Translate( −5, −5, −5.1 );
    // Now the glass box.
    define_centered_cube( GlassBox, LightBlue, 8 );
    // Finally define a cube that "stands on its diagonal":
    define_centered_cube( Exhibit, Yellow, 4.6 );
    Exhibit.Rotate( Zaxis, 45 );
}   Exhibit.Rotate( Xaxis, Deg( atan( sqrt( 2 ) ) ) );

}
```

```
void Scene::Draw( )
{
   Desk.Shade( );
   // Draw the wire frame of the glass box in black
   GlassBox.ChangeColor( Black );
   GlassBox.WireFrame( false, MEDIUM );
   // Draw the transparent "upright" cube:
   SetOpacity( 0.7 );
   Exhibit.SetSolid( false );
   Exhibit.ShadeBackfaces( );
   Exhibit.SetSolid( true );
   Exhibit.Shade( );
   // Plot the transparent glass box:
   SetOpacity( 0.3 );
   GlassBox.ChangeColor( LightBlue );
   GlassBox.Shade( );
   SetOpacity( 1 );
}
```

If you want to create oblique boxes, you can interpret them as an oblique prism. (See the following section.)

5.2 Prisms and Pyramids

OPEN GEOMETRY uses a type *RegFrustum* (regular frustum), which is the parent class of *RegPyramid* (regular pyramid) and *RegPrism* (regular prism). Cone frustums, cones, and regular cylinders fit into that scheme (we just increase the order of the corresponding type). A cylinder of revolution is interpreted as a regular prism with an order of, say, 50 or more.

class *RegFrustum*; → declaration in "pyrprism.h"

> Describes a frustum in 3-space. Inherits the methods and operators of *O23d* and *O3d*.

Constructors:

> *RegFrustum( );* // Default constructor
> *RegFrustum(Color* col,
>   *Real* r1, // radius of the base circle
>   *Real* r2, // radius of the top circle
>   *Real* height, // the height of the frustum
>   **int** n, // the "order," i.e., the number of points on the circles
>   SolidOrNot = *SOLID*, // alternative HOLLOW
>   **const** *StrL3d* &axis = *Zaxis*);

Definitions:

> **void** Def(*Color* col, *Real* r1, *Real* r2, *Real* height,
>   **int** n, SolidOrNot = *SOLID,* **const** *StrL3d* &axis = *Zaxis*);
> // See constructor.

Additional or overwriting methods and operators:

> **void** Shade(*FlatOrSmooth* smooth = *SMOOTH,*
>   *Boolean* reflect = **true**);
> **void** WireFrame(*Boolean* remove_hidden_lines,
>   *ThinOrThick* thick,
>   *Real* offset = *STD_OFFSET*); /* const */
> **void** Outline(*Color* col, *ThinOrThick* style,
>   *Real* offset = *STD_OFFSET*);
>   // as an example, see Figure 5.7
> **int** GetOrder( ); // Returns the order of the frustum.
> *Boolean* HasApex( ); // Returns true if the frustum is a pyramid.
> **void** TranslateTop(**const** *V3d* &t);
>   // Makes object oblique.
> **void** RotateTop(**const** *StrL3d* &axis, *Real* angle_in_deg);
>   // Rotates top circle.
> *Polyhedron* * **operator** ( ) (**void**);
>   // Converts the frustum into an "ordinary"
>   // polyhedron and returns a pointer to this polyhedron.
> *StrL3d* GetGeneratingLine(**int** i);
>   // Returns the i-th generating line (Figure 4.15)

Listing (Figure 5.3):

RegFrustum pyramid(*Orange,* 6, 3, 8, 40, *HOLLOW*);
// Ordinary shading

FIGURE 5.3. Solid and nonsolid frustums (shaded or wire frame).

```
pyramid.Translate( −12, 0, 0 );
pyramid.Shade( );
// Black-white wireframe (hidden lines removed)
pyramid.Translate( 12, 0, 0 );
pyramid.ChangeColor( Black );
pyramid.WireFrame( true, THIN, 1e−3 );
// Shaded pyramid with black painted edges
pyramid.Translate( 12, 0, 0 );
pyramid.WireFrame( false, THIN, 1e−3 );
pyramid.ChangeColor( Orange );
pyramid.Shade( );
```

Listing (Figure 5.4):

```
// Figure 5.4
RegFrustum G( Green, 5, 2, 7, 100, SOLID );
StrL3d axis( P3d( 0, 0, 7 ), Xdir );
G.RotateTop( axis, −30 );
G.TranslateTop( V3d( 0, 5, 0 ) );
G.Shade( );
G.Rotate( Zaxis, 180 );
G.Shade( );
```

By means of the methods TranslateTop( ) and RotateTop( ), the shape of the frustum can be changed (Figure 5.4). If you only use TranslateTop( ), the frustum will stay convex. The function RotateTop( ) should be applied with caution: it

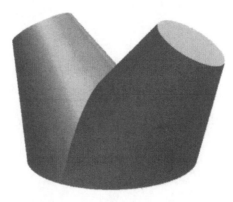

FIGURE 5.4. Convex polyhedra derived from frustums.

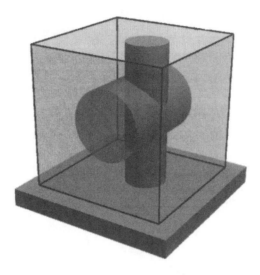

FIGURE 5.5. Solid and transparent cylinder.

may easily be that the object is not convex anymore. In this case, the new object should be triangulated, which can be done by means of the ( ) operator. (More about that when we talk about the class *Polyhedron*.)

The classes *RegPyramid* and *RegPrism* do not differ essentially from the parent class *RegFrustum*. They have only one parameter less in the definition. In both cases, the radius r2 is skipped since it is zero for a pyramid and is equal to r1 for a prism.

We just want to show how to paint a transparent cylinder. Please look at the code that is to be inserted to a previous code (the exhibit in a transparent cube, remember?) and the corresponding image. Again, the realism of the image is not perfect: there are no calculated refractions. On the other hand, the intersection line between the cylinders comes out quite well. This is due to the fact that we painted the upright cylinder "in between" (Figure 5.5).

Listing of program book/solid_and_transp_cyl.cpp (Figure 5.5):

```
RegPrism HorizontalCylinder( Yellow, 2, 6, 50, SOLID, Xaxis ),
         UprightCylinder( Brown, 1.2, 8, 50, SOLID, Zaxis );
UprightCylinder.Translate( 0, 0.7, −4 );
HorizontalCylinder.Translate( −3, 0, 0 );
HorizontalCylinder.SetSolid( false );
SetOpacity( 0.7 );
HorizontalCylinder.ShadeBackfaces( );
SetOpacity( 1 );
```

```
UprightCylinder.Shade( );
SetOpacity( 0.7 );
HorizontalCylinder.Shade( );
```

5.3 Spheres

<u>class</u> *Sphere*; → declaration in `"sphere.h"`

Describes a sphere in 3-space. Inherits the methods and operators of *Circ3d* and therefore also from *O3d*, etc.

Constructors:

Sphere( ); // Default constructor.
Sphere(*Color* col, *P3d* &center, *Real* radius,
    int points_on_contour = 100,
    int points_on_meridian = 0,
    int order = 0);
// If the number of points on the meridian and the
// order is not specified, the program tries to optimize
// these numbers. In general, one should increase the
// numbers for larger spheres. The same is true for the
// number of points on the contour (which is usually a
// small circle).

Definitions:

void Def(*Color* col, *P3d* &center, *Real* radius,
    int points_on_contour = 100,
    int points_on_meridian = 0,
    int order = 0);
// See constructor.

Additional or overwriting methods and operators:

void Draw(*Color* col, *ThinOrThick* thick,
    Real offset = *STD_OFFSET*);
// Draws the silhouette, i.e., the image of the contour.
void Shade(*Shininess* reflect = *REFLECTING*);
// Ordinary shading.
void WireFrame(*Color* col, *ThinOrThick* style,
    int n1 = 0, **int** n2 = 0,
    Real offset = *STD_OFFSET*);
// Draws a wire frame with n1 meridians
// and n2 parallel circles.

void Scale(*Real* k);
  // Only one parameter. Other scalings are not allowed.
  // Ellipsoids can be plotted as parameterized surfaces.
P3d GetCenter( ) **const**;
Real GetRadius( ) **const**;
void GetContour(*Circ3d* &c);
Plane PolarPlane(*P3d* &P) **const**;
  // Returns the polar plane of a point P.
Boolean SectionWithPlane(*Plane* &e, *Circ3d* &c,
          int size_of_section = 100) **const**;
  // Returns true if there is a section.
  // The intersection circle c is calculated (default: 100 points).

Listing of program book/some_planet.cpp (Figure 5.6):

```
#include "opengeom.h"
#include "defaults3d.h"
Sphere SomePlanet, Moon, Earth;
StrL3d EarthAxis;
void Scene::Init( )
{
  SomePlanet.Def( Blue, P3d( 6, 0, 0 ), 4, 100, 32, 32 );
    // The bigger the sphere, the more points we need.
  Moon.Def( Orange, Origin, 1 );
    // take default parameters.
  Earth.Def( NoColor, Origin, 4, 100, 32, 32 );
    // Move earth and its axis to its position in space.
```

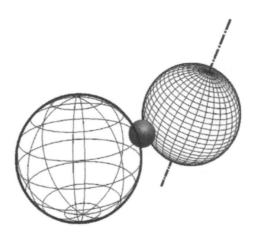

FIGURE 5.6. Some planets.

```
    Real delta = −23.5; // Ecliptic
    Earth.Rotate( Xaxis, delta );
    Earth.Translate( −6, 0, 0 );
    EarthAxis = Zaxis;
    EarthAxis.Rotate( Xaxis, delta );
    EarthAxis.Translate( −6, 0, 0 );
}
void Scene::Draw( )
{
    SomePlanet.Draw( Black, THICK ); // Silhouette
    SomePlanet.WireFrame( Black, THIN, 8, 8 );
    Moon.Shade( );
    Earth.WireFrame( Black,THIN, 20, 20 );
        // The offset is comparatively large.
    Earth.Shade( );
        // Since the earth has no color, this just has
        // the effect of a hidden line removal
    Earth.Draw( Black, THICK );
    EarthAxis.LineDotted( Black, −8, 8, 20, THICK );
}
```

Another example (Figure 5.7) shows how we can work with polar planes, intersecting circles, etc., in order to get a tangential cone. The corresponding code looks like this:

Listing of program book/tangential_cone.cpp (Figure 5.7):

```
#include "opengeom.h"
#include "defaults3d.h"
void Scene::Init( )
```

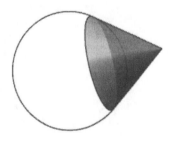

FIGURE 5.7. We calculate and display a tangential cone.

```
{
}
void Scene::Draw( )
{
    Sphere S( Orange, Origin, 4, 200 );
    P3d P( −2, 6, 2 );
    Plane sigma = S.PolarPlane( P );
    Circ3d circle;
    S.SectionWithPlane( sigma, circle );
    StrL3d axis( S.GetCenter( ), P );
    RegPyramid Cone( Green, circle.rad,
        sigma.OrientedDistance( P ), 100, HOLLOW, axis );
    Cone.Translate( circle.GetCenter( ) );
    SetOpacity( 1 ):
    S.Draw( Black, MEDIUM );
    Cone.Outline( Black, MEDIUM );
    SetOpacity( 0.7 );
    Cone.Shade( ):
}
```

As a final example, we show how we can use texture maps in order to let spheres appear like planets. Note that the contours of the spheres are conics. In order to paint the background black, we use the method SetBackgroundColor( ) of the class Scene. The three parameters are the red-green-blue components of the background color $(0 \le r, g, b \le 1)$.

Listing of program book/earth.cpp (Figure 5.8):

```
#include "opengeom.h"
#include "defaults3d.h"

Sphere TheEarth, TheMoon;
TextureMap
    EarthPhoto( "bmp/earth.bmp" ),
    MoonPhoto( "bmp/moon.bmp" );
void Scene::Init( )
{
    TheEarth.Def( LightBlue, P3d( 0, 2, 5 ), 2 );
    TheMoon.Def( Gray, P3d( 0, 0, −30 ), 30, 150 );
    SetBackgroundColor ( 0, 0, 0 );
}
void Scene::Draw( )
```

FIGURE 5.8. Once again a scene in orbit: the earth—seen from the moon.

```
{
    Circ3d contour;
    TheEarth.GetContour( contour );
    contour.ChangeColor( NoColor );
    contour.ShadeWithTexture( EarthPhoto );
    TheMoon.GetContour( contour );
    contour.ChangeColor( NoColor );
    contour.ShadeWithTexture( MoonPhoto );
}
```

5.4 Groups of 3D Objects

When a 3D scene consists of subscenes that are built up in the same way, we can use the OPEN GEOMETRY class *O3dGroup*:

class *O3dGroup*; → declaration in `"groups.h"`

Describes groups of objects in 3-space.

Constructor:

O3dGroup(**int** N = 0); // N is the number of elements

Operator:

O3d ∗ **operator** [ ] (**int** i);
// returns an O3d-pointer to the i-th element.

Additional methods:

> **void** Def(**int** N); // Allows to operate with N elements
> **void** AddMember(**int** i,   *O3d* &obj); // adds an O3d
> **void** AddChild(**int** i, *O3dGroup* &obj); // adds another group
> **void** Elem(**int** i, **int** j, *Real* x, *Real* y, *Real* z) ;
>   // set coords of the j-th point of the i-th object.
> **int** N( ); // returns the number of elements

Additional member functions are the usual transformation methods like Translate( ), Rotate( ), Scale( ), etc.

The following listings show how object groups can be implemented. Since no drawing routines can be predefined, these routines have to be implemented by the user. As one can see, this requires a bit of experience and knowledge about syntax with pointers of different types. Once a group is fully implemented, however, it is very convenient to work with. Thus, you can derive a new class from *O3dGroup* when you work more frequently with special conglomerates of different objects.

Listing of program book/object_group (Figure 5.9):

```
#include "opengeom.h"
#include "defaults3d.h"
class SubScene: public O3dGroup
{
public:
   void Draw( );
};
class WholeScene: public O3dGroup
```

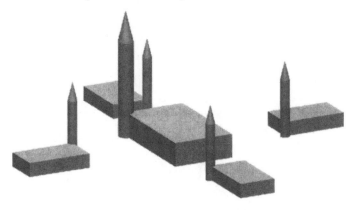

FIGURE 5.9. A scene consisting of similar subscenes.

```
{
public:
   void Draw( );
};
void SubScene::Draw( )
{
   (( Box *) Elem( 1 ) )->Shade( );
   (( RegPrism *) Elem( 2 ) )->Shade( );
   (( RegPyramid *) Elem( 3 ) )->Shade( );
}
void WholeScene::Draw( )
{
   for ( int i = 1; i <= N( ); i++ )
      ( ( SubScene *) Elem( i ) )->Draw( );
}
const int N = 5;
Box B [N + 1];
RegPrism C [N + 1];
RegPyramid P [N + 1];

SubScene Part [N + 1];
WholeScene All;
void Scene::Init( )
{
   All.Def( N );
   for ( int i = 1; i <= N; i++ )
   {
      B [i].Def( Gray, 7, 4, 1.5 );
      B [i].Translate( -3.5, -2, 0 );
      C [i].Def( Gray, 0.5, 6, 40 );
      C [i].Translate( -3.5, -2, 0 );
      P [i].Def( Gray, 0.5, 2, 40 );
      P [i].Translate( -3.5, -2, 6 );
      SubScene &Sub = Part [i];
      Sub.Def( 3 );
      Sub.AddMember( 1, B [i] );
      Sub.AddMember( 2, C [i] );
      Sub.AddMember( 3, P [i] );
      if ( i > 1 )
      {
         Sub.Scale( 0.6 );
         Sub.Translate( 9, 0, 0 );
      }
      Sub.Rotate( Zaxis, 90 * i );
      All.AddChild( i, Sub );
```

```
        }
    }
    void Scene::Draw( )
    {
        All.Draw( );
    }
```

5.5 The Virtual Camera

The projection of 3-space and the mapping onto the screen is done by the efficient OPENGL routines. We have introduced a class *Projection* that comes with a number of methods.

One global instance of this class is used for handling the most frequent projecting tasks in 3-space. This instance is called **TheCamera**. It works similar to an ordinary camera, as you can

- change the position (eye point) and/or the target point,

- move around in space by means of rotations and translations,

- change the focus (zoom in and out),

- switch between perspective and orthogonal projection,

- choose special views like top view, front view, etc.,

- turn the depth-buffer on and off (and define clipping planes),

- change the light direction,

- determine projection rays and projections of points, etc.

We give a short description of the most frequent methods:

class *Projection;* $\rightarrow$ declaration in `"camera.h"`
───────────
        Describes the projection of 3-space (virtual camera).

    Methods:

```
        // Define camera:
            void Def( );
                // This member function has to be implemented by the user
            void Def( Real eye_x, Real eye_y, Real eye_z,
                    Real target_x, Real target_y, Real target_z,
                    Real fovyAngle = 20 );
                // fovy ... field of vision angle ( 1 < fovy < 65 )
```

```
            void DefaultCamera( Real eye_x, Real eye_y, Real eye_z );
                // Perspective: eye( x, y, z ), target( 0, 0, 0 ),
                // fovy = 20 (focus = 50).
        // Change camera lens (zoom in and out with factor k)
                // k = 1 ... no effect; k = 1.05 ... 5% magnification, etc.
            void ZoomIn( Real k );
            void ZoomOut( Real k );
            void ChangeFocus( Real focus_in_deg );
                // Default is 50 ... ordinary camera lens
                // 15 <= focus <= 35 ... wide angle
                // focus >= 70 ... tele−objective lens
        // Change eye point:
            void ChangePosition( const P3d &NewEye );
            void ChangePosition( Real eye_x, Real eye_y, Real eye_z );
        // Rotate camera (target unchanged)
            void RotateVertically( Real angle_in_deg );
                // Rotate about z-parallel axis through target point.
            void RotateHorizontally( Real angle_in_deg );
            void AutoRotation( Boolean switch_on );
                // Starts or stops vertical autorotation (1 degree per frame).
        // Change target point:
            void ChangeTarget( const P3d &NewTarget );
            void ChangeTarget( Real target_x, Real target_y, Real target_z );
        // Rotate camera (eye unchanged)
            void TargetLeftRight( Real angle_in_deg );
            void TargetUpDown( Real angle_in_deg );
        // Move camera (change eye and target point)
            void Translate( Real dx, Real dy, Real dz );
            void Forward( Real translation );
            void Backward( Real translation );
            void UpDown( Real translation );
            void LeftRight( Real translation );
        // Twist camera:
            void Roll( Real angle_in_deg );
            void ChangeTwist( Real angle_in_deg );
        // Special views
            void TopView( );
            void FrontView( );
            void RightSideView( );
            void SpecialView( char c );
                // '1' = top view, '2' = front view, '3' = right side view
                // '4' = bottom view, '5' = back view, '6' = left side view
        // Switch from perspective to orthoprojection and vice versa:
            void SwitchProjection( );
            void SwitchToNormalProjection( );
```

```
// Control depth buffering
    void Zbuffer( Boolean on_off );
    void ClearZBuffer( );
    void SetDepthRange( Real z_min, Real z_max );


// Get data from class (all angles are returned in degrees):
    Real GetAzim( ) const;
    Real GetElev( ) const;
    Real GetFocus( ) const;
    Real GetFovy( ) const;
    Real GetTwist( ) const;
    P3d GetPosition( ) const;
    P3d GetTarget( ) const;
    Plane GetProjPlane( ) const;
    Real GetDist( ) const;
    Boolean IsActive( ) const;
    Boolean IsOrthoProj( ) const;
    Boolean IsSpecialView( ) const;
    void GetDepthRange( Real &z_min, Real &z_max );
// Save data to file 'tmp.dat'
    void SaveEyeAndLight( );
// Change Light (only parallel light allowed):
    void ParallelLight( Real x, Real y, Real z );
// Intersection of the proj. ray with the image plane.
    P3d ProjectPoint( const P3d &P );
// Pixel coords. in the current window.
    P3d CoordsInScreenSystem( const P3d &P );
        // The z-coord. of the result is a depth value (for z-buffering).
// Projection ray in direction eyepoint
    V3d GetProjRay( const P3d &P ) const;
    V3d GetNormalizedPrincipalRay( ) const;
// Make light heliocentric instead of geocentric:
    void Heliocentric( Boolean on_off );
// Save and restore camera temporarily
    void Save( );
    void Restore( );
```

When and where can the camera be changed, and where does it make sense?

The favorite location is the implementation of the routine Projection::Def( ). This routine is called by OPEN GEOMETRY before a new frame is drawn, and it has to be implemented by the user in each application. (The implementation may be hidden in the header file `defaults3d.h`.) In Projection::Def( ), you can write whole animations for the camera. We gave an example for this in Section 2.3. Here again is the listing:

```
void Projection::Def( )
{
   if ( FrameNum( ) == 1 ) // Initialization of the camera
   {
      DefaultCamera( 18, 10, 8 );
      ParallelLight( 2, 3, 4 );
      SetDepthRange( −5, 5 ); // this helps to improve z-buffering
   }
   int f = ( FrameNum( ) − 1 ) % 120;
   if ( f < 60 )
      RotateHorizontally( 2 );
   else if ( f < 70 )
      RotateVertically( 2 );
   else if ( f < 80 )
      ZoomIn( 1.02 );
   else if ( f < 90 )
      ZoomOut( 1.02 );
   else if ( f < 100 )
      RotateVertically( −2 );
   else
  *   LightDirection.Rotate( Zaxis, 5 );
}
```

The call of the function **SetDepthRange( )** sometimes helps to improve depth-buffering. The default values are $[-40, 40]$.

The variable **LightDirection** is a global instance of the class *LightSource* which is declared in `light.h`. Its methods are

```
void Def( Real x, Real y, Real z );
void Indicate( ); // Show axes and light direction
void Rotate( const StrL3d &a, Real w );
```

Besides in Projection.Def( ), you can change the camera in the implementation of Scene::Draw( ) or in Scene::Animate( ). Anywhere else is also possible as long as the changes are done in the infinite loop between these three routines. In Scene::Draw( ) or Scene::Animate( ), the virtual camera has to be called by its full name. As an example, we show that instead of moving an object in space, one can also change the camera. In this case, we need the method Heliocentric( ) in order to get a correct image (Figure 5.10, right); otherwise, the result is not shaded as we had wanted (Figure 5.10, left). In other cases, e.g., when three or four views of a scene are to be displayed at different locations in one and the same image, a geocentric light source may be preferred.

FIGURE 5.10. Simulation of a moving object by means of changing the camera. Left: light source is geocentric. Right: light source is heliocentric.

Listing of program book/change_camera.cpp (Figure 5.10):

```
#include "opengeom.h"
#include "defaults3d.h"

Sphere S;

void Scene::Init( )
{
   S.Def( Pink, P3d( 6, 0, 0 ), 0.7 );
}
void Scene::Draw( )
{
   TheCamera.Save( );
   TheCamera.Heliocentric( true );
   LightSource L = LightDirection;
      // the direction is changed because of 'Heliocentic( )'
   for ( int k = 0; k < 90; k++ )
   {
      TheCamera.RotateHorizontally( 4 );
      TheCamera.RotateVertically( 10 * sin ( Arc( 4 * k ) ) );
      S.Shade( );
   }
   TheCamera.Restore( );
   LightDirection = L;
}
```

Figure 5.11 illustrates how the projection works in space. The corresponding OPEN GEOMETRY program is listed below. (If you are a beginner, skip the code for the time being.)

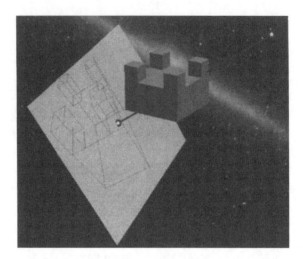

FIGURE 5.11. The virtual camera and the projection in space.

Listing of program book/change_camera2.cpp (Figure 5.11):

```
#include "opengeom.h"
#include "defaults3d.h"

Box box[5]; // The object consists of 5 boxes.
void DefineAndShowObjects( )
{
    box[0].Def( Yellow, 4, 4, 2 );
    box[1].Def( Yellow, 1, 1, 1 ); box[1].Translate( 0, 0, 2 );
    box[2].Def( Yellow, 1, 1, 1 ); box[2].Translate( 3, 0, 2 );
    box[3].Def( Yellow, 1, 1, 1 ); box[3].Translate( 3, 3, 2 );
    box[4].Def( Yellow, 1, 1, 1 ); box[4].Translate( 0, 3, 2 );
    for ( int i = 0; i < 5; i++ )
        box[i].Shade( );
}
void FakeNewCamera( )
{
    TheCamera.Save( );
    // Install a new camera
    P3d NewPosition( −1, 8, 5 );
    TheCamera.ChangePosition( NewPosition );
    P3d NewTarget( 2, −2, −2 );
    TheCamera.ChangeTarget( NewTarget );
    for ( int i = 0; i < 5; i++ )
        for ( int j = 1; j <= 8; j++ )
```

```
                box[i][j] = TheCamera.ProjectPoint( box[i][j] );
        // Define a rectangle that represents the proj. plane
        V3d x, y;
        TheCamera.GetNormalizedPrincipalRay( ).OrthoBase( x, y );
        x *= 9; y *= 5;
        Poly3d ProjPlane( Gray, 4 );
        ProjPlane[1] = NewTarget + x + y;
        ProjPlane[2] = NewTarget − x + y;
        ProjPlane[3] = NewTarget − x − y;
        ProjPlane[4] = NewTarget + x − y;


        // Switch to original camera
        TheCamera.Restore( );
        // Show everything in original camera position.
        NewPosition.Mark( PureRed, 0.2, 0.1 );
        NewTarget.Mark( PureRed, 0.2, 0.1 );
        StraightLine3d( PureRed, NewPosition, NewTarget, MEDIUM );
        ProjPlane.Shade( );
        for ( i = 0; i < 5; i++ )
            box[i].WireFrame( false, THIN );
    }
    void Scene::Init( )
    {
        SetBackgroundTexture( "e:/opengeom/BMP/stars.bmp" );
    }
    void Scene::Draw( )
    {
        DefineAndShowObjects( );
        FakeNewCamera( );
    }
```

So far we only talked about 3-space. In 2-space, things are of course much less complicated. The OPEN GEOMETRY class *Wdw* handles a "virtual 2D camera":

class *Wdw;* → declaration in `"wdw.h"`

      Describes the drawing area in 2-space (virtual 2D camera).

   Methods:

        void Def(*Real* x1, *Real* x2, *Real* y1, *Real* y2);
           // Define a preferred area in which you want to draw.
        void Clear(*Real* r = 1, *Real* g = 1, *Real* b = 1);
           // Clear window with RGB color r,g,b.
        void ShowRaster(*Color* col, *Real* dx, *Real* dy, *Real* opacity = 0.5);

```
    // Show raster with width dx (dy), by default half-transparently.
void DottedRaster( Color col, Real dx, Real dy, Real opacity = 0.5 );
    // Show dotted raster with width dx (dy).
void Zoom( Real k );
    // Zoom in ( k > 1 ) or out ( 0 < k < 1 )
void Translate( Real delta_x, Real delta_y );
    // Move 2D-drawing area.
```

The only global instance of this class is named TheWindow. In the same routines where you can change the 3D camera, you can change TheWindow, e.g., by means of TheWindow.Clear(0.2, 0.7, 1).

6

Complex Surfaces

In this chapter, we will learn how to decribe and display more complicated surfaces. Among these surfaces we will mainly speak about "mathematical surfaces," i.e., surfaces that are described by mathematical equations. We also introduce "swept surfaces," i.e., surfaces that are swept when a space curve is somehow moved in space.

6.1 Parameterized Surfaces

Mathematical surfaces are sometimes given by implicit equations:

$$F(x, y, z) \equiv 0. \tag{1}$$

Implicit equations are very important for theory. Algebraic implicit equations, for example, allow you to determine the order of the surface (i.e., the maximum number of possible intersection points with a straight line).

Computer programs, however, prefer parameterized equations of a surface:

$$\vec{x}(u, v) = \begin{pmatrix} x(u, v) \\ y(u, v) \\ z(u, v) \end{pmatrix} \quad \text{with} \quad u \in [u_1, u_2], v \in [v_1, v_2]. \tag{2}$$

Once we have such an equation, the surface can be displayed immediately.

A torus (Figure 6.1), for example, can be described by the parameterization

$$\vec{x}(u, v) = \begin{pmatrix} (a + b \cos v) \cos u \\ (a + b \cos v) \sin u \\ b \sin v \end{pmatrix} \quad \text{with} \quad u \in [0, 2\pi], \ v \in [0, 2\pi]. \tag{3}$$

The parameters u, v can be eliminated, which leads to

$$F(x, y, z) = (a - \sqrt{x^2 + y^2})^2 + z^2 - b^2 \equiv 0 \tag{4}$$

or to the implicit algebraic equation of degree 4

$$F(x, y, z) = (x^2 + y^2 + z^2 + a^2 - b^2)^2 - 4a^2(x^2 + y^2) \equiv 0. \tag{5}$$

Thus, a torus turns out to be an algebraic surface of order 4.

In OPEN GEOMETRY, the corresponding class is *ParamSurface*. It had to be implemented abstractly, since at the time the methods were implemented, the parametric equations were not yet known. (We had the same problem with *ParamCurve2d* and *ParamCurve3d*.) This class works with the purely virtual functions SurfacePoint( ) and SweepFunction( ). In order to determine a surface of your own, you have to derive a new class from *ParamSurface* and implement either SurfacePoint( ) or SweepFunction( ).

Here are the most important methods of *ParamSurface*:

class *ParamSurface*; → declaration in `"paramsurface.h"`
　　　　Describes a parameterized mathematical surface. Abstract class (no instances!). Inherits the methods and operators of *O3d*.

Constructor:

　　ParamSurface( ); // Default constructor

Definitions:

　　void Def(*Color* col, **int** n1, **int** n2,
　　　　　　　Real u1, *Real* u2, *Real* v1, *Real* v2);
　　　// n_1 ... number of v-lines(u = const),
　　　// n_2 ... number of u-lines(v = const),
　　　// parameter ranges $u_1 \leq u \leq u_2, v_1 \leq v \leq v_2$.
　　　// The virtual function SurfacePoint( ) has to be adapted.
　　void Def(*Color* col, **int** n, *Real* v1, *Real* v2, *L3d* &k);
　　　// Sweeping of a 3D curve k (n positions).
　　　// The virtual function SweepFunction( ) has to be adapted.

Additional or overwriting methods and operators:

int NumOfULines( ); // Returns the number of u-lines.
int NumOfVLines( ); // Returns the number of v-lines.
void Shade(*FlatOrSmooth* smooth, Shininess reflecting,
       FaceMode which_faces = *ALL_FACES*) **const**;
  // Par.1: *FLAT OR SMOOTH*
  // Par.2: *MATTE, REFLECTING*, etc.
  // which_faces may also be
  //   *ONLY_BACKFACES, ONLY_FRONTFACES*
void WireFrame(*Color* c, **int** n1, **int** n2, *ThinOrThick* style,
       Real offset = *STD_OFFSET*) **const**;
  // Draws a wire frame with n1 u-lines (v = const)
  // and n2 v-lines (u = const). Due to problems with
  // the z-buffer, we have to introduce an "offset."
void ULines(*Color* c, **int** n, *ThinOrThick* style,
       Real offset = *STD_OFFSET*) **const**;
  // Same as wire frame, but only the n u-lines are plotted.
void VLines(*Color* col, **int** n, *ThinOrThick* style,
       Real offset = *STD_OFFSET*) **const**;
  // Same as wire frame, but only the n v-lines are plotted.
void DrawBorderLines(*Color* col, *ThinOrThick* style,
       Boolean u_lines = true, *Boolean* v_lines = true,
       Real offset = *STD_OFFSET*);
  // Draws only the bordering u-lines (if u_lines is true)
  // and v-lines (if v_lines is true).
void Contour(*Color* col, *ThinOrThick* style,
       Real offset = $10 * STD\_OFFSET$);
  // Draws the outline (silhouette). Since the planes of tangency are
  // projecting in contour points, the offset is by default larger.
void GetULine(*L3d* &uline, **const** *Real* v0,
       Color col = *Black*, **int** size = 0);
  // Calculates a specific u-line (v = v0) which has to be passed
  // as first parameter. Color and size can be chosen (the default
  // color is *Black*). If no size is chosen, the "usual" size
  // (i.e., the parameter n1 in Def( )) is taken.
void GetVLine(*L3d* &vline, **const** *Real* u0,
       Color col = *Black*, **int** size = 0);
  // The same for a specific v-line (u = u0). Default size is
  // the parameter n2 in Def( ).
V3d NormalVector(*Real* u, *Real* v);
  // Returns the normalized surface normal in the point (u, v).
StrL3d Normal(*Real* u, *Real* v);
  // Returns the normal in the point (u, v).
Plane TangentPlane(*Real* u, *Real* v);

```
// Returns the tangent plane in the point (u, v).
```
virtual *P3d* SurfacePoint(*Real* u, *Real* v); // Pure virtual!
```
    // When you derive a new class from ParamSurface, you have to
    // implement this function when working with parameter equations.
```
virtual *P3d* SweepFunction(*Real* v, *P3d* P); // Pure virtual!
```
    // When you derive a new class from ParamSurface, and you want
    // to define the surface as a swept surface, you have to implement
    // this virtual function.
```

As a first sample program, we derive a new class from *ParamSurface* that describes a torus (Figure 6.1). We then shade the surface, draw some parameter lines, and the contour. Here is the code:

Listing of program X/3D/paramsurf.cpp (Figure 6.1):

```cpp
#include "opengeom.h"
#include "defaults3d.h"
// The following example shows how we can easily display
// a parameterized surface. In this case here, we draw a torus.
class MySurface: public ParamSurface
{
public:
    virtual P3d SurfacePoint( Real u, Real v )
    {
        // This is the parameterized equation of a torus:
        const Real a = 9, b = 6;
        Real r = a + b * cos( v );
```

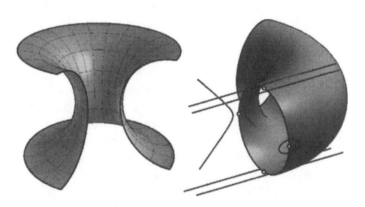

FIGURE 6.1. Parts of a torus. Listing for the left image see below. Right: indicatrices in points of different type (elliptic, parabolic, and hyperbolic). Corresponding OPEN GEOMETRY program X/SURF/mathsurf.cpp

```
        Real x, y, z;
        x = r * cos( u );
        y = r * sin( u );
        z = b * sin ( v );
        return P3d( x, y, z );
    }
};
MySurface Torus; // An instance of the class.
void Scene::Init( )
{
    int n_rot_circ = 64, n_parallel_circ = 25;
    Real u1 = PI / 2, u2 = 2 * PI; // Range of parameter u
    Real v1 = PI / 2, v2 = v1 + PI; // Range of parameter v
    Torus.Def( Orange, n_rot_circ, n_parallel_circ, u1, u2, v1, v2 );
    Torus.PrepareContour( );
    // This is a bit time-consuming, but it has to be done only once.
}
void Scene::Draw( )
{
    Torus.Shade( SMOOTH, REFLECTING );
    Torus.Contour( Black, THICK ); // The outline (silhouette).
    Torus.WireFrame( Black, 9, 10, THIN );
    // Nine u-lines (v = const), i.e., parallel circles,
    // and ten v-lines (u = const), i.e., meridian circles.
    Torus.DrawBorderLines( Black, MEDIUM );
}
```

Before we continue with other examples, we give some additional general comments that you should keep in mind when you start to write more sophisticated applications:

- Of course, when a surface is plotted, it is first triangulated. If the parameters n_1 and n_2 in the definition of the surface are given, the program approximates the surface by means of a polyhedron with $2n_1n_2$ triangular faces.

  If the parametric equations of the surface are given, the surface normals can be determined with high accuracy. This leads to good results if the surface is "smooth-shaded."

  Both z-buffering (for hidden surface removal) and smooth shading (Gouraud shading) are done very efficiently by OPENGL routines.

- Since the surface is only approximated, and, additionally, since the accuracy of z-buffering is restricted, this leads to an annoying fact: when we plot a curve on the surface (which is again approximated by a polygon), the z-buffer will "swallow" some pixels. In order to avoid this syndrome, we have introduced a so-called "offset": The parameter offset is usually a default parameter at the end of most function calls that deal with lines or polygons. In general, do not experiment with offset at the beginning— leave the default values (STD_OFFSET is set to 10^{-4}). The best results are achieved if normal projection is chosen. The results get worse if extreme perspectives (with large field-of-vision angles) are used. We are working on this problem.

- Contour lines can support imagination on shaded images, and they are essential on line drawings. These contour lines are interpreted as contour polygons of the approximating polyhedron. This has two consequences:

  First, the accuracy of the approximating contour line heavily depends on the accuracy of the polyhedral approximation (i.e., on the parameters n1 and n2 in the definition of the surface). On the other hand, these numbers should not be increased too much, as the calculation time increases with the square of n1 and n2.

  Second, the *fast* determination of the approximating contour requires a lot of information about the approximating polyhedron. The corresponding preparations are done in the routine PrepareContour( ). This routine should be called in the *initialization part* of the program. It is one of the most time-consuming routines of Open Geometry: usually it will consume parts of a second for up to several seconds for higher parameters n1 and n2.

  If you do not need the contour, do not call this function. Calls of Contour( ) will then be ignored.

But now back to our examples. Parameterized surfaces have been fascinating mathematicians and geometrists for centuries. And now we can create them almost interactively!

A sphere can be interpreted as a special case of a torus ($a = 0$ in Equations (3) and (5)). Similar to Equation (3) is the parameterization

$$\vec{x}(u,v) = \begin{pmatrix} r\sin v \cos u \\ r\sin v \sin u \\ r\cos v \end{pmatrix} \quad \text{with} \quad u \in [0, 2\pi],\ v \in [0, \pi]. \tag{6}$$

We now generalize this equation as follows:

$$\vec{x}(u,v) = \begin{pmatrix} r\sin v \cos u \\ r\sin v \sin u \\ r\cos v + cu + d\log\tan ev \end{pmatrix} \quad (\tan ev > 0). \tag{7}$$

In order to get equations for whole families of surfaces, for $c = d = 0$ we still have the sphere (Figure 6.2a). For $c \neq 0, d = 0$, we get a family of circular helical

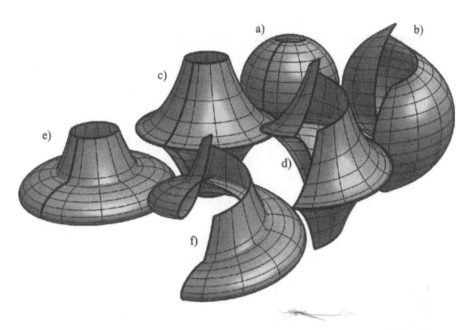

FIGURE 6.2. Surfaces corresponding to the variations of the constants in Equation (7).

surfaces (Figure 6.2b: $d = 1$). For $c = 0, d \neq 0$, we get a family of surfaces of revolution (Figure 6.2c,d), among them the "pseudosphere" ($d = r, e = \frac{1}{2}$). Its meridian is a so-called traktrix (Figure 6.2d). The most general case ($c \neq 0, d \neq 0$) leads to combinations of these surfaces (Figure 6.2e,f).

The OPEN GEOMETRY-code to create these surfaces looks like this:

Listing of program BOOK/pseudosphere.cpp (Figure 6.2):

```
#include "opengeom.h"
#include "defaults3d.h"
// This is another example for displaying a math surface. The
// formulae were found at the Internet—location www.mhri.edu.au—
// and slightly modified. Thanks to the author Paul Bourke.
char Figure;
class PseudoSphere: public ParamSurface
{
public:
    P3d SurfacePoint( Real u, Real v )
    {
        Real r = 6, c, d, e;
        if ( Figure == 'a' )
            c = 0, d = 0, e = 0.5; // Figure 6.2a
```

```
         else if ( Figure == 'b' )
            c = 1, d = 0, e = 0.5; // Figure 6.2b
         else if ( Figure == 'c' )
            c = 0, d = r, e = 0.5; // Figure 6.2d
         else if ( Figure == 'd' )
            c = 1, d = r, e = 0.5; // Figure 6.2f
         else if ( Figure == 'e' )
            c = 0, d = r, e = 0.25; // Figure 6.2c
         else if ( Figure == 'f' )
            c = 1, d = r, e = 0.25; // Figure 6.2e
         Real x, y, z;
         x = r * cos( u ) * sin( v );
         y = r * sin( u ) * sin( v );
         z = r * cos( v ) + c * u + d * Log( tan( e * v ) );
            // Open Geometry function Log( ) involves security check!
         return P3d( x, -y, -z );
      }
};
PseudoSphere Surf[6];
void Scene::Init( )
{
   int n1 = 64, n2 = n1;
   const Real delta = 0.3;
   const Real size[6] = { 2.5, 4, 3.2, 4, 3, 3.2 };
   for ( int i = 0; i < 6; i++ )
   {
      Figure = ( char ) ('a' + i );
      Surf[i].Def( LightYellow, n1, n2, 0, 2 * PI, delta, 3.14 - delta );
      Surf[i].FitIntoSphere( size[i] );
      Surf[i].Translate( 7 * ( i / 2 - 1 ), 6 * ( i % 2 ) - 3, 0 );
      Surf[i].PrepareContour( );
   }
}
void Scene::Draw( )
{
   for ( int i = 0; i < 6; i++ )
   {
      Surf[i].Shade( SMOOTH, REFLECTING );
      Surf[i].Contour( Black, MEDIUM );
      Surf[i].DrawBorderLines( Black, MEDIUM );
      Surf[i].WireFrame( Black, 12, 12, THIN );
   }
}
```

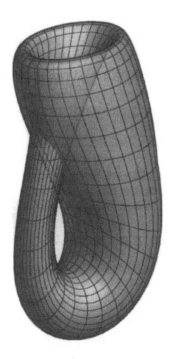

FIGURE 6.3. To illustrate the hidden parts of a surface (as in the case of a KLEIN bottle), it can be helpful to make the surface transparent.

We will now explain a little trick that allows us to make surfaces transparent. This can be a nice feature when we display complicated surfaces where the interior is not "trivial." Please have a look at the implementation of Scene::Draw( ) in the following listing.

The surface itself is the famous KLEIN bottle that cannot be oriented (i.e., there is no inside and no outside).

Listing of program X/SURF/klein_bottle.cpp (Figure 6.3):

```
#include "opengeom.h"
#include "defaults3d.h"

// KLEIN_BOTTLE

// This is another example for displaying a mathematical surface.
// The formulae were found at the Internet location
// www.mhri.edu.au
// and slightly modified. Thanks to the author Paul Bourke.
```

```
class KleinBottle: public ParamSurface
{
public:
    P3d SurfacePoint( Real u, Real v )
    {
        Real r = 5 *( 1 − cos( u ) / 2 );
        Real x, y, z;
        const Real a = 4, b = 15;
        if ( u < PI )
        {
            x = a * cos( u ) * ( 1 + sin( u ) ) + r * cos( u ) * cos( v );
            y = b * sin( u ) + r * sin( u ) * cos( v );
        }
        else
        {
            x = a * cos( u ) * ( 1 + sin( u ) )
                − r * ( 1 − (u − 2 * PI ) * ( u − PI ) / 10 ) * cos( v );
            y = b * sin( u );
        }
        z = r * sin( v );
        const Real k = 0.5;
        return P3d( k * x, k * z, − k * y );
    }
};

KleinBottle Bottle;

void Scene::Init( )
{
    int n_rot_circ = 61, n_parallel_circ = 61;
    Real u1 = 0, u2 = u1 + 2 * PI;
    Real v1 = −PI, v2 = v1 + 2 * PI;
    Bottle.Def( Green, n_rot_circ, n_parallel_circ, u1, u2, v1, v2 );
    Bottle.PrepareContour( );
}

void Scene::Draw( )
{
    // First, the bottle is shaded and equipped with
    // contour lines and parameter lines as usual.
    Bottle.Shade( SMOOTH, SUPER_REFLECTING );
    Bottle.Contour( Black, THICK );
    Bottle.WireFrame( Black, 30, 30, THIN );
    // Second, we redraw the surface transparently
    // (z-buffer deactivated)
```

```
        SetOpacity( 0.1 );
        TheCamera.Zbuffer( false );
        Bottle.Shade( SMOOTH, REFLECTING );
        Bottle.Contour( Black, MEDIUM );
        Bottle.WireFrame( Black, 30, 30, THIN );
        Bottle.ULines( Black, 2, MEDIUM );
        // reset defaults
        SetOpacity( 1.0 );
        TheCamera.Zbuffer( true );
    }
```

Figure 6.3 shows the result: usually invisible parts of the surface (including curves on the surface) can be seen through the visible parts of the surface. You can, of course, vary the degree of transparency, until you are satisfied with the result.

6.2 Swept Surfaces

So far we have given explicit parameterized equations for a surface. Now we give some examples where we prescribe an arbitrary parameterized line in 3-space and a "sweep-function." Though one can always easily find a parameterization when a generating curve and sweep function is given, this kind of definition can sometimes be clearer.

As a first example, we generate a parboloid (elliptic or hyperbolic) by means of translating one parabola along another (Figure 6.4).

Listing of program BOOK/paraboloid.cpp (Figure 6.4):

```
#include "opengeom.h"
#include "defaults3d.h"


Real K = 1;
class Parab: public ParamCurve3d
{
    virtual P3d CurvePoint( Real u )
    {
        return P3d( 2 * u, 0, u * u + K ); // Parabola in the xz-plane.
    }
};
class Paraboloid: public ParamSurface
{
    virtual P3d SweepFunction( Real v, P3d P)
```

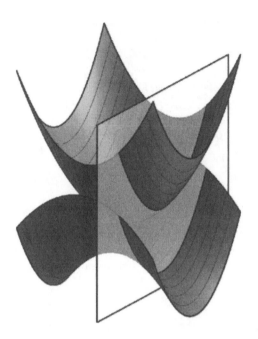

FIGURE 6.4. Elliptic and hyperbolic paraboloid as swept surfaces.

```
    {
        // Sweeping can be quite general. It may also deform the space
        // curve. In our simple case, we want to sweep one parabola along
        // another in order to get a paraboloid.
        P.Translate( 0, 2 * v, K * v * v ); // Parabola in yz-plane.
        return P;
    }
};


Paraboloid Surf[2];
Rect3d Rect;
L3d SampleSweptCurve[2];

void Scene::Init( )
{
    int n1 = 61, n2 = 61, u1 = −2, u2 = 2, v1 = −2, v2 = 2;
    Real u0 = 1;
    Parab parabola;
    for ( int i = 0; i < 2; i++ )
    {
        K = ( i == 0 ? 1 : −0.6 );
        Surf[i].Def( Yellow, n1, n2, u1, u2, v1, v2, parabola );
```

```
            Surf [i].GetULine( SampleSweptCurve [i], u0, Black ) ;
            Surf [i].PrepareContour( ) ;
        }
    Rect.Def( LightBlue, 12, 10 ) ;
    Rect.Rotate( Xaxis, 90 ) ;
    Rect.Translate( −6, 2 ∗ u0, −2 ) ;
}

void Scene::Draw( )
{
    for ( int i = 0; i < 2; i++ )
    {
        Surf [i].Shade( SMOOTH, REFLECTING) ;
        Surf [i].ULines( Black, 20, THIN ) ; // 20 swept parabolas
        Surf [i].WireFrame( Black, 2, 2, MEDIUM ) ; // bord. parabolas
        Surf [i].Contour( Black, MEDIUM ) ;
        SampleSweptCurve [i].Draw( MEDIUM ) ; // the one in the rect.
    }
    Rect.ShadeTransparent( LightBlue, 0.7, Black, MEDIUM ) ;
}
```

As a second example, we create a PLÜCKER surface (Figure 6.5): a straight line rotates about an axis. At the same time, it swings harmonically along this axis. The parameterized straight line is derived from *ParamCurve3d*.

Listing of program BOOK/pluecker.cpp (Figure 6.5):

```
#include "opengeom.h"
#include "defaults3d.h"

// Pluecker conoid and generalizations:
// A straight line rotates about z and moves along z harmonically
class Rule: public ParamCurve3d
{
    virtual P3d CurvePoint( Real u )
    {
        return P3d ( u, 0, 0 ); // Straight line
    }
};
Real N = 2;
class Conoid: public ParamSurface
{
```

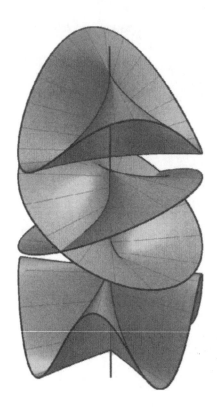

FIGURE 6.5. PLÜCKER conoid and related harmonic conoidal surfaces.

```
virtual P3d SweepFunction( Real v, P3d P)
{
    P.Rotate( Zaxis, Deg( v ) );
    P.Translate( 0, 0, 3 * sin ( N * v ) ); // harmonical movement
    return P;
}
};

Conoid Surface [3];
void Scene::Init( )
{
    Rule c;
    N = 2; // Pluecker conoid
    Surface [0].Def( LightCyan, 30, 91, −6, 6, 0, PI, c );
    Surface [0].Translate( 0, 0, 7 );
    N = 1;
    Surface [1].Def( LightCyan, 30, 91, −6, 6, 0, 2 * PI, c );
```

```
      N = 4;
      Surface[2].Def( LightCyan, 30, 91, −6, 6, 0, PI, c );
      Surface[2].Translate( 0, 0, −7 );
      for ( int i = 0; i < 3; i++ )
          Surface[i].PrepareContour( );
}
void Scene::Draw( )
{
    Zaxis.Draw( Black, −12, 12, MEDIUM );
    for ( int i = 0; i < 3; i++ )
    {
        Surface[i].Shade( SMOOTH, REFLECTING );
        Surface[i].ULines( DarkGray, 15, THIN );
        Surface[i].VLines( Black, 2, MEDIUM );
        Surface[i].Contour( Black, MEDIUM );
    }
}
```

A final example shows how to create a surface of revolution by rotating a meridian about an axis (Figure 6.6). Additionally, the surface is then inverted at a sphere (with a center that does not lie on the rotation axis).

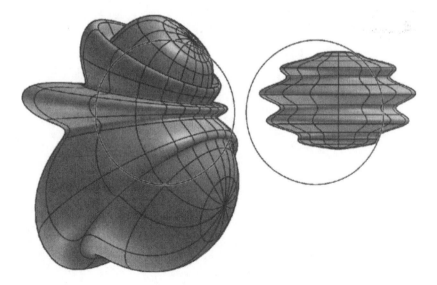

FIGURE 6.6. A surface of revolution (right) and its inverted surface (left).

Listing of program BOOK/funny_surf.cpp (Figure 6.6):

```cpp
#include "opengeom.h"
#include "defaults3d.h"

class SomeMeridian: public ParamCurve3d
{
    virtual P3d CurvePoint( Real u )
    {
        return P3d ( ( 1 + 0.15 * sin( 10 * u ) ) * 3 * cos( u ),
                     0,  1 + 2 * sin( u ) );
        // Meridian of a surface of revolution in the xz-plane.
    }
};

Sphere InvertingSphere;
Boolean Invert = false;

class FunnySurface: public ParamSurface
{
    virtual P3d SweepFunction( Real v, P3d P)
    {
        P.Rotate(Zaxis, Deg( v ) );
        // So far, we have a surface of revolution.
        // An inversion makes things more complicated.
        if ( Invert )
            P.Inversion( InvertingSphere );
        return P;
    }
};

FunnySurface Surface[2];
void Scene::Init( )
{
    P3d center( -0.5, -1, 0.5 );
    InvertingSphere.Def( Yellow, center, 3, 200 );
    SomeMeridian c;
    int n = 135;
    Surface[0].Def( LightBlue, n, n, -1.57, 1.57, 0, 2 * PI, &c );
    Invert = true;
    Surface[1].Def( LightBlue, n, n, -1.57, 1.57, 0, 2 * PI, &c );
    for ( int i = 0; i < 2; i++ )
        Surface[i].PrepareContour( );
    Surface[1].Translate( 0, -6.5, 0 );
}
```

```
void Scene::Draw( )
{
    for ( int i = 0; i < 2; i++ )
    {
        Surface[i].Shade( SMOOTH, REFLECTING );
        Surface[i].WireFrame( Black, 15, 15, THIN );
        Surface[i].Contour( Black, MEDIUM );
        Zbuffer( false );
        CreateAura( MEDIUM );
        InvertingSphere.Draw( Black, THIN );
        InvertingSphere.Translate( 0, −6.5, 0 );
        Zbuffer( true );
    }
    InvertingSphere.Translate( 0, 13, 0 );
}
```

6.3   Surfaces of Revolution

The third example of a swept surface showed how a surface of revolution can be created by rotating a meridian about an axis (Figure 6.6). We also showed how a surface of revolution can be described by parameterized equations (Figure 6.1), but since surfaces of revolution are such an important special case of surfaces, we introduced a class *SurfOfRevol*.

Due to historical reasons, we implemented many methods for these surfaces, with many of them being very specific. In this context, we just introduce some kinds of definitions and the corresponding constructors:

class *SurfOfRevol*;   → declaration in `"revol.h"`

> Describes a surface of revolution. No abstract class. Derived from *ParamSurface*.

Constructors:

> SurfOfRevol(**const** *StrL3d* &a = *Zaxis*);
> SurfOfRevol(*Color* c, *Boolean* isSolid, **int** rot_zahl, *Spline3d* &k,
>   *Real* w1 = 0, *Real* w2 = 360);
> SurfOfRevol(*Color* c, *Boolean* solid, **int** n_vertices,
>   *Coord3dArray* points_on_meridian,
>   **int** fine, **int** order, *Real* w1 = 0, *Real* w2 = 360);

Definitions:

> **void** Def(**const** *StrL3d* &a = *Zaxis*);
> **void** Def(*Color* c, *Boolean* isSolid, **int** rot_zahl, *Spline3d* &k,

$$Real\ \text{w}1 = 0,\ Real\ \text{w}2 = 360\ );$$
void Def(*Color* c, *Boolean* solid, **int** n_vertices,
Coord3dArray points_on_meridian,
int fine, **int** order, *Real* w1 = 0, *Real* w2 = 360);

In practice, curves are frequently only given by a discrete number of points. The listing for Figure 6.7 shows how we can describe a meridian of a surface of revolution by a few points, smoothen it by means of cubic splines, and then rotate it about an axis.

Listing of program BOOK/revol.cpp (Figure 6.7):

```cpp
#include "opengeom.h"
#include "defaults3d.h"

SurfOfRevol Surf[2];

void Scene::Init( )
{
    Coord3dArray P =   // 8 points on the meridian
```

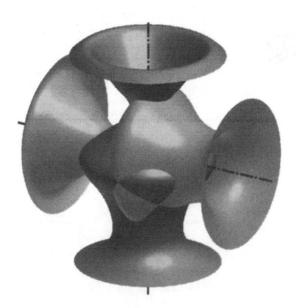

FIGURE 6.7. A smooth surface of revolution created by only a few points on the meridian. The second surface is congruent. Since the two surfaces touch several times, we have double points on the intersection lines.

```
   {
      { 6, 0, −9 }, { 3, 0, −7 }, { 4, 0, −3 }, { 5.4, 0, 0 },
      { 1.6, 0, 3 }, { 3, 0, 6 }, { 4.8, 0, 8.6 }, { 6.4, 0, 8 }
   };
   int order = 120, fine = 15;
   Color col [ 2 ] = { Blue, LightOrange };
   for ( int i = 0; i < 2; i++ )
      Surf [i].Def( col [i], HOLLOW, 8, P, fine, order );
   Surf [ 1 ].Rotate( Xaxis, 90 );
}
void Scene::Draw( )
{
   for ( int i = 0; i < 2; i++ )
   {
      Surf [i].Shade( SMOOTH, REFLECTING );
      Surf [i].GetAxis( ).LineDotted( Black, −12, 12, 21, THICK );
   }
}
```

6.4 Helical Surfaces

When we apply a rotation about an axis, a, and—at the same time—a proportional translation along a, points move along helices. The proportionality factor p is called the parameter of the helical motion. For $p = 0$, we have a pure rotation; for $p = \infty$, we have a pure translation.

class *HelicalSurface;* → declaration in `"revol.h"`

        Describes a helical surface. No abstract class. Derived from *ParamSurface.*

    Additional Definition:

        void Def(*Color* c, *Real* **param**, **int** order, *Spline3d* &k,
                             Real w1, *Real* w2);
        // Rotation angles w1 and w2 degrees.

The additional definition method allows us to pass splines as parameters. As an example, we passed a circle (Figure 6.8 left and Figure 6.9 left). In the corresponding images to the right, we first applied the helical motion to the points of the spline in such a way that the points are transformed into the base plane ($z = 0$). The result is, of course, the same surface. The borders, however, are different.

FIGURE 6.8. A circle is transformed by means of a helical motion. In this special case, the result is a tubular surface. In the image to the right, the points of the generating curve are first transformed into the base plane.

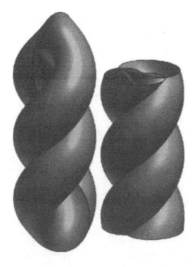

FIGURE 6.9. The same task as in the previous image. This time, however, the generating circle is vertical and symmetrical to the helical axis.

Listing of program BOOK/helical.cpp (Figure 6.8):

```
#include "opengeom.h"
#include "defaults3d.h"


HelicalSurface Surf[2];


void Scene::Init( )
{
    const Real H = 6, parameter = H / ( 2 * PI );
    const int N = 12;
    L3d circle( Gray, N );  // We define a circle
    P3d P( 0, 2, 0 );
    for ( int i = 1; i <= N; i++ )
    {
        circle[i] = P;
        P.Rotate( Xaxis, 360. / ( N - 1 ) );
    }
    CubicSpline3d m;
    Real r = 3;
    circle.Translate( 0, r, 0 );
    circle.Rotate( Yaxis, Deg( parameter / r ) );
    m.Def( Black, 5, circle );
    Surf[0].Def( Green, parameter, 200, m, -360, 270 );
    Surf[0].Translate( 0, -5, 0 );
    // Now transform the spline into the base plane
    for ( i = 1; i <= m.Size( ); i++ )
    {
        m[i].Rotate( Zaxis, -Deg( m[i].z / parameter ) );
        m[i].z = 0;
    }
    Surf[1].Def( Green, parameter, 200, m, -360, 270 );
    Surf[1].Translate( 0, 5 , 0 );
}
void Scene::Draw( )
{
    for ( int i = 0; i < 2; i++ )
        Surf[i].Shade( SMOOTH, REFLECTING );
}
```

6.5   Tubular Surfaces

Other special surfaces that are implemented in OPEN GEOMETRY are the tubular surfaces. They are swept by a sphere (Figure 6.10–6.12).

class *TubularSurface*;   → declaration in `"tubular.h"`

> Describes a tubular surface. No abstract class. Derived from *Param-Surface*.

Additional Definition:

> **void** Def(*Color* c, **int** n, *Coord3dArray* P, **int** fine, *Real* fi1, *Real* fi2,
>   **int** n1, **int** n2, *Real* radius);
> // n is the number of given points, P are the given points.
> // fine is the number of in between points.
> // fi1, fi2 are the parameters for the great circle of the sphere
> // (usually 0, 2π).
> // n1 is the number of points on the great circle.
> // n2 is the number of points on the center line.
> // radius is the radius of the sweeping sphere (and the great circle).

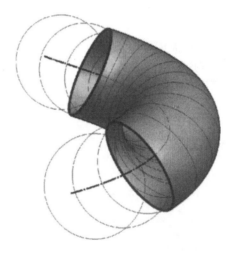

FIGURE 6.10. A tubular surface is swept by a sphere. The surface consists of great circles of the sphere.

Listing of program `BOOK/tubular.cpp` (Figure 6.11):

```
#include "opengeom.h"
#include "defaults3d.h"
```

FIGURE 6.11. Four examples for tubular surfaces, among them a helical surface.

```
void coords( Real &x, Real &y, Real &z, Real u, int i )
    // This is an aux. function in order to get points on a smooth curve
{
    switch ( i )
    {
    case 0:
        x = 3 * cos ( 2 * u ) + 3 * cos ( 3 * u );
        y = 3 * sin ( 2 * u ) + 3 * sin ( 3 * u );
        z = 3 * sin ( 2 * cos ( u − PI / 4 ) );
        break;
    case 1: // helix
        u *= 2;
        x = 4 * cos( u );
        y = 4 * sin( u );
        z = 0.5 * u;
        break;
    case 2:
        x = −cos( u ) + 3 * cos( u ) + 4 * cos( −2 * u );
        y = −sin( u ) + 3 * sin( u ) + 4 * sin( −2 * u );
        z = 4 * sin( 4 * cos ( u − PI / 8 ) );
        break;
    case 3:
        x = 3 * cos( 2 * u ) − 2 * cos ( u ) − 1;
        y = 4 * sin( 2 * u );
        z = 4 * sin( 4 * cos ( u − PI / 8 ) );
        break;
    }
}
TubSurf Surf[4];
```

```
void Scene::Init( )
{
    const int size = 20;
    Real P [size] [3];
    for ( int i = 0; i < 4; i++ )
    {
        Real u = 0, du = 2 * PI / ( size − 1 );
        for (int k = 0; k < size; k++, u += du )
            coords( P [k] [0], P [k] [1], P [k] [2], u, i );
        int n1 = 20, n2 = 200;
        Surf [i].Def( Yellow, size, P, 10, 0, 2 * PI, n1, n2, 0.5 );
        Surf [i].Translate( ( i % 2 ) * 12 − 6, ( i / 2 ) * 12 − 6, 0 );
    }
}


void Scene::Draw( )
{
    for ( int i = 0; i < 4; i++ )
        Surf [i].Shade( SMOOTH, REFLECTING);
}
```

FIGURE 6.12. Top view of the four surfaces of Figure 6.11.

6.6 Function Graphs

As a last example, we show how function graphs are implemented in OPEN GEOMETRY. For a function graph, we can find at least one parallel projection, where all projection rays intersect the surface at most at one point, without being tangent to it. If such a projection direction is given by the z-axis of a Cartesian (x, y, z) coordinate system, the surface Φ may be written as $z = z(x, y)$, i.e., as a graph of a bivariate function f, defined over some domain D in the xy-plane.

class *FunctionGraph*; $\rightarrow$ declaration in `"paramsurface.h"`

Describes a function graph. Abstract class. Derived from *ParamSurface*.

Additional Method:

void ShadeSolidBlockUnderGraph(*Color* c, *Real* zmin);

This class is abstract due to the fact that the equation $z = z(x, y)$ had to be implemented as a purely virtual function:

virtual *Real* z(*Real* x, *Real* y) = 0;

Thus, the user has to derive a new class from *FunctionGraph*, as in the following listing:

Listing of program `X/Surf/fctgraph.cpp` (Figure 6.13):

```
#include "opengeom.h"
#include "defaults3d.h"

class SomeGraph: public FunctionGraph
{
```

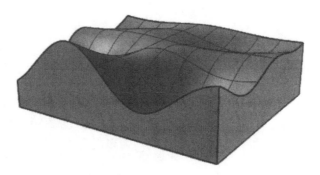

FIGURE 6.13. A function graph above a rectangular domain in the xy-plane. By means of the method ShadeSolidBlockUnderGraph( ), it can be interpreted as a solid.

```
virtual Real z( Real x, Real y )
{
    // Apply some weared functions.
    x *= 0.3; y *= 0.3;
    Real z = ( y + sin( y ) − 2 * sin( 2 + y ) );
    z *= ( 2 * sin( 0.9 * x ) − 1 );
    z *= exp( −( 0.8 * x + 0.4 * y − 1 ) / 20 );
    z *= 0.3 * cos( x + 0.7 * y − 1 );
    return z + 2;
}
};
SomeGraph F;
void Scene::Init( )
{
    int n = 60;
    F.Def( Green, n, n, −7.5, 9, −9, 11 );
    F.PrepareSmoothShading( );
    F.PrepareContour( );
}
void Scene::Draw( )
{
    F.Shade( SMOOTH, REFLECTING );
    F.WireFrame( Black, 10, 6, THIN );
    F.WireFrame( Black, 2, 2, MEDIUM );
    F.Contour( Black, MEDIUM );
    F.ShadeSolidBlockUnderGraph( Gray, −3 );
}
```

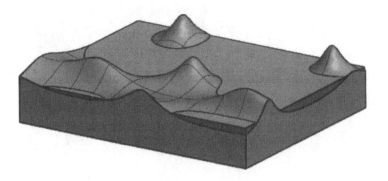

FIGURE 6.14. A flooded landscape.

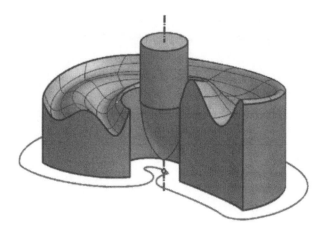

FIGURE 6.15. Milling of a function graph by means of a rotating cutter [18].

Finally two more images: Figure 6.14 shows how landscapes can be created with function graphs (program **X/Surf/sealevel.cpp**); Figure 6.15 shows the milling process of a sculptured surface (program **X/MILLING/sculpt_surf.cpp**).

Solids

In this chapter, we talk about how solids can be stored in computer files so that sufficient information is provided for a wide range of geometrical questions concerning these solids. In particular, polyhedral solids are treated. We focus on their boundary representation since it is mainly in OPEN GEOMETRY that this model is used. At the end of this chapter, the difficulties are addressed that can naturally arise from Boolean products of polyhedra.

7.1 What Is a Solid?

For simulating the real world on the computer, it is important to treat solids beside curves and surfaces. Intuitively, a solid is a bounded, closed point set of the Euclidean 3-space satisfying some restrictions that catch our idea of "solidity." In particular, a solid is "all material"; there is no single point, line, or two-dimensional area missing. In the language of point-set topology, a solid $\mathbf{S}$ equals the closure of its interior, i.e., $\mathbf{S} = clos(int\mathbf{S})$.

A solid $\mathbf{S}$ may be disconnected, but the boundary of each component $\mathbf{S}_i$ is a compact connected and orientable two-dimensional manifold $\partial\mathbf{S}_i$. However, for solids generated from basic solids by Boolean operations, this property can sometimes be disturbed. There might be exceptional points or line segments where $\partial\mathbf{S}_i$ touches itself. We have to be aware of this fact, even when we confine ourselves solely to polyhedral solids later on.

7.2   How to Represent Solids

For the representation of solids, we have to encode the infinite point set in a finite amount of computer storage. This should be done in such a complete way that arbitrary geometric questions about this solid can be answered algorithmically. Three classes of representations can be distinguished:

1. *Decomposition models*: The solid is seen as the union of a collection of primitive object types. Frequently, the basic building blocks are tiny cubes from a regular subdivision of space.

2. *Constructive models*: The basis consists of *primitives* that can be arbitrarily scaled and displaced in space. The solid is obtained from these primitives by Boolean operations.

3. *Boundary models*: The closed solid **S** is defined by its boundary ∂**S**. This is a collection of faces that, in the most general form, are portions of parametric surfaces. Each face has a boundary in the form of a curve.

The advantages and disadvantages of these three classes will be briefly outlined below.

Decomposition Model

If a bounding box of the solid is given, then the basis cubes can be stored in a three-dimensional array of binary data. As the storage requirements rise sharply with increased resolution, a recursive subdivision is used. This then leads to the *octree representation*. The algorithms for handling such structures are extremely simple, but slow because of the mere size of the objects. For example, the Boolean operations are just bitwise operations of "and" and "or." Any decomposition model of a solid (see Figure 7.1) is approximated, and its relation to the solid is not invariant against rotations.

The "voxelized" model has become standard in digital tomography and image scanning devices. For a concise summary on recent visualization techniques in medical imaging, the reader is referred to [13], pp. 303–328. New fast rendering techniques brought significant improvements, and many other application areas are beginning to appreciate the benefits of this kind of volumetric modeling.

For FEM (Finite Element Method), another decomposition model is used, the *cell decomposition*. Here the solid is decomposed into an array of cubes with curved edges and with disjoint interior.

Constructive Model

The most important example is the *CSG tree*, where CSG stands for "Constructive Solid Geometry": The solid is the root of a binary tree. The leaves are given

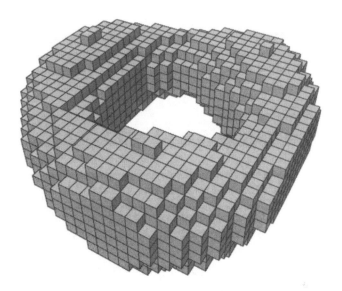

FIGURE 7.1. Voxelized toroidal solid

basis solids, so-called *primitives*. Hence, each leaf consists of a type identifier and a sequence of dimension parameters. The interior nodes express Boolean operations or displacements (cf. [17], see Figure 7.2). This kind of model[1] is user-friendly, as it utilizes the geometric description of the solid that is usually much shorter and clearer than explicit lists of data.

There are some algorithms developed for this type of representation. The *set-membership classification* for determining whether a given point X is *in* a given

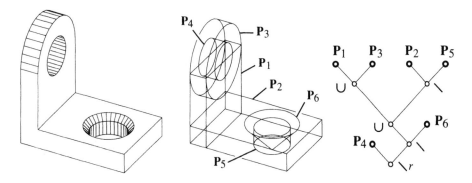

FIGURE 7.2. 3D object and its CSG tree. The primitives $\mathbf{P}_1, \mathbf{P}_2$ are boxes, $\mathbf{P}_3, \mathbf{P}_4, \mathbf{P}_5$ are cylinders, and $\mathbf{P}_6$ is a cone. The notation $\mathbf{L} \setminus_r \mathbf{R}$ stands for $\mathbf{R} \setminus \mathbf{L}$.

---

[1]The CSG tree of any object is obviously not unique, but this does not cause any troubles.

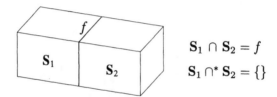

$$\mathbf{S}_1 \cap \mathbf{S}_2 = f$$
$$\mathbf{S}_1 \cap^* \mathbf{S}_2 = \{\}$$

FIGURE 7.3. Boolean intersection versus set-theoretic intersection.

solid S or *on* the solid (i.e., $X \in \partial\mathbf{S}$) or *out* of S, is rather easy because X can be transferred back to the involved primitives. However, some care is necessary for the following reason: primitives are closed point sets. Therefore, the *Boolean intersection* of two solids $\mathbf{S}_1$ and $\mathbf{S}_2$ actually means

$$\mathbf{S}_1 \cap^* \mathbf{S}_2 := clos(int\mathbf{S}_1 \cap int\mathbf{S}_2). \tag{1}$$

For example, the Boolean intersection $\mathbf{S}_1 \cap^* \mathbf{S}_2$ of the two bricks displayed in Figure 7.3 is empty, while the intersection $\mathbf{S}_1 \cap \mathbf{S}_2$ of the closed point sets gives the common rectangular face f. However, for the sake of simplicity, we will only use the symbol $\cap$ instead of $\cap^*$ in the sequel.

The CSG tree of a Boolean product of two solids is obtained by joining the two given trees together with a node combining the original roots. The CSG tree of a solid can immediately be used for obtaining a ray-traced image since all the Boolean operations now have to be executed on the one-dimensional ray only (cf. [22]).

Constructive models have the virtue that they can be converted into any other representation. The conversion from the CSG tree to the boundary model is called the *boundary evaluation* and is an essential part in almost all CSG modelers. So the applicability of this truly economical CSG model is not as restricted as it might look. This model, as well as the following boundary model are exact, up to the restricted precision of the involved floats.

Boundary Model

The explicit representation of the boundary has the advantage that most of the solid's volumetric data is immediately available. The integration of area and volume is easy, the set-membership classification is a standard routine. Hidden-line algorithms for boundary models often run with hardware support. However, the data structure of the boundary model is rather complex. Concerning the validity of boundary models, expensive tests would be necessary to guarantee the geometric integrity. There might be self-intersections. In particular, CSG objects might have no convenient representation as boundary models. This deficiency may cause problems, but experienced users can avoid such objects.

Set operations for boundary models are computationally expensive (see the following sections) and sensitive for numerical problems. Therefore, boundary model description mechanisms based on the CSG conversion of set operations are always vulnerable.

Constructive models can be converted into decomposition models approximately as easily as CSG models. But this makes little sense: if the exact information is already available, why attempt its reconstruction? The *inverse boundary evaluation*, i.e. the conversion from a boundary representation to a CSG model, still remains an unsolved problem.

7.3 Boundary Representation of Polyhedral Models

There are different ways of representing the boundary when the faces are portions of parametric surfaces. However, from now on we restrict to polyhedral models with faces as portions of planes. Also many commercial modellers use this kind of approximation for real objects (compare Figure 7.4).

The boundary $\partial \mathbf{P}$ of a polyhedron $\mathbf{P}$ contains vertices, edges, and faces. An *edge e* is a closed line segment bounded by two vertices. A *face f* is a closed subset of the spanned plane $[f]$ consisting of one or more polygonal disks with a disjoint interior. These polygons need not be simply connected: there might be holes. Each polygon is defined by its boundary, the so-called *loops*. We use a

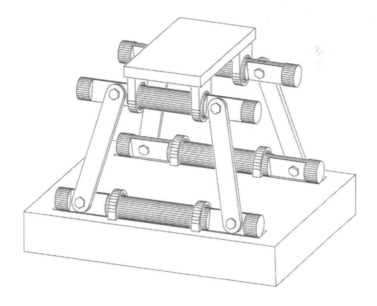

FIGURE 7.4. Polyhedral approximation of a compliance element that provides an infinitesimal spherical mobility of degree 2.

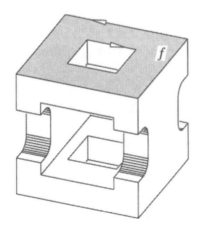

FIGURE 7.5. Orientation of loops.

vertex-based boundary model; so each loop $\mathcal{L}$ is a cyclic sequence of vertices.[2] For each polygon of the face f, the neighboring interior of the polyhedron $\mathbf{P}$ is on the same side of the plane $[f]$. This side (with or without the points of $[f]$) is called the (closed or open) *inside halfspace* of f, the other being called the *outside halfspace*. It might happen that two faces f_1, f_2, of $\mathbf{P}$, share the same spanned plane $[f_1] = [f_2]$; but then the corresponding inside halfspaces must differ.

Each loop of face f has an unambiguous *orientation* that obeys the following rule (see Figure 7.5): When looking from outside onto f and running the loop in the given order, then the (two-dimensional) interior of the face lies on the left side.

The vertices of $\mathbf{P}$ together with the list of faces, each given by its consistently ordered vertex loops, define a polyhedron uniquely. The coordinates of the vertices are sometimes called the "geometrical data" of $\mathbf{P}$. The lists of loops are called "topological data," as they define the face-edge-vertex adjacencies and the orientations. For the polyhedron displayed in Figure 7.6 the data is as follows:

Vertex list:

$$\vec{v}_1 = (24.0, 28.0, \ 0.0) \qquad \vec{v}_2 = (48.0, 28.0, \ 0.0) \qquad \vec{v}_3 = (24.0, 48.0, \ 0.0)$$
$$\vec{v}_4 = (24.0, \ 0.0, 25.7) \qquad \vec{v}_5 = (48.0, \ 0.0, 25.7) \qquad \vec{v}_6 = (48.0, \ 0.0, 10.2)$$
$$\vec{v}_7 = (24.0, \ 0.0, 10.2) \qquad \vec{v}_8 = (48.0, \ 5.9, 42.1) \qquad \vec{v}_9 = (48.0, 48.0, 26.8)$$
$$\vec{v}_{10} = (24.0, 48.0, 26.8) \qquad \vec{v}_{11} = (\ 0.0, \ 0.0, \ 0.0) \qquad \vec{v}_{12} = (\ 0.0, \ 0.0, 70.0)$$
$$\vec{v}_{13} = (48.0, \ 0.0, \ 0.0) \qquad \vec{v}_{14} = (48.0, \ 0.0, 70.0) \qquad \vec{v}_{15} = (48.0, 48.0, 70.0)$$
$$\vec{v}_{16} = (\ 0.0, 48.0, \ 0.0) \qquad \vec{v}_{17} = (\ 0.0, 48.0, 70.0) \qquad \vec{v}_{18} = (24.0, \ 5.9, 42.1)$$

---

[2]Concerning different databases like edge-based loop lists, the winged-edge structure, or the half-edge structure, the reader is asked to refer to [16].

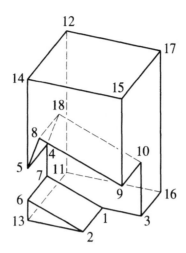

FIGURE 7.6. Geometrical and topological data of a polyhedron.

Faces with loops:

f_1: $(12, 14, 15, 17)$ f_2: $(1, 2, 13, 11, 16, 3)$

f_3: $(4, 5, 14, 12, 11, 13, 6, 7)$ f_4: $(15, 14, 5, 8, 9)(13, 2, 6)$

f_5: $(16, 17, 15, 9, 10, 3)$ f_6: $(17, 16, 11, 12)$

f_7: $(5, 4, 18, 8)$ f_8: $(9, 8, 18, 10)$

f_9: $(2, 1, 7, 6)$ f_{10}: $(18, 4, 7, 1, 3, 10)$

The following examples reveal that other databases of polyhedra may cause ambiguities:

- It is surprising that the *lists of vertices and edges* together need not be sufficient for defining a polyhedron uniquely. A standard example of three polyhedra with a common wire-frame model is displayed in Figure 7.7.

- In [19], two distinct polyhedra that share all *vertices* as well as all *oriented planes* spanned by their faces are presented. One is the union of the five left tetrahedra inscribed into a regular pentagon-dodecahedron. The second is its mirror image (see Figure 7.8; the shaded faces at the two polyhedra span the same plane).

What could be done in order to test whether a given boundary representation defines any polyhedron? One necessary condition is that each edge has two neighboring faces. This is, of course, not sufficient enough to prevent from self-intersections. However, self-intersections could be detected when one completes the boundary by replacing the polyhedron **P** by **P** ∪ **P** (or **P** ∩ **P**), where the boundary representation of the Boolean product is determined according to Chapter 8.

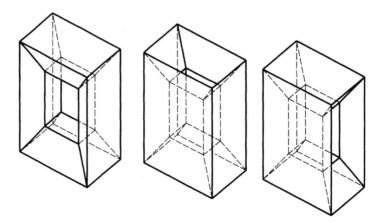

FIGURE 7.7. Three polyhedra with the same edges.

Even for a connected polyhedron, it would be neither necessary nor sufficient to check the consistency of the given boundary representation by computing the EULER characteristic according to the formula

$$\chi(\mathbf{P}) := n_v - n_e + n_f = 2 - 2g,$$

where n_v, n_e, n_f are the numbers of vertices, edges, and faces of $\mathbf{P}$, and g denotes its genus. This formula is only true when there are no holes in the faces. Note the counter example in Figure 7.9 which is a topological sphere (see [2]).

For further details on the evaluation of polyhedra, refer to [1].

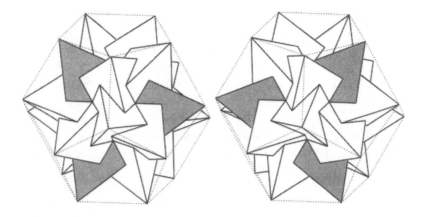

FIGURE 7.8. Two polyhedra sharing all vertices and oriented bounding planes.

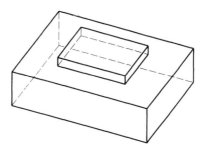

FIGURE 7.9. A topological sphere **P** with $n_v - n_e + n_f = 16 - 24 + 11 = 3 \neq \chi(\mathbf{P})$.

7.4 Polyhedra in OPEN GEOMETRY

When OPEN GEOMETRY is treating any polyhedron **P**, then the vertices as well as the faces are stored in linked lists. Each face contains a list of loops. Each loop is stored as a linked list of vertex pointers. For many procedures on polyhedra, it is recommendable to use more data than the bare minimum. So we associate with each face f the *normal unit vector* $\vec{n}_f$ pointing outside, i.e., away from the material. And we associate the linear equation of $[f]$. We have to be aware of the fact that due to floating-point rounding off, the points of f will only more or less obey this equation (cf. [1]).

It is not possible to require a particular order of the loops in the faces. Therefore, some care is necessary when the normal unit vector $\vec{n}_f$ of face f is computed from the given loops of f. We start with a vertex V (coordinate vector $\vec{v}$) [3] with extreme coordinates, e.g., with a minimal x-coordinate and—in case of an ambiguity—with a minimal y- or z-coordinate, too. This implies that $\vec{v}$ belongs to an outside loop $\mathcal{L}$ with an anticlockwise orientation, if seen from outside. Additionally, the inside angle of $\mathcal{L}$ at $\vec{v}$ must be less than 180 degrees.

Then we specify two other vertices $\vec{v}_1$, $\vec{v}_2$, in the loop $\mathcal{L}$ such that the order of $\vec{v}_1$, $\vec{v}$, $\vec{v}_2$ is compatible with the cyclic order in $\mathcal{L}$ (see Figure 7.10a,b). Additionally, what we require for the vector-product $\vec{p} := (\vec{v}_2 - \vec{v}) \times (\vec{v}_1 - \vec{v})$ is that the squared norm obeys

$$|\vec{p}|^2 = \vec{p} \cdot \vec{p} = (\vec{v}_2 - \vec{v})^2 (\vec{v}_1 - \vec{v})^2 - \left[(\vec{v}_2 - \vec{v}) \cdot (\vec{v}_1 - \vec{v}) \right]^2 > \varepsilon^2$$

for given small positive ε. Then we obtain

$$\vec{n}_f := \frac{\vec{p}}{|\vec{p}|}. \tag{2}$$

---

[3]In the following we frequently identify points with their coordinate vector. There will be no confusion, though contrary to the point V its coordinate vector $\vec{v}$ strongly depends on the choice of the coordinate system.

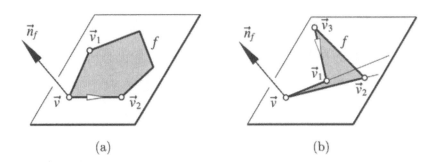

FIGURE 7.10. Computation of the outside normal vector of a face.

How do we figure out appropriate vertices $\vec{v}_1$, $\vec{v}_2$, in the face f? We start with the neighbors of $\vec{v}$ in the loop $\mathcal{L}$. Suppose $|\vec{p}| < \varepsilon$ for this choice. Then Figure 7.10b shows an example where the results for $\vec{n}_f$ according to (2) differ when either $\vec{v}_1$ or $\vec{v}_2$ is replaced by the neighbor $\vec{v}_3 \neq \vec{v}$; the vectors $(\vec{v}_2 - \vec{v}) \times (\vec{v}_3 - \vec{v})$ and $(\vec{v}_3 - \vec{v}) \times (\vec{v}_1 - \vec{v})$ point into opposite directions. We notice that $\vec{v}_1$ and $\vec{v}_3$ are on the same side of the line $[\vec{v}\vec{v}_2]$. On the other hand, $\vec{v}_2$ and $\vec{v}_3$ are separated by $[\vec{v}\vec{v}_1]$, and this causes the reversion of the vector product.

So the strategy must be, replace $\vec{v}_2$ by the next vertex $\vec{v}_2^*$ in the loop $\mathcal{L}$, provided that $\vec{v}_2$ and $\vec{v}_2^*$ are on the same side of the line $[\vec{v}\vec{v}_1]$. Iterate as long as points $\vec{v}_2^*$ are available until $\vec{p}$ meets the condition $|\vec{p}| > \varepsilon$. If this fails, then go the other way round: replace $\vec{v}_1$ repeatedly by its forerunner $\vec{v}_1^*$ in the loop $\mathcal{L}$ without crossing the line $[\vec{v}\vec{v}_2]$, until the normalization of $\vec{p}$ works.

This method must lead to a triangle $\vec{v}_1 \vec{v} \vec{v}_2$ of a better shape, provided $\mathcal{L}$ contains a vertex in the exterior of the sector enclosed by the halflines $[\vec{v}\vec{v}_1]$ and $[\vec{v}\vec{v}_2]$. Otherwise, the whole loop $\mathcal{L}$ is almost aligned. In this case, one may still succeed by replacing either $\vec{v}_1$ or $\vec{v}_2$ by any point of another loop in f^1, if available. However, one can't rule out that a Boolean product of two polyhedra contains poorly shaped faces with nearly aligned vertices and $|\vec{p}| < \varepsilon$ for each choice.

Here, we are facing another subtle numerical problem that will appear several times in the sequel: due to the floating-point rounding off, we need an absolute limit ε. However, after a regular affine transformation of the polyhedron, e.g., after a similarity transformation with a rather small dilatation factor, it might happen that in a face there are no more three vertices $\vec{v}, \vec{v}_1, \vec{v}_2$, that obey the condition $|\vec{p}| > \varepsilon$. So, there is an immanent discrepancy between our model with a fixed precision approximation and the *ideal world of geometry*. In our model, the property of being a triangle is not generally invariant under all regular affine transformations, and this makes all algorithms unstable in a certain sense.

It turns out that it is also useful to provide a *list of edges* as redundant data of **P**. We extract this linked list from the given loop lists. With each edge e, we associate pointers to its endpoints and to the neighboring faces. The order of the end points orientates the edge e. And this implies an order for the neighboring

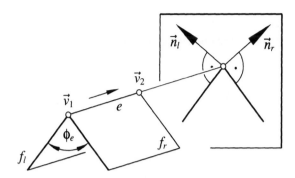

FIGURE 7.11. Characterization of convex edges.

faces: one face lies left, the other on the right, when looking from the outside and running from the first vertex torwards the second.

In addition, it is helpful to indicate whether an edge e is *convex* (inside angle $\varphi_e < 180°$) or *concave* ($\varphi_e > 180°$). Let $\vec{n}_r, \vec{n}_l$ denote the normal unit vectors of the left and right face of edge e with endpoints $\vec{v}_1, \vec{v}_2$. Then (see Figure 7.11) edge e is convex if and only if

$$\det\left(\vec{v}_2 - \vec{v}_1, \vec{n}_l, \vec{n}_r\right) > 0 \,. \tag{3}$$

The following diagram shows roughly how in OPEN GEOMETRY the types vertex, edge, face, and polyhedron are defined:

```
typedef struct Vertex
{
    long id;   // Index used in the loops
    coord3 pnt;   // The coordinates
    struct Vertex *next; // Pointer to next vertex
} Vertex;

typedef struct Face
{
    double dist;   // x.n > dist  <=>  x outside
    coord3 normal_vector;
    Boolean vis;   // visibility
    listelement *first_Loop;
    struct Face *next;
} Face;

typedef struct Edge
{
    Vertex *iV, *eV;  // bounding points
    Face *lF, *rF;   // left and right face
```

```
        Boolean concave;
        struct Edge *next;
    } Edge;

    typedef struct Polyhedron
    {
        Boolean connected, convex;
        unsigned short id, color;
        Vertex *first_Vertex;
        Edge *first_Edge;
        Face *first_Face;
        box bounding_box;
        struct Polyhedron *next;
    } Polyhedron;
```

When a polyhedron is transformed under a *regular affine transformation*, then the vertices are mapped according to

$$\vec{v} \;\mapsto\; \vec{v}' = \vec{a} + A\vec{v} \tag{4}$$

with a regular 3×3 matrix A and a constant vector $\vec{a}$. Let A^T denote the transposed matrix of A. Then the normal vectors $\vec{n}, \vec{n}'$ of corresponding faces obey

$$\vec{n} \;\mapsto\; \vec{n}' = \frac{\vec{n}^*}{|\vec{n}^*|}, \quad \text{where} \quad \vec{n}^* = A^{T-1}\vec{n}, \tag{5}$$

as $(\vec{v}_2' - \vec{v}_1') \cdot \vec{n}^* = (\vec{v}_2 - \vec{v}_1) \cdot \vec{n}$ for all $\vec{v}_1, \vec{v}_2, \vec{n} \in \mathbf{R}^3$. In the particular case of a motion, the matrix A is orthogonal, i.e., $A^T = A^{-1}$; then the normalization of $\vec{n}^*$ can be omitted.

Note that affine transformations with $\det A < 0$ do not preserve the orientation. Therefore, in this case all loops have to be reversed in order to meet the rules defined above.[4] And for each edge, the left and right face have to be interchanged when the order of the vertices is retained. The transformation of normal vectors given in (5) remains valid in any case.

7.5 Consistency Conditions for Polyhedra

Polyhedra can be more "pathological" than one might expect, thinking on regular polyhedra or prisms only (cf. [11]). We have already pointed out that the boundary of a polyhedron obtained by Boolean operations need not be a mani-

---

[4]When a linked list is to be reversed, then each element becomes the successor of the next element. And the original initial element gets **NULL** as its next.

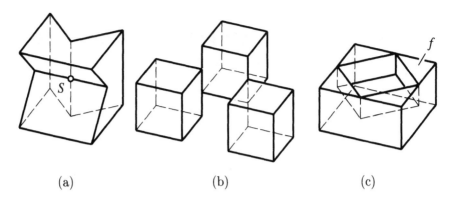

FIGURE 7.12. Some "pathological" polyhedra.

fold, even when only primitives like boxes or cylinders are used. Figure 7.12a shows a polyhedron **P** with a point S where the boundary touches itself. Hence, $\partial \mathbf{P}$ is no manifold; there is no two-dimensional open neighborhood of S on the $\partial \mathbf{P}$ homeomorphic to the open unit disk. The following definition is an attempt to meet the demands of Constructive Solid Geometry:

Under the following conditions, a polyhedron **P** is called *consistent*:

(C1) Each face f is bounded by loops of edges and vertices. Consecutive edges in a loop can be aligned, provided either the second neighboring faces or the corresponding loops differ. Two distinct edges of f are not allowed to cross, i.e., their (one-dimensional) interiors must be disjoint. Two distinct loops in f can only share single points. When vertex $\vec{v}$ is common for the two loops $\mathcal{L}_1, \mathcal{L}_2$ in f, then $\mathcal{L}_1$ lies either inside or outside $\mathcal{L}_2$, as otherwise the orientation of the loops would fail.

(C2) Let f_l and f_r be the two neighboring faces of edge e. Then the spanned planes $[f_l]$ and $[f_r]$ must be different. When e is convex, then the intersection of the two (open or closed) inside halfspaces of f_r and f_l is called the (*open* or *closed*) *inside wedge* of e, otherwise their union. The boundary of this inside wedge consists of two halfplanes called the *inside halfplanes* of f_l and f_r with respect to edge e.

An edge of **P** with more than two neighboring faces is called *multiple edge*. Such an edge is quoted repeatedly in the list of edges, and we suppose that the corresponding open inside wedges are disjoint. In order to avoid self-intersections of $\partial \mathbf{P}$, the (two-dimensional) interiors of each two faces must be disjoint.

(C3) Each vertex $\vec{v}$ defines a set of edges ending at $\vec{v}$ and a set of corresponding neighboring faces. The faces can be ordered into loops such that consecutive faces are neighbors of an edge through $\vec{v}$. These cyclic sequences of edges and faces represent the neighborhood of vertex $\vec{v}$ and they define pyramids

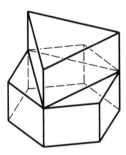 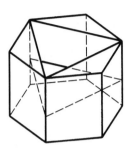

FIGURE 7.13. Coinciding vertices and edges.

with vertex $\vec{v}$, the so-called *vertex pyramids*. We suppose that each vertex
pyramid contains at least three different faces.

Note that the considered polyhedra obviously need not be convex. A vertex
may be located in faces or edges that do not belong to the corresponding vertex
pyramid. An edge e may be located in a face that is no neighboring face of e. Two
distinct edges may have a common point that is not a vertex of the polyhedron
(Figure 7.12a or b). There may be *multiple vertices* with more than one vertex
pyramid. Examples with such particularities can also be seen in [11] or [12], p. 38.

When in a face there are touching loops, then the definition of the loops can
be ambiguous, for example, the top face f of the polyhedron displayed in Figure 7.12c can either be seen as four pairwise touching triangles or as a square
with a hole (compare also Figure 7.13).

When working with OPEN GEOMETRY, one should avoid such pathologies for
the following reasons: On the one hand, the hidden lines algorithm might fail
because of numerical inaccuracies. On the other hand, our data structure can
imply logical errors. Look at the polyhedron **P** of Figure 7.12c: According to
(3), the vertical edges e of the deepening are concave, and the angle of the
inside wedge is $> 180°$. But at **P**, the interior of e actually consists of two
convex wedges. OPEN GEOMETRY does not provide such sophisticated control
mechanims that move the vertices of the inside loop in the top face a little bit
off from the outside loop. This is left to the user.

8

Boolean Operations

Boolean set operations have their prominent position in solid modeling. The algorithms behind are fairly nontrivial programs, and their proper treatment leads easily to a very hairy case analysis. This analysis must be based on various tests for the identity of points or vectors, for linear dependence, complanarity, and intersection, which are difficult to implement robustly in the presence of numerical errors.

In this chapter we start with a detailed exposition of the algorithm. For each case, we distinguish between the so-called generic case, where no particular positions occur, and the special cases. The latter may be omitted on first reading.

8.1 Types of Boolean Operations

Why Boolean operations?

Even for simple polyhedra, the boundary representation is rather complex. For example, the data of the polyhedron in Figure 7.6 is given on page 185. Instead of generating this data by hand, it is much more convenient to implement only the geometric description of this polyhedron. For example, the polyhedron in Figure 7.6 is obviously the difference of two particular prisms, and this information should be sufficient for obtaining its data.

Hence, all we need is
- a certain stock of primitives that can be scaled and located arbitrarily,
- a CSG tree of the required polyhedron **R**, and

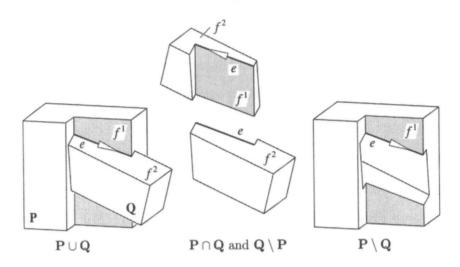

FIGURE 8.1. Boolean products of the prismatic polyhedra **P** and **Q**.

- an algorithm for carrying out the boundary evaluation.

Apart from displacements of polyhedra, this conversion consists of iterated computations of the boundary representation of a Boolean product of two polyhedra. Therefore, Boolean operations are inevitable for generating the boundary representation of complex polyhedra.

There are three types of Boolean operations: the *union* **P** ∪ **Q**, the *intersection* **P**∩**Q** in the sense of equation (7.1), and the *subtraction* **P****Q** (see Figure 8.1 with prisms **P**, **Q**). The exact meaning of the latter again differs from the set-theoretic meaning, as the difference polyhedron is exactly

$$\mathbf{P} \setminus^* \mathbf{Q} := clos[int(\mathbf{P} \setminus \mathbf{Q})]. \tag{1}$$

However, for the sake of brevity, we again write "\" instead of "*".

In order to reduce the subtraction to an intersection, we define the *complement* of a polyhedron **Q** as

$$\overline{\mathbf{Q}} := clos\{X \mid X \ out \ of \ \mathbf{Q}\}. \tag{2}$$

For example, the complement $\overline{\mathbf{Q}}$ of a cube **Q** consists of the complete space from which just the interior of cube **Q** is removed. We see that **Q** and $\overline{\mathbf{Q}}$ share their boundary $\partial\mathbf{Q} = \partial\overline{\mathbf{Q}}$, but for each face the inside and the outside halfspace have to be exchanged. This implies that a polyhedron can be complemented in the following four steps:

(i) Reverse all loops.

(ii) For each face f, replace the normal vector $\vec{n}_f$ by $-\vec{n}_f$.

(iii) For each edge, permutate the two neighboring faces f_l, f_r.

(iv) For each edge, permute the edge attributes *"convex"* and *"concave."*

However, we have to pay attention to the fact that the complement $\overline{\mathbf{Q}}$ of a bounded polyhedron $\mathbf{Q}$ is an unbounded point set.

By virtue of the complementation, we can replace the Boolean subtraction of polyhedra by the intersection according to

$$\mathbf{P} \setminus \mathbf{Q} = \mathbf{P} \cap \overline{\mathbf{Q}}. \tag{3}$$

Hence, there remain only two Boolean operations to execute. We could even replace the union by

$$\mathbf{P} \cup \mathbf{Q} = \overline{\overline{\mathbf{P}} \cap \overline{\mathbf{Q}}} \tag{4}$$

but then the intersection of two unbounded polyhedra would be required. Otherwise, it turns out that the algorithms for the union and the intersection of two polyhedra differ by only a few steps. Therefore, it does not essentially lengthen the program code when both Boolean operations are treated simultaneously.

8.2 Three Main Steps

Let the boundary representations of two consistent polyhedra $\mathbf{P}^1$ and $\mathbf{P}^2$ be given.[1] We compute the boundary either of $\mathbf{P}^1 \cap \mathbf{P}^2$ or of $\mathbf{P}^1 \cup \mathbf{P}^2$ in three steps:

Step 1: Intersect each face f^1 of $\mathbf{P}^1$ with each face f^2 of $\mathbf{P}^2$. The edges of intersection will be called *mixed edges* in the sequel, since the two neighboring faces f^1, f^2 originate from distinct polyhedra.

Step 2: Merge in all faces f of $\mathbf{P}^1$ and $\mathbf{P}^2$ the given loops with all mixed edges with f as one neighboring face.

Step 3: Check for each loop $\mathcal{L}$ of $\mathbf{P}^1$ or $\mathbf{P}^2$ that is not met by any mixed edge, whether $\mathcal{L}$ is part of the resulting polyhedron $\mathbf{R}$.

The most time-consuming step is the first one. The intersection of two faces has to be executed $(n_f^1 \times n_f^2)$ times when n_f^i denotes the number of faces of $\mathbf{P}^i$. One can perhaps save time by checking the bounding boxes of $\mathbf{P}^1$ and $\mathbf{P}^2$ first.

---

[1]From now on we consequently use the superscripts 1 and 2 in order to distinguish between elements of the two given polyhedra.

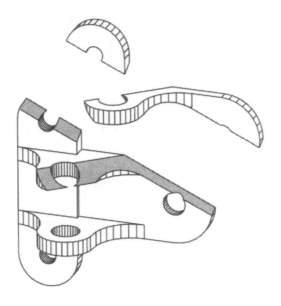

FIGURE 8.2. A split polyhedron.

When there is a separating plane between the boxes, then $\mathbf{P}^1 \cap \mathbf{P}^2$ is empty and $\mathbf{P}^1 \cup \mathbf{P}^2$ can be obtained by unifying the lists of vertices, faces, and edges. However, this database might be nonconsistent, as the oriented planes spanned by the faces $f^1 \subset \partial \mathbf{P}^1$ and $f^2 \subset \partial \mathbf{P}^2$ may be identical. So, even for disjointed bounding boxes, a comparison of faces is recommendable.

Finally, it should also be pointed out that the *splitting* of a polyhedron into two parts by any given plane α (cf. Figure 8.2) can be seen as the composite of two Boolean operations: in this case one "polyhedron" is specified as one of the two closed halfspaces of α. This *halfspace-polyhedron* is unbounded with an empty vertex list and with a face list containing just one face in α without any loop. It is not hard to adapt the general algorithm so that also this type of polyhedron can be treated. In any case, remember that we have to be aware of complemented and therefore unbounded polyhedra when according to (3), the difference of two polyhedra is computed.

Points X of the boundary $\partial \mathbf{R}$ are characterized by the property that each open neighborhood of X contains points of the interior $int\mathbf{R}$ as well as points out of $\mathbf{R}$. This implies the following fundamental rules for the boundaries of $\mathbf{P}^1 \cup \mathbf{P}^2$ and $\mathbf{P}^1 \cap \mathbf{P}^2$. For the sake of brevity, we denote with N_X^i the open (or closed) *polyhedral neighborhood* of X with respect to $\mathbf{P}^i$. This means for $X \in int f^i$, the open (closed) inside halfspace of face f^i, for $X \in e^i$, the open (closed) inside wedge of edge e, and finally for the vertex $X \in \mathbf{P}^i$, its vertex pyramid, seen as an open (closed) solid:

$$X \in \partial(\mathbf{P}^1 \cup \mathbf{P}^2) \iff \begin{cases} X \in \partial\mathbf{P}^1 \text{ and } X \notin clos\mathbf{P}^2 \text{ or} \\ X \in \partial\mathbf{P}^2 \text{ and } X \notin clos\mathbf{P}^1 \text{ or} \\ X \in (\partial\mathbf{P}^1 \cap \partial\mathbf{P}^2) \text{ and the two sets } closN_X^1, \\ \quad closN_X^2 \text{ do not cover the whole space.} \end{cases} \quad (5)$$

$$X \in \partial(\mathbf{P}^1 \cap \mathbf{P}^2) \iff \begin{cases} X \in \partial\mathbf{P}^1 \text{ and } X \in int\mathbf{P}^2 \text{ and} \\ X \in \partial\mathbf{P}^2 \text{ and } X \in int\mathbf{P}^1 \text{ and} \\ X \in (\partial\mathbf{P}^1 \cap \partial\mathbf{P}^2) \text{ and } (intN_X^1 \cap intN_X^2) \neq \{\}. \end{cases}$$

8.3   Intersection of Faces, Generic Case

We execute step 1 of the general algorithm in the following way:

```
f1 = P1->first_Face;
while ( f1 != NULL )
{
    if ( !empty_intersection( f1, P2->bounding_box ) )
    {
        f2 = P2->first_Face;
        while ( f2 != NULL )
        {
            intersect( f1, f2 );
            f2 = f2->next;
        }
    }
    f1 = f1->next;
}
```

If the plane $[f^1]$ does not intersect with the bounding box of $\mathbf{P}^2$, then we can skip the comparison of f^1 with all faces of $\mathbf{P}^2$.

The intersection of two faces is a set of mixed edges e of the resulting polyhedron $\mathbf{R}$. All these edges are located on the line of intersection $s := [f^1] \cap [f^2]$. In the generic case, which is treated first, each mixed edge e contains interior points of f^1 and f^2. For $\mathbf{R} = \mathbf{P}^1 \cap \mathbf{P}^2$, the inside wedge of all e on s is the intersection of the inside halfspaces of the given faces f^1, f^2. For $\mathbf{P}^1 \cup \mathbf{P}^2$, the union of these halfspaces makes the inside wedge.

Figure 8.3 reveals that in the generic case, the mixed edge e must be convex for the intersection $\mathbf{P}^1 \cap \mathbf{P}^2$ and concave for the union $\mathbf{P}^1 \cup \mathbf{P}^2$. Let $\vec{n}^i$ denote the (outside) normal unit vector of face f^i, $i = 1, 2$. Then for all edges e on line s,

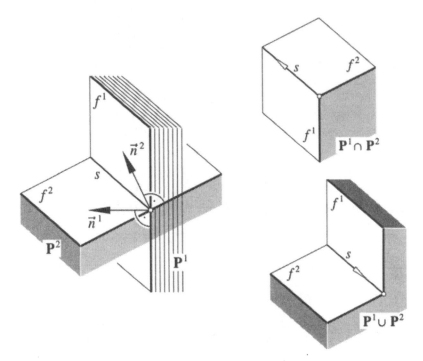

FIGURE 8.3. Orientation of the mixed edge e with respect to f^1—generic case.

the orientation with respect to f^1 is given by

$$\vec{s} := \begin{cases} \vec{n}^1 \times \vec{n}^2 & \text{for} \quad \mathbf{P}^1 \cap \mathbf{P}^2 \\ -\vec{n}^1 \times \vec{n}^2 & \text{for} \quad \mathbf{P}^1 \cup \mathbf{P}^2. \end{cases} \tag{6}$$

We start the algorithmic determination of $f^1 \cap f^2$ with the computation of the vector product $\vec{s}$. For $|\vec{s}| \leq \varepsilon$, we check the identity of the planes $[f^1]$ and $[f^2]$. The cases of direct or indirect identity of the oriented planes, i.e., of $|\vec{n}^1 - \vec{n}^2| < \varepsilon$ or $|\vec{n}^1 + \vec{n}^2| < \varepsilon$, will be treated later. For $|\vec{s}| > \varepsilon$, we compute an arbitrary point $\vec{s}_0$ on the line s and introduce a coordinate ξ on s according to

$$\vec{x} = \vec{s}_0 + \xi \vec{s} \ \mapsto \ \xi.$$

The intersection $s \cap f^i$ consists of disjointed line segments. Based on our coordinate system on line s, this set can be represented as the union of closed intervals

$$\mathcal{I}^i := [a_1^i, b_1^i] \cup \ldots \cup [a_{k_i}^i, b_{k_i}^i] \text{ for } i = 1, 2.$$

Whenever two consecutive vertices $\vec{v}_j, \vec{v}_k$ of any loop of f^1 are on distinct sides of s, then the joining edge $\vec{v}_j \vec{v}_k \subset f^1$ penetrates $s \subset f^2$. Let $l(\vec{x}) = 0$ denote the linear equation of $[f^2]$. Then the point $\vec{y}$ of intersection $[\vec{v}_j \vec{v}_k] \cap s$ obeys

$$\vec{y} = \vec{v}_j + \xi(\vec{v}_k - \vec{v}_j) \text{ for } \xi = -\frac{l(\vec{v}_j)}{l(\vec{v}_j) - l(\vec{v}_k)}$$

which results in

$$\vec{y} = \frac{l(\vec{v}_j)\vec{v}_k - l(\vec{v}_k)\vec{v}_j}{l(\vec{v}_j) - l(\vec{v}_k)} . \tag{7}$$

The ξ-coordinates of all points of intersection between the edges of f^1 and the plane $[f^2]$ must be put in natural order. When the polyhedron $\mathbf{P}^1$ is unbounded, then we add $-\infty$ at the beginning and ∞ at the end. By subdividing this sequence into pairs of consecutive coordinates, we obtain a set of intervals. The union $\mathcal{I}^1$ of these intervals represents $f^1 \cap [f^2]$. The same procedure for the loops of f^2 gives $f^2 \cap [f^1]$ and the corresponding subset $\mathcal{I}^2$ of $\Re$.

After these computations, the intersection $\mathcal{I}^1 \cap \mathcal{I}^2$ defines the common segments of f^1 and f^2 and therefore all mixed edges with the neighboring faces f^1 and f^2, independent from whether the intersection $\mathbf{P}^1 \cap \mathbf{P}^2$ or the union $\mathbf{P}^1 \cup \mathbf{P}^2$ is required (see Figure 8.1). Only the orientation of the mixed edges differs according to (6). However, it will turn out later that only in the generic case the sets of mixed edges for $\mathbf{P}^1 \cap \mathbf{P}^2$ and $\mathbf{P}^1 \cup \mathbf{P}^2$ are equal.

Step 1 ends up with a list of mixed edges. In the next step, these edges have to be merged with the loops of $\mathbf{P}^1$ and $\mathbf{P}^2$. For this purpose, the relative position of each mixed edge with respect to both polyhedra is needed. The exact type definition of mixed edges must cover all particular cases. The next sections will explain in detail that the bounding points of mixed edges can be located on edges of the given polyhedra or may even coincide with vertices of $\mathbf{P}^1$ or $\mathbf{P}^2$. Hence, the type of a mixed edge reads as follows:

> **typedef struct** *neighbors*
> {
>   *Vertex* ∗fore, ∗ident, ∗next;
> } *neighbors*;
>
> **typedef struct** *mixedEdge*
> {
>   *Vertex* ∗iV, ∗eV;
>   *Face* ∗lF, ∗rF;
>   *neighbors* iV_lF_nb, iV_rF_nb, eV_lF_nb, eV_rF_nb;
> } mixedEdge;

For the orientation given in (6), the left face of the mixed edge e is located in $[f^1]$, the right in $[f^2]$. When the initial point iV of e is a boundary point of f^1, then we store in iV_IF_nb its predecessor and its follower in the loop that passes through. Otherwise, the pointers fore and next are set as NULL. When the initial vertex iV of e happens to coincide with a vertex of f^1, then this pointer is the entry of ident in iV_IF_nb. Otherwise, iV_IF_nb->ident is set as NULL. The other "neighborhoods" iV_rF_nb, eV_IF_nb and eV_rF_nb are treated analogously.

For the resulting polyhedron $\mathbf{R}$, one has to expect three types of vertices: some originate from $\mathbf{P}^1$, some from $\mathbf{P}^2$; but the vertex list of $\mathbf{R}$ must also contain all bounding points of mixed edges. So the listing of mixed edges goes hand in hand with the generation of the vertex list of $\mathbf{R}$. And for each new edge, one has to check whether its initial point or its endpoint has already been stored among the vertices of $\mathbf{R}$.

While intersecting the faces, we also detect all pairs (f^1, f^2) of faces with $[f^1] = [f^2]$. In view of the future steps 2 and 3 in our algorithm, we provide a list of all pairs of coplanar faces.

8.4 The Geometry of Particular Cases

When the given polyhedra $\mathbf{P}^1$ and $\mathbf{P}^2$ have aligned edges or coplanar faces, then some of the general rules about Boolean operations can fail. Therefore, it is necessary to look for such particular instances. Due to our restricted precision, these events depend on an arbitrary ε, and we have already pointed out that this can cause trouble. However, we prefer this treatment since the alternative avoidance of all particularities by slight local modifications of the polyhedra $\mathbf{P}^1, \mathbf{P}^2$ may disturb essential geometric properties of the resulting polyhedron.

In this section we discuss the pure geometric background. The algorithmic aspect will be adressed in the next section.

Classification of Particular Cases

The following cases have to be distinguished:

P1	vertex in face	P5	edge in face
P2	intersecting edges	P6	aligned edges
P3	vertex on edge	P7	coinciding faces—equal orientation
P4	coinciding vertices	P8	coinciding faces—opposite orientation

With the order of these cases, a certain priority is expressed: each particular event has to be treated under its highest number. If, for example, the edges $e^1 \in \mathbf{P}^1$ and $e^2 \in \mathbf{P}^2$ have a common endpoint, then look at case P4 instead of P2 or P3. Additionally, if e^1 and e^2 happen to share a neighboring face, then the necessary criteria can be found under P7 or P8, but not under P2.

This classification will help to break the treatment of particular cases into simpler subproblems.

The Cases P1–P4

Let the vertex $\vec{v}^1 \in \mathbf{P}^1$ be located in the interior of the face $f^2 \in \mathbf{P}^2$. Then $\vec{v}^1$ is a vertex of the Boolean product $\mathbf{R}$ if and only if $[f^2]$ splits a vertex pyramid of $\vec{v}^1$ into two or more parts. We assume that no edge adjacent to $\vec{v}^1$ lies in f^1; this will be discussed in case P5. So there is an even number of $\mathbf{P}^1$ faces that intersect f^2 along a line segment bounded by $\vec{v}^1$. If the number of these edges is greater than two, then they have to be coupled into pairs of consecutive edges in view of the loops of $\mathbf{R}$ (see the object displayed in Figure 8.4a, which is the union of a truncated hollow cube $\mathbf{P}^1$ and a box $\mathbf{P}^2$).

In case P2, the edges $e^1 \in \mathbf{P}^1$ and $e^2 \in \mathbf{P}^2$ are supposed to meet at an interior point $\vec{v}$. Then $\vec{v}$ is a vertex of $\mathbf{R}$ if and only if the inside wedges of e^1 and e^2 are penetrating. Under this condition, $\vec{v}$ terminates at least four mixed edges of $\mathbf{R}$ (see Figure 8.4b). When the two open inside wedges are disjoint, then at least one of the edges must be convex.

In case P3, the vertex $\vec{v}^1$ is assumed in the interior of the edge e^2. Then $\vec{v}^1$ is a vertex of $\mathbf{R}$ if and only if a neighboring face f_l^2 or f_r^2 of e^2 splits a vertex pyramid of $\vec{v}^1$ into two or more parts. If this condition is given and e^2 contains no interior points of this vertex pyramid, then the edge e^2 can also be found at the union $\mathbf{R} = \mathbf{P}^1 \cup \mathbf{P}^2$. But ambiguity will arise when the edges in $[f_l^2]$ and $[f_l^2]$ have to be sorted into loops. One solution treats this case as if the vertex $\vec{v}^1$ of $\mathbf{R}$ is not

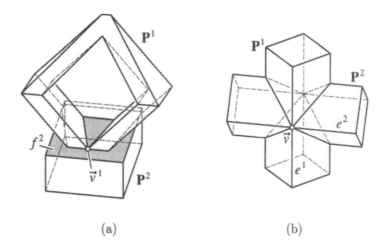

(a)   (b)

FIGURE 8.4. (a) Vertex $\vec{v}^1$ in face f^2. (b) Intersecting edges e^1, e^2.

located on e^2. We prefer the other solution where $\mathbf{R}$ contains two aligned edges on $[e^2]$ that share the endpoint $\vec{v}^1$ and the planes spanned by the neighboring faces. In this sense, we define four loops in the top face f of the polyhedron in Figure 7.12c on page 191 instead of only two.

In case P4, we suppose $\vec{v}^1 = \vec{v}^2$. This point is a vertex of $\mathbf{R}$ if and only if $\mathbf{R}$ is the union $\mathbf{P}^1 \cup \mathbf{P}^2$ or the interiors of vertex pyramids of $\vec{v}^1$ and of $\vec{v}^2$ are not disjoint. Examples with coinciding vertices are displayed in Figure 7.13 on page 192 when the polyhedra are seen as Boolean products of two prisms. However, these pairs of polyhedra also meet the conditions of case P6.

The Case P5

The following two cases are much more complex. It turns out that because of these particularities, the mixed edges of $\mathbf{P}^1 \cup \mathbf{P}^2$ may differ from that of $\mathbf{P}^1 \cap \mathbf{P}^2$—contrary to the general case. Moreover, the existence of mixed edges cannot be decided purely from the intersection of two faces f^1, f^2, but the 3D neighborhoods of the faces with respect to their polyhedra have to be taken into consideration too.

Suppose $e^1 \subset [f^2]$ and $int\, e^1 \cap int\, f^2 \neq \{\}$: then three subcases have to be distinguished:

(i) $[f^2]$ separates the inside halfplanes of the neighboring faces f_l^1, f_r^1 of e^1 properly (see Figure 8.5a). Then each connected component of $e^1 \cap f^2$ is a mixed edge of $\mathbf{R}$ with one neighboring face in $[f^2]$.

(ii) The inside wedge of e^1 lies *"face to face"* to $\mathbf{P}^2$, i.e., one neighboring plane of e^1, say $[f_r^1]$, is equal to $[f^2]$, but the orientations differ. One obtains mixed edges on e^1 in two cases: either e^1 is convex and $\mathbf{R}$ is the union $\mathbf{P}^1 \cup \mathbf{P}^2$ (Figure 8.5b), or e^1 is concave and $\mathbf{R}$ is the intersection $\mathbf{P}^1 \cap \mathbf{P}^2$ (Figure 8.5c).

No other case with $[f^2] = [f_r^1]$ gives rise to mixed edges.

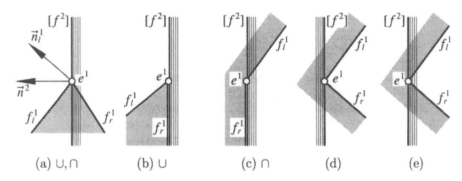

FIGURE 8.5. Case P5: edge e^1 in face f^2.

(iii) e^1 is concave and $[f^2]$ does not separate the open inside halfplanes of f_l^1 and f_r^1. Then it depends on the type of operation ($\cap$ or $\cup$) and on the orientation of f^2 whether e^1 contains an edge of **R** or not. However, this edge is never mixed (see Figure 8.5d).

In the case of $\mathbf{R} = \mathbf{P}^1 \cap \mathbf{P}^2$, an ambiguity seems to arise at a concave e^1, where the inside halfspace of f^2 is not a subset of the inside wedge of e^1 (see Figure 8.5e). Then e^1 could be seen as a double edge of **R** where both wedges have a bounding plane in $[f^2]$. But this version with two coincident edges of **R** in $[f^2]$ would contradict the consistency condition (C1) in section 7.5, page 191. So we better imagine that e^1 is translated a little towards the inside halfspace of f^2.

The Case P6

Let the edges e^1, e^2, be aligned, i.e., $[e^1] = [e^2]$ and $(inte^1 \cap inte^2) \neq \{\}$. In the following three cases, the segment $e^1 \cap e^2$ belongs[2] to a mixed edge e of **R**:

(i) At e^1 and e^2, the inside halfplanes of the neighboring faces separate each other, i.e. (see Figure 8.6a), for one neighboring face of e^2, the open inside

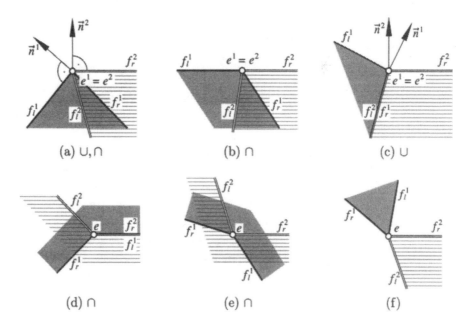

(a) $\cup, \cap$ (b) $\cap$ (c) $\cup$

(d) $\cap$ (e) $\cap$ (f)

FIGURE 8.6. Case P6: aligned edges e^1, e^2.

[2] Finally, this mixed edge e can be longer than $e^1 \cap e^2$ or even longer than $e^1 \cup e^2$.

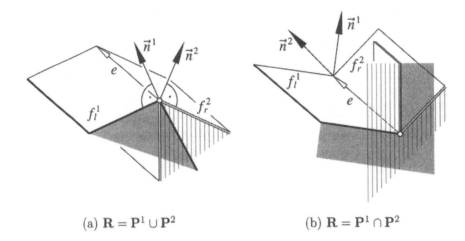

(a) $\mathbf{R} = \mathbf{P}^1 \cup \mathbf{P}^2$ (b) $\mathbf{R} = \mathbf{P}^1 \cap \mathbf{P}^2$

FIGURE 8.7. Orientation of the mixed edge e in the particular case P6.

halfplane lies in the open inside wedge of e^1, whereas for the other neighboring face, the inside halfplane is a subset of the open outside wedge of e^1, and vice versa. Under this condition, the union (intersection) of the open inside wedges gives the open inside wedge of e with respect to $\mathbf{R} = \mathbf{P}^1 \cup \mathbf{P}^2$ ($\mathbf{R} = \mathbf{P}^1 \cap \mathbf{P}^2$).

It can be excluded here that due to coplanar bounding planes (see Figure 8.6b), e vanishes since the inside wedge of e degenerates into a halfspace. This case will be treated under P7.

(ii) The inside wedges of e^1 and e^2 are face to face, and either $\mathbf{R}$ is the union and the open inside wedges of e^1 and e^2 are disjoint (Figure 8.6c), or $\mathbf{R}$ is the intersection and the open outside wedges are disjoint (Figure 8.6d). Again, the degenerate cases with coplanar neighboring planes of e will be discussed in P7.

(iii) At e^1 and e^2, the inside halfplanes do not separate, $\mathbf{R}$ is the intersection, and the outside wedges of e^1 and e^2 are disjoint (see Figure 8.6e). Then e is a double edge of $\mathbf{R}$. The open inside wedges of e are the two connected components of the intersection of the open inside wedges of e^1 and e^2. Obviously, e^1 or e^2 must be concave.

The case with not separating inside halfplanes and with disjoint inside wedges (see Figure 8.6f) gives no mixed edge, neither at $\mathbf{P}^1 \cup \mathbf{P}^2$ nor at $\mathbf{P}^1 \cap \mathbf{P}^2$.

Let the intersection $f^1 \cap f^2$ contain a mixed edge e originating from aligned edges e^1, e^2. Then one has to take into account that the formula (6) for the orientation of e with respect to f^1 (cf. Figure 8.3) fails if

- either $\mathbf{R}$ is the union and e is convex (Figure 8.7a)
- or $\mathbf{R}$ is the intersection and e is concave (see Figure 8.7b).

8.5   Intersection of Faces, Particular Cases

Improper Points and Improper Segments of Intersection

In Section 8.3, we described how in the general case the intersection $f^1 \cap f^2$ can be computed: we intersect the edges of f^1 with the plane $[f^2]$, and vice versa. The intersections $f^1 \cap [f^2]$ and $f^2 \cap [f^1]$ consist of disjoint closed line segments that finally have to be merged. This is carried out by determining the intersection $\mathcal{I}^1 \cap \mathcal{I}^2$ of the corresponding sets of ξ-coordinates.

Let the consecutive vertices $\vec{v}_j^1, \vec{v}_k^1$ of a loop $\mathcal{L}^1$ in f^1 be located on different sides of $[f^2]$, i.e., $l(\vec{v}_j^1) \cdot l(\vec{v}_k^1) < 0$ for $l(\vec{x}) = 0$ denoting the equation of $[f^2]$. Then we obtain a *"proper point of intersection"* according to equation (7). But now, in view of the particular cases P1, P5, P6 in the table on page 200, we have also to deal with the case $\vec{v}_i^1 \in [f^2]$. Such points of intersection will be called *"improper."*

The following criteria for an improper point $\vec{v}_i^1$ of intersection are based on the predecessor and the follower in the loop $\mathcal{L}^1$ through $\vec{v}_i^1$. So we must start our run through $\mathcal{L}^1$ at a point outside $[f^2]$.

Suppose $|l(\vec{v}_i^1)| < \varepsilon$: when $\vec{v}_{i-1}^1$ and $\vec{v}_{i+1}^1$ are on distinct sides of $[f^2]$ (see Figure 8.8a), i.e., $l(\vec{v}_{i-1}^1) \cdot l(\vec{v}_{i+1}^1) < 0$, then $\vec{v}_i^1$ bounds a segment of intersection between f^1 and $[f^2]$. In the case $l(\vec{v}_{i-1}^1) \cdot l(\vec{v}_{i+1}^1) > 0$, a loop of f^1 only touches $[f^2]$ at $\vec{v}_i^1$. However, under $|l(\vec{v}_{i+1}^1)| < \varepsilon$, the whole edge $\vec{v}_i^1 \vec{v}_{i+1}^1$ lies in $[f^2]$. Then according to P5 and P6, it depends not only on f^1 and f^2 but on the relative position of the inside wedges or halfspaces whether $\vec{v}_i^1 \vec{v}_{i+1}^1$ becomes a mixed edge of the Boolean product **R** or not. We call $\vec{v}_i^1 \vec{v}_{i+1}^1$ an *"improper segment of intersection,"* as opposed to *"proper"* segments, which contain interior points of the face f^1.

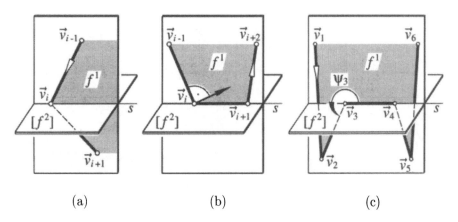

(a)	(b)	(c)

FIGURE 8.8. Improper points of intersection—improper and proper segments of intersection.

Proper segments of intersection are pairwise disjoint. We see in Figure 8.8b,c that improper segments can share a bounding point with other segments. While computing the intersection $f^1 \cap [f^2]$, we are unable to decide which portions of $\vec{v}_i^1 \vec{v}_{i+1}^1$ coincide with an edge of f^2, i.e., which parts of $\vec{v}_i^1 \vec{v}_{i+1}^1$ have to be handled according to P5 and which according to P6. We must postpone this decision after both intersections $f^1 \cap [f^2]$ and $f^2 \cap [f^1]$ have been determined and the sets of segments are going to be merged. But then we need the information as to which segments of intersection are proper and which are improper.

Whenever in this merging process an improper segment is treated, the criteria of P5 or P6 have to be applied carefully. It is obvious that distinct portions of $\vec{v}_i^1 \vec{v}_{i+1}^1$ have to be handled separately, as the relative position of the inside wedge of $\vec{v}_i^1 \vec{v}_{i+1}^1$ with respect to $\mathbf{P}^2$ may change (see Figure 8.9).

In a case with only proper intersections, all segments of intersection are enclosed by pairs of consecutive points of intersection. We see in Figure 8.8b,c that at improper points of intersection both can happen. Some terminate a proper segment too, some do not. Hence, an additional criterion is required

We learn from Figure 8.8c that the inside angle ψ_i of f^1 at $\vec{v}_i^1$ is decisive: the vertex $\vec{v}_i^1$ is a common bound for a proper and an improper segment of intersection if and only if $\psi_i > 180°$. Under $\psi_i = 180°$, the adjacent edges of $\vec{v}_i^1$ in f^1 are aligned and $\vec{v}_i^1$ bounds two improper segments of intersection. When ψ_i is acute (Figure 8.8b), then $\vec{v}_i^1$ only terminates the improper segment $\vec{v}_i^1 \vec{v}_{i+1}^1$.

In order to figure out whether ψ_i is acute or obtuse, let $\vec{n}^1$ denote the outside normal vector of f^1. Then we get (compare equation (7.2))

$$\det \left(\vec{n}^1, (\vec{v}_i^1 - \vec{v}_{i-1}^1), (\vec{v}_{i+1}^1 - \vec{v}_i^1) \right) \begin{cases} > 0 & \Leftrightarrow & \psi_i < 180° \\ < 0 & \Leftrightarrow & \psi_i > 180°. \end{cases} \qquad (8)$$

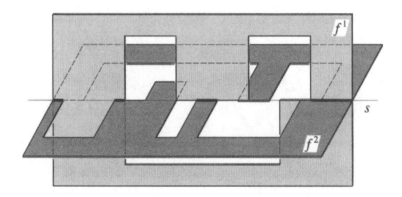

FIGURE 8.9. Mixed edges composed from proper and improper segments of intersection.

Before we merge the sets $f^1 \cap [f^2]$ and $f^2 \cap [f^1]$, we must know for each proper or improper point of intersection whether a point running along the oriented line $s = [f^1] \cap [f^2]$ is entering or leaving a proper or an improper segment of intersection.

One should also mention that at each proper point $\vec{y}$ of intersection between an edge $\vec{v}_k \vec{v}_{k+1} \subset f^1$ and $[f^2]$, it is possible to decide whether a proper segment is starting or ending there. We need in f^1 a vector perpendicular to $\vec{v}_k \vec{v}_{k+1}$ pointing to the inside halfplane of f^1 (compare Figure 8.8b). The dot product of this vector $\vec{n}^1 \times (\vec{v}_{k+1} - \vec{v}_k)$ and the direction vector $\vec{s}$ of s leads to the equivalence

$$d := \det \left(\vec{n}^1, (\vec{v}_{k+1} - \vec{v}_k), \vec{s} \right)$$

$$
\begin{matrix} d > 0 \\ d < 0 \end{matrix} \iff \vec{y} \text{ is } \begin{matrix} \text{initial} \\ \text{end-} \end{matrix} \text{ point of a } \begin{Bmatrix} \text{proper segment} \\ \text{of intersection.} \end{Bmatrix}
\tag{9}
$$

Algorithmic Treatment of the Cases P5 and P6

The particular cases P5 and P6 require some additional remarks since these cases have to be detected and handled while faces are intersected.

Suppose that in step 1 of the general algorithm the edge e^1 with the two neighboring faces f_l^1 and f_r^1 turns out to lie in $[f^2]$. Can the pairs (f_l^1, f^2) or (f_r^1, f^2) be neighbors of a mixed edge on e^1?

Let f^1 denote any neighboring face of f^1 at $\mathbf{P}^1$. Then we learn from Figure 8.5a,b,c that the following two conditions are necessary and sufficient:

(R1) Equation (6) gives a direction vector $\vec{s}$ for mixed edges on the line $s = [f^1] \cap [f^2]$, when seen as edges in a loop of $[f^1]$. When s and e^1 are equally oriented, then $f^1 = f_l^1$ is necessary; otherwise, $f^1 = f_r^1$.

(R2) The open inside halfplanes of f_l^1 and f_r^1 are either separated by $[f^2]$, or the neighboring face of e^1 which is different from f^1 coincides with $[f^2]$, but the outside normal vectors are opposite.

Let the edges $e^1 \in \mathbf{P}^1$ and $e^2 \in \mathbf{P}^2$ share the line segment $e := e^1 \cap e^2$. Then the line $[e]$ appears four times in step 1 as a line of intersection between two planes $[f^1], [f^2]$, since there are two neighboring planes at each polyhedron. Which pair (f^1, f^2) finally gives a mixed edge at $\mathbf{R}$? How can the rules of case P6 be executed?

An analysis of the cases depicted in Figure 8.6a,...,e reveals that for equally oriented e^1 and e^2 (as supposed in Figure 8.6), the following two conditions are necessary and sufficient:

(R3) The faces f^1 and f^2 are on distinct sides of e, i.e., f^1 is the (left) right neighboring face of e^1, and f^2 the (right) left neighboring face of e^2.

(R4) For $\mathbf{P}^1 \cup \mathbf{P}^2$, the open inside halfplane of f^1 and the open inside wedge of e^2 must be disjoint, and vice versa.

For $\mathbf{P}^1 \cap \mathbf{P}^2$, the opposite must be true, i.e., the open inside halfplane of f^1 must be a subset of the open inside wedge of e^2, and vice versa.

In the cases displayed in Figure 8.6c and d, the rule (R3) together with the first condition of (R4), respectively, is already sufficient.

The rules (R1) and (R2) as well as (R3) and (R4) are self-symmetric in the following sense: they must be preserved under complementation since a mixed edge remains mixed, while due to 4 "$\cap$" and "$\cup$" commute under this operation.

After all proper and improper segments of intersection between f^1 and $[f^2]$ on the one hand, and between f^2 and $[f^1]$ on the other, have been determined, these sets have to be merged: we obtain a mixed edge with neighboring faces in $[f^1]$ and $[f^2]$ if and only if it is a subset of either

(i) proper line segments in both intersections, or

(ii) a proper segment in one intersection and an improper segment in the other and it obeys the rules (R1) and (R2), or

(iii) two improper segments, and it obeys the rules (R3) and (R4).

When the intersection $f^1 \cap f^2$ yields two mixed edges that share a bounding point, then they should be combined to one edge (compare Figure 8.9) due to the consistency condition (C1), page 191.

Joint Edges

After all pairs (f^1, f^2) of faces $f^i \subset \mathbf{P}^i$ are intersected, we are able to figure out aligned edges e^1, e^2 with neighboring faces that are pairwise coplanar and equally oriented, e.g., $[f_l^1] = [f_l^2]$ and $[f_r^1] = [f_r^2]$. Such incidences happen frequently; see, for example Figure 7.3 or Figure 8.12. Unexpectedly, it is *not* generally true that the union (intersection) of these edges will appear as an edge of the union $\mathbf{P}^1 \cup \mathbf{P}^2$ (intersection $\mathbf{P}^1 \cap \mathbf{P}^2$) of the given polyhedra.

A counter-example can be found in Figure 8.10 where a simplified staircase $\mathbf{P}^1$ and a box $\mathbf{P}^2$ are given, with $\mathbf{P}^2$ representing exactly the lower part of $\mathbf{P}^1$: the first of the aligned edges e^1, e^2 is subset of the second. However, $e^1 = e^1 \cap e^2$ is an edge of the union $\mathbf{P}^1 \cup \mathbf{P}^2 = \mathbf{P}^1$, and $e^2 = e^1 \cup e^2$ is showing up at the intersection $\mathbf{P}^1 \cap \mathbf{P}^2 = \mathbf{P}^2$. This paradox is caused by the concave edge that follows e^1 in the loop of f^1.

Edges e that result from aligned edges e^1, e^2, with identical inside wedges will be called *joint edges* of the Boolean product $\mathbf{R}$ in the sequel. In Figure 8.11a, there are examples of this type. They will help to find an answer to the following

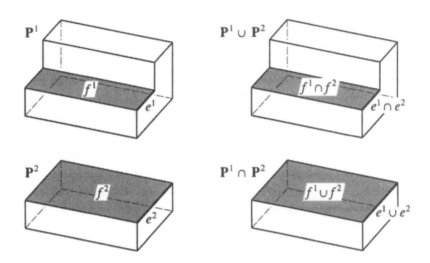

FIGURE 8.10. Paradox behavior of aligned edges e^1, e^2, with identical inside wedges.

question: which segments e on the line $l = [e^1] = [e^2]$ will become a joint edge of **R**?

According to (5), for a test point X on the line l, the rules are as follows:

$$X \in e \subset \mathbf{P}^1 \cap \mathbf{P}^2 \iff X \in e^i \text{ and } \begin{cases} X \in e^j \text{ or } X \in int f^j \text{ or} \\ X \in int\mathbf{P}^j, \ i \neq j \end{cases}$$

$$X \in e \subset \mathbf{P}^1 \cup \mathbf{P}^2 \iff X \in e^i \text{ and } \begin{cases} X \notin int f^j \text{ and} \\ X \notin int\mathbf{P}^j, \ i \neq j \end{cases} \tag{10}$$

Here f^j denotes a neighboring face of e^j on $\mathbf{P}^j$.

How can we figure out that $X \in int f^j$ or $X \in int f^j$ holds true, without using expensive inclusion tests for "point in polygon" or "point in polyhedron" (cf. section 8.2)? The examples in Figure 8.11a reveal the following equivalent propositions for the point X running along l: immediately after having left edge e^j at vertex $\vec{v}^j$, point X is *in* the face f^j if and only if the inside angle ψ^j at $\vec{v}^j$ is obtuse (compare (8)). And X is *in* $\mathbf{P}^j$ if and only if the neighboring edge of e^j at $\vec{v}^j$ in the loop $\mathcal{L}^j$ is concave.

When does the running point X leave the *"in-interval"* (i.e., *in* f^j or *in* $\mathbf{P}^j$)? There is either an additional edge e'^j on l, or the coincident edge e^i of the other polyhedron $\mathbf{P}^i$ is ending earlier or, finally (see Figure 8.11a, left, $(j, i) = (1, 2)$), X is leaving the in-interval before e^i ends. However, in the last case there must be any mixed edge e_m in one neighboring face of e^i with a bounding point $\vec{v}_m$ on l.

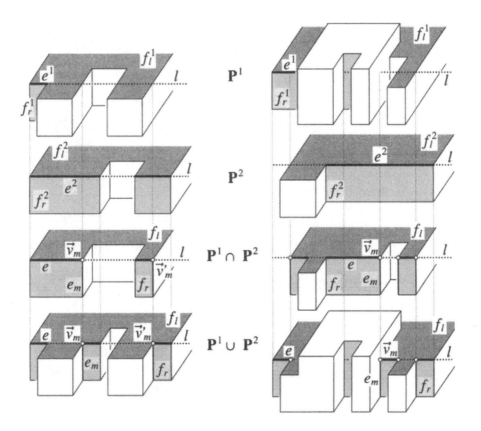

(a)   Edges $e^1 \in \mathbf{P}^1$, $e^2 \in \mathbf{P}^2$, and e of $\mathbf{P}^1 \cap \mathbf{P}^2$ and $\mathbf{P}^1 \cup \mathbf{P}^2$ on the line l.

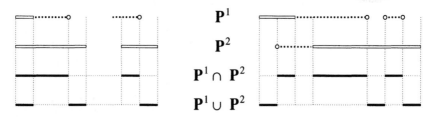

(b)   The "on-intervals" (double line) and the "in-intervals" (dotted) of $\mathbf{P}^1$, $\mathbf{P}^2$, $\mathbf{P}^1 \cap \mathbf{P}^2$, and $\mathbf{P}^1 \cup \mathbf{P}^2$ on l.

FIGURE 8.11. Aligned edges e^1, e^2 with identical inside wedges and the resulting joint edges e at $\mathbf{P}^1 \cap \mathbf{P}^2$ and $\mathbf{P}^1 \cup \mathbf{P}^2$.

There might even more such endpoints $\vec{v}'_m$ located on l, without any edge $e^j \in \mathbf{P}^j$ between. For this case it is sufficient to know whether $\vec{v}'_m$ is the initial point or the endpoint of an in-interval with respect to $\mathbf{P}^j$; the exact endpoint is not needed since the coinciding edge $e^i \in \mathbf{P}^i$ must end earlier. This requested property of $\vec{v}'_m$ can be figured out with the scalar product between a direction vector $\vec{s}$ of l and the outside normal vector of the l intersecting face f'^j according to (9).

Hence, we start the algorithm by collecting all edges e^1 along l and all endpoints of mixed edges on l. After sorting, we get a sequence of *"on-intervals"* (i.e., X on $e^1 \subset l$) and in-intervals. The same is done for $\mathbf{P}^2$. Then we merge according to the rules given in (10), which can be summarized briefly as

$$X \in e \subset \mathbf{P}^1 \cap \mathbf{P}^2 \iff on^i \text{ and } \left(on^j \text{ or } in^j \right), \; i \neq j$$
$$X \in e \subset \mathbf{P}^1 \cup \mathbf{P}^2 \iff on^i \text{ and not } in^j, \; i \neq j.$$

Here "on^i" stands for $X \in e^i$, and "in^i" for $X \in int f^i$ or $X \in int \mathbf{P}^i$.

This is illustrated in Figure 8.11a. The intervals along the line l are displayed in Figure 8.11b. On-intervals are indicated by double lines, in-intervals by dashed lines, and the endpoints of mixed edges are encircled.

8.6 Steps Two and Three

According to the definition of the main steps in section 8.2, the second step in our algorithm for carrying out the Boolean operations is devoted to the merging of mixed edges with the loops of the given polyhedra $\mathbf{P}^1, \mathbf{P}^2$. Afterwards when there is a loop remaining that is not met by any mixed edge, then in step 3 we have to decide whether this loop belongs to the resulting polyhedron $\mathbf{R}$ or not (see, for example, the top face of $\mathbf{P}$ in Figure 8.1).

Generic Case

Step 1 ends up with a list of mixed edges. For each such edge e, the left face $f_l = f^1$ stems from $\mathbf{P}^1$, the right face $f_r = f^2$ from $\mathbf{P}^2$. For the bounding points iV, eV of e, we have stored the adjacent vertices in f^1 and f^2 under the variables iV_lF_nb, eV_lF_nb and iV_rF_nb, eV_rF_nb, respectively.

Now we run all faces of $\mathbf{P}^1$ and $\mathbf{P}^2$. For each face f, we pick out those mixed edges e for which f is any neighbor. For the faces $f \subset \mathbf{P}^1$, edge e has already the right orientation: the neighbors of the initial point $\vec{a}$ of e can be found under iV_lF_nb, for the endpoint $\vec{b}$ of e under eV_lF_nb. However, for $f \subset \mathbf{P}^2$, we have to note that this time f is the right neighbor. Hence, we must reverse the orientation of the mixed edge e. Now eV_rF_nb gives the neighbors of the initial point $\vec{a}$ and iV_rF_nb that of the endpoint $\vec{b}$.

After these preparations of the mixed edges e in f, we start with a list of the *"old"* loops in f. During the merging process, we generate the list of *"new"* loops, the loops in $[f]$ that will belong to the resulting polyhedron **R**. In between, we also use a third list of *"split"* loops that, in general, are not closed. The list of the new loops and that of split loops are, of course, empty at the beginning.

The iterated algorithm for the insertion of e in the face f reads as follows:

(a) Suppose the initial point $\vec{a}$ of e is located on any edge $\vec{v}_i\vec{v}_{i+1}$ of f. Then we insert $\vec{a}$ on this edge in the following way: when the side $\vec{v}_i\vec{v}_{i+1}$ is found in any (old or new) loop, then we split this loop into the sequence $S_a := (\vec{a}, \vec{v}_{i+1}, \ldots, \vec{v}_i, \vec{a})$ and transfer it from the list of loops into the list of split loops.[3] When $\vec{v}_i\vec{v}_{i+1}$ is found in any split loop, then we split this loop once more into two sequences and insert $\vec{a}$ in both parts: the first part $S_a := (\ldots, \vec{v}_i, \vec{a})$ is added to the list of split loops. The second sequence $(\vec{a}, \vec{v}_{i+1}, \ldots)$ replaces the original split loop.

(b) Suppose $\vec{a}$ is not located on the boundary of f: then we look for any split loop ending with $\vec{a}$. If there is such a loop, then this is again denoted by S_a. Otherwise, we generate a new split loop S_a that consists of $\vec{a}$ only.

So, in any case, there is a split loop S_a with $\vec{a}$ at its end. After the edge $\vec{v}_i\vec{v}_{i+1}$ is subdivided into the two segments $\vec{v}_i\vec{a}$ and $\vec{a}\vec{v}_{i+1}$, we must pay attention to the fact that for all further mixed edges of f, the vertices $\vec{v}_i$, $\vec{v}_{i+1}$ are no more consecutive in any old, new, or split loop. Therefore, we have to update the neighbors and to replace one of them by $\vec{a}$ whenever another mixed edge in f has a bounding point between $\vec{v}_i$ and $\vec{v}_{i+1}$.

With the endpoint $\vec{b}$ of the mixed edge e, we proceed in a similar way:

(a) Suppose $\vec{b}$ has neighbors on any edge of f. When these neighbors are found in any (old or new) loop, we then insert $\vec{b}$ two times, split this loop into the sequence $S_b := (\vec{b}, \ldots, \vec{b})$, and cancel it from the looplist. When the pair of neighbors is found in any split loop S, we then subdivide this loop once more into two sequences. The first part ends with the inserted $\vec{b}$ and remains where it is. The second part starts with $\vec{b}$ and is called S_b.

(b) Suppose $\vec{b}$ has no neighbors: then we look for any split loop starting with $\vec{b}$. If there is such a loop, then this is canceled from the list of split loops and again denoted by S_b. Otherwise, a new sequence S_b is generated, consisting of $\vec{b}$ only.

There are two cases when the inserted mixed edge $e = \vec{a}\vec{b}$ closes a new loop: either under a) the split loop S, which was finally subdivided, has been equal to

---

[3]Here and in all other cases, we must insert $\vec{a}$ twice. This is to guarantee that both segments $\vec{v}_i\vec{a}$ and $\vec{a}\vec{v}_{i+1}$ are still available for the insertion of further mixed edges.

$\mathcal{S}_a$; or under b) $\mathcal{S}_b$ coincides with $\mathcal{S}_a$. In both cases, the sequence $\mathcal{S}_b$ with $\vec{b}$ at its end becomes a loop and has to be added to the list of new loops.

In all other cases, the sequence $\mathcal{S}_a$ remains a split loop but it is extended After its final element $\vec{a}$, we add the sequence $\mathcal{S}_b$ that starts with $\vec{b}$.

After this process, all mixed edges are inserted and all loops of $\mathbf{P}^1$ and $\mathbf{P}^2$ that are met by any mixed edge are modified into loops of the Boolean composite $\mathbf{R}$. The remaining loops of $\mathbf{P}^1$ and $\mathbf{P}^2$ have to be treated in the following step 3:

Suppose loop $\mathcal{L}^1 \subset \mathbf{P}^1$ is not met by any mixed edge. Then—in the generic case—no edge of $\mathcal{L}^1$ intersects $\mathbf{P}^2$. So $\mathcal{L}^1$ is either in the interior of $\mathbf{P}^2$ or totally outside. Therefore we proceed as follows:

(a) Specify any vertex $\vec{v}^1$ of $\mathcal{L}^1$ and check whether $\vec{v}^1$ is in $\mathbf{P}^2$ or outside.

(b) $\vec{v}^1 \in int\mathbf{P}^2 \implies \mathcal{L}^1 \subset (\mathbf{P}^1 \cap \mathbf{P}^2)$ and $\mathcal{L}^1 \not\subset (\mathbf{P}^1 \cup \mathbf{P}^2)$.
$\vec{v}^1 \in int\overline{\mathbf{P}^2} \implies \mathcal{L}^1 \subset (\mathbf{P}^1 \cup \mathbf{P}^2)$ and $\mathcal{L}^1 \not\subset (\mathbf{P}^1 \cap \mathbf{P}^2)$.

The loops of $\mathbf{R}$ are sufficient to define the boundary representation of the resulting polyhedron.

Particular Cases

During the elimination of loops mentioned above it can happen in particular cases that the vertex $\vec{v}^1$ is located on the boundary of $\mathbf{P}^2$. This might be caused by the fact that the loop $\mathcal{L}^1$ touches $\partial\mathbf{P}^2$ along any vertex or edge (particular cases P1, P3, P5, or P6 according to the table in section 8.4). Then it is sufficient to replace $\vec{v}^1 \in \mathcal{L}^1$ by any other vertex in $\mathcal{L}^1$. But it can also happen that the whole loop $\mathcal{L}^1$ is located in any face f^2 of $\mathbf{P}^2$ (particular cases P7 or P8). Then the treatment of steps 2 and 3 is much more complex. In the following we give only a brief introduction without going into details.

Suppose the faces $f^1 \subset \mathbf{P}^1$ and $f^2 \subset \mathbf{P}^2$ are coplanar with equal inside half-spaces (case P7). Then the loops in the plane $\varphi := [f^1] = [f^2]$ have to be merged with the coincident mixed edges simultaneously.[4] However, this merging process needs some preparation:

(a) There can be *"crossing points"* between loops $\mathcal{L}^1 \subset f^1$ and $\mathcal{L}^2 \subset f^2$: A *proper* crossing point X (see Figure 8.12), where the final loop changes over from $\mathcal{L}^1$ to $\mathcal{L}^2$, is always the endpoint of any mixed edge $e \not\subset \varphi$. So, the determination of crossing points starts with the search for mixed edges with exactly one endpoint X lying in φ. Note that the edges $e^1 \in \mathcal{L}^1$ and $e^2 \in \mathcal{L}^2$ that intersect at X need not be the traces of the neighbor faces of

---

[4]Note that in φ the closure of the resulting face of $\mathbf{P}^1 \cup \mathbf{P}^2$ ($\mathbf{P}^1 \cap \mathbf{P}^2$) need not be the union (intersection) of the closures of f^1 and f^2 (see shaded faces in Figure 8.10).

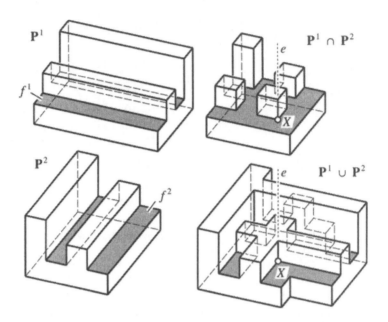

FIGURE 8.12. Coplanar and equally orientated faces with a crossing point X

the mixed edge e. But e^1 (e^2) must be reached; when starting from e we run around the vertex pyramid of $\mathbf{P}^1$ $(\mathbf{P}^2)$ at X.

Crossing points can be seen as mixed edges of zero length. So the merging of the crossing points with the loops of f^1 and f^2 in φ works in the same way as that of mixed edges.

(b) There are also *improper* crossing points: The loops $\mathcal{L}^1$ and $\mathcal{L}^2$ can have overlapping aligned edges or they share one or more consecutive edges. At such a common sequence, the loop of $\mathbf{R}$ can pass over from $\mathcal{L}^1$ to $\mathcal{L}^2$. Therefore, a particular treatment of the endpoints Y of such overlapping or coinciding edges is necessary, similar to that in section 8.5.

Suppose that at Y the following edges of $\mathcal{L}^1$ and $\mathcal{L}^2$ are different. Then for $\mathbf{R} = \mathbf{P}^1 \cap \mathbf{P}^2$, the edge with the smaller interior angle at Y has to be selected, provided this edge is convex. If it is concave, then the other edge has to be taken. A similar rule holds for $\mathbf{R} = \mathbf{P}^1 \cup \mathbf{P}^2$.

(c) As already explained in section 8.5, aligned edges with identical inside wedges need a particular treatment, too. On $\mathbf{R}$ such *joint edges* e_1, e_2 with $close_1 \cap close_2 \neq \{\}$ must be combined (consistency condition C1 on page 191). Joint edges can serve as transitions from $\mathcal{L}^1$ and $\mathcal{L}^2$. So these also have to be determined in advance, before the merging process can start in the plane φ.

Finally, when a loop $\mathcal{L}^1 \subset f^1 \subset \mathbf{P}^1$ is not met by any proper mixed edge or joint edge and it does not contain any crossing point, then again we have to apply an inclusion test for figuring out whether $\mathcal{L}^1$ is

(i) in $clos\, f^2$

(ii) in the exterior of $\mathbf{P}^2$

(iii) coinciding with any loop $\mathcal{L}^2 \subset f^2$.

In case (i) we apply the following rules:

The edges of $\mathcal{L}^1$ are convex[5] $\implies$ $\mathcal{L}^1 \subset (\mathbf{P}^1 \cap \mathbf{P}^2)$ and $\mathcal{L}^1 \not\subset (\mathbf{P}^1 \cup \mathbf{P}^2)$.

The edges of $\mathcal{L}^1$ are concave $\implies$ $\mathcal{L}^1 \subset (\mathbf{P}^1 \cup \mathbf{P}^2)$ and $\mathcal{L}^1 \not\subset (\mathbf{P}^1 \cap \mathbf{P}^2)$.

Case (ii) follows the rules stated in the generic case of step 3. In case (iii) we have to take into consideration whether the orientations of $\mathcal{L}^1$ and $\mathcal{L}^2$ are equal or different. Under equal orientation, only one of these loops remains on $\mathbf{R}$. Under different orientation, the two loops reduce to zero, independent from the fact whether the inside wedges of the edges with respect to $\mathbf{P}^1$ and $\mathbf{P}^2$ are disjoint, face to face, or overlapping.

Finally we assume that the faces $f^1 \subset \mathbf{P}^1$ and $f^2 \subset \mathbf{P}^2$ are coplanar, but the inside halfspaces are different (case P8). Then the merging in f^1 is performed separately from that in f^2, as on $\mathbf{R}$ the faces resulting from f^1 and f^2 are different. For loops $\mathcal{L}^1$ of f^1 step 3 is performed in the following way: under $\mathcal{L}^1 \subset \overline{\mathbf{P}^2}$ we follow the rules of the generic case. When $\mathcal{L}^1$ contains a vertex $\vec{v}^1 \in int f^2$, then loop $\mathcal{L}^1$ has to be cancelled; the edges of $\mathcal{L}^1$ are mixed edges of the type in Figure 8.5b or c with f^2, as one neighbor.

Coincident loops $\mathcal{L}^1$ and $\mathcal{L}^2$ are treated in step 3 as follows: when the orientations of $\mathcal{L}^1$ and $\mathcal{L}^2$ are opposite, both loops reduce to zero. Along each edge the neighbor faces must be complanar, since otherwise there would be mixed edges of the type in Figure 8.6c or d. Under equal orientation both loops $\mathcal{L}^1 \subset f^1$ and $\mathcal{L}^2 \subset f^2$ become loops of the Boolean composite too, provided along each edge the inside wedges are disjoint according to Figure 8.6f (with $[f_r^1] = [f_r^2]$).

8.7 Practical Applications

The implementation of the Boolean operations among solids is one of the best things that OPEN GEOMETRY offers. You can define "solids", i.e., closed polyhedra, and then apply operations like union, difference, and intersection by means of a simple '$+$', '$-$' or '$*$'. The result is a *pointer* to a new solid. To make code

---

[5]Since $\mathcal{L}^1$ is not met by any mixed edge, $\mathcal{L}^1$ cannot contain convex and concave edges simultaneously.

more readable, we define

>   **typedef** *Solid* ∗ *BoolResult*;

The class *Solid* is derived from *Obj3d* and inherits methods like Translate( ), Rotate( ), Scale( ), etc. A *Solid* consists of "complex polygons." OPENGL can draw such polygons correctly, but at the cost of computation time. Thus, solids cannot be displayed as quickly as "ordinary polyhedra" that are considered to consist of convex polygons. Still, the results are very satisfying.

OPEN GEOMETRY is compatible with the CAD3D system (you will find a copy of the DOS version of CAD3D on the enclosed CD). It can read solids generated by CAD3D, and it can store new results in CAD3D-compatible files. These files should have the suffix ∗.llx.

Here are the most important methods of the class *Solid*:

class *Solid*;   → declaration in "solid.h"
>   Derived from *Obj3d*.

Constructors:

>   *Solid*( ); // default constructor
>   *Solid*(*RegFrustum* &frustum);
>   *Solid*(*Box* &box);
>   *Solid*(*Polyhedron* &phdr); // Polyhedron must be closed!
>   *Solid*(*ParamSurface* &ClosedSurf, *Boolean* IsSurfOfRevol);
>   *Solid*(*FunctionGraph* &Graph);
>   *Solid*(**const char** ∗name); // Name of a CAD3D File

Operators (the classical Boolean operations: union, difference, intersection):

>   **friend** *BoolResult* **operator** + (**const** *Solid* &One, **const** *Solid* &Two);
>   // Union of two solids.
>   **friend** *BoolResult* **operator** − (**const** *Solid* &One, **const** *Solid* &Two);
>   // First difference.
>   **friend** *BoolResult* **operator** ∗ (**const** *Solid* &One, **const** *Solid* &Two);
>   // Second difference.
>   **friend** *BoolResult* **operator** ∗ (**const** *Solid* &Total, **const** *Plane* &plane);
>   // Intersection with a plane.

Methods:

>   // Define solid by means of previously defined primitives or closed (!) surfaces
>   **void** Def(*RegFrustum* &frustum);
>   **void** Def(*Box* &box);
>   **void** Def(*Polyhedron* &phdr);
>   **void** Def(*ParamSurface* &ClosedSurf, *Boolean* IsSurfOfRevol);
>   **void** Def(*FunctionGraph* &Graph);
>   **void** Def(**const char** ∗name); // name of CAD3D file

```
void Shade( ) const;
void WireFrame( Color c, Boolean remove_hidden_lines, ThinOrThick thick,
    Real offset = STD_OFFSET );
// Compatability to CAD3D
void ReadFrom_CAD3D_File( const char *name );
void SaveAs_CAD3D_File( const char *name );

int NoOfPolys( ) const; // Returns number of faces.
void SetColor( Color c, int n1 = 0, int n2 = 0 );
    // You can assign color c to the faces with index n1...n2 . If you do not
    // specify any number, all faces are painted in the given color.
```

Figure 8.13 shows the logo of the CAD3D system. And here is the corresponding OPEN GEOMETRY code to draw this image:

Listing of program `X/Boole/cad3logo2.cpp` (Figure 8.13):

```cpp
#include "opengeom.h"
#include "defaults3d.h"

Solid SomeObject( "DATA/cad3logo.l1x" );

void Scene::Init( )
{
    SomeObject.FitIntoSphere( 15 );
}
void Scene::Draw( )
{
    SomeObject.Shade( );
}
```

FIGURE 8.13. The logo of the CAD3D system.

FIGURE 8.14. We read a CAD3D object and cut out a part of it.

CAD3D and OPEN GEOMETRY work with different drawing units and different origins of the Cartesian coordinate system. The method FitIntoSphere( ) helps to center the objects around the origin and to scale them in a convenient way.

The next listing shows how we can read a CAD3D file and apply Boolean operations to the objects (Figure 8.14). The result is stored in a new CAD3D file.

Listing of program X/Boole/tube2.cpp (Figure 8.14):

```
#include "opengeom.h"
#include "defaults3d.h"

Solid SomeObject( "DATA/tube.11x" );
BoolResult Result; // Remember: Result is a pointer to a Solid

void Scene::Init( )
{
   SomeObject.FitIntoSphere( 10 );
   Box box( Green, 20, 20, 20 );
   box.Translate( 0, 0, -10 );
   // Now we subtract the part of the object that lies inside the box.
   Result = SomeObject - Solid( box ); // Uses constructor
   Result->SaveAs_CAD3D_File( "DATA/tube_minus_box.11x" );
}
```

```
void Scene::Draw( )
{
    Result->Shade( );
}
```

In the third example, we show how to generate solids via OPEN GEOMETRY—without the help of CAD3D: We define a cube and subtract (add) a cylinder (Figure 8.15):

Listing of program X/Boole/cyl_x_cube.cpp (Figure 8.15):

```
#include "opengeom.h"
#include "defaults3d.h"

BoolResult Union, Difference;

void Scene::Init( )
{
    // Define a first solid by means of a cube
    Box cube;
    cube.Def( Gray, 6, 6, 6 );
    cube.Translate( -3, -1, -3 );
    cube.Rotate( Xaxis, 65 );
```

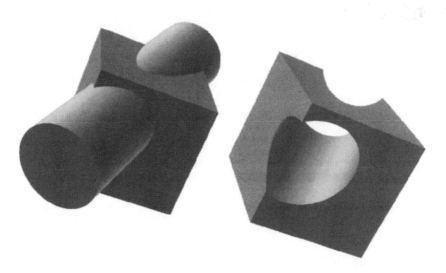

FIGURE 8.15. How to generate solids via OPEN GEOMETRY.

```
        cube.Rotate( Zaxis, 30 );
        Solid FirstSolid( cube );
        // Define a second solid by means of a cylinder
        RegPrism cyl;
        cyl.Def( Gray, 2, 14, 100, SOLID, Zaxis );
        cyl.Translate( -3, 1, -7 );
        cyl.Rotate( Yaxis, 90 );
        Solid SecondSolid( cyl );
        // Now define union and difference
        Union = SecondSolid + FirstSolid;
        Union->Translate( 0, -5, 0 );
        Difference = FirstSolid - SecondSolid;
        Difference->Translate( 0, 5, 0 );
    }

    void Scene::Draw( )
    {
        Union->Shade( );
        Difference->Shade( );
    }
```

So far, we have only generated solids by means of primitives, and then created a "Boolean result" (which is a pointer to a *Solid*). When we build differences or unions of Boolean results, we must not forget the syntax for pointers (see the following listing). Additionally, to shading we can also draw wireframes of our solids. Together with the shading, the hidden surface removal works fine. When the color of the object is *NoColor*, we get a wireframe with removed edges without any shading (exactly this is done when you let the second parameter of WireFrame( ) be true).

In the following example (Figure 8.16), a cube and a regular six-sided prism are both united and subtracted. The two results are united to the Boolean result WholeScene. This result is not only shaded but is also drawn with thin invisible and thicker visible edges.

Listing of program X/Boole/tree_house.cpp (Figure 8.16):

```
#include "opengeom.h"
#include "defaults3d.h"

BoolResult WholeScene;

void Scene::Init( )
```

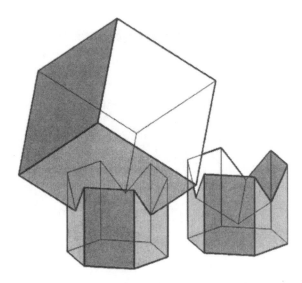

FIGURE 8.16. In this scene, visible and invisible edges can be seen (drawn with different line style).

```
{
    Box Cube( AlmostWhite, 10, 10, 10 );
    Cube.Translate( −5, −5, −5 ),
    Cube.Rotate( Zaxis, 45 );
    Cube.Rotate( Xaxis, Deg( atan( sqrt( 2 ) ) ) );
    RegPrism Prism;
    Prism.Def( AlmostWhite, 4, 8, 6 );
    Prism.Translate( 0, 0, −10 );
    BoolResult Union = Solid( Cube ) + Solid( Prism );
    Union−>Translate( 0, −5, 0 );
    BoolResult Difference = Solid( Prism ) − Solid( Cube );
    Difference−>Translate( 0, 5, 0 );
    WholeScene = *Union + *Difference;
}
void Scene::Draw( )
{
    WholeScene−>Shade( );
    Zbuffer( false );
    WholeScene−>WireFrame( Black, false, THIN );
    Zbuffer( true );
    WholeScene−>WireFrame( Black, false, MEDIUM );
}
```

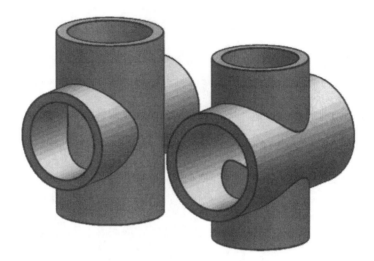

FIGURE 8.17. When we apply Boolean operations to Boolean results, the objects soon become complex.

The next example shows how to create more complex objects by applying several Boolean operations in the correct order.

Listing of program X/Boole/tubes.cpp (Figure 8.17):

```
#include "opengeom.h"
#include "defaults3d.h"

BoolResult Tube1, Tube2;

void Scene::Init( )
{
    // Define two cylinders as usual
    RegPrism Cyl1, Cyl2;
    Cyl1.Def( LightGray, 3, 10, 50 );
    Cyl1.Translate( 0, 0, −5 );
    Cyl2.Def( LightGray, 2.7, 10, 50 );
    Cyl2.Translate( 0, 0, −5 );
    Cyl2.Rotate( Yaxis, 90 );
    // Calculate the union of the two cylinders
    BoolResult Exterior = Cyl1 + Cyl2;
    // Now shrink the cylinders
    Real s = 0.8;
    Cyl1.Scale( s, s, 1.1 );
```

```
    Cyl2.Scale( 1.1, s, s );
    // Calculate the union of the two smaller cylinders
    BoolResult Interior = Cyl1 + Cyl2;
    // Get the difference, i.e., the tube
    Tube1 = *Exterior - *Interior;
    Tube1->Translate( 0, -5, 0 );
    Tube2 = *Exterior - *Interior;
    Tube2->Rotate( Yaxis, 90 );
    Tube2->Translate( 0, 5, 0 );
}


void Scene::Draw( )
{
    Tube1->Shade( );
    Tube1->WireFrame( Black, false, MEDIUM );
    Tube2->Shade( );
    Tube2->WireFrame( Black, false, MEDIUM );
}
```

Solid primitives can be more complicated than just cylinders or boxes. You can define closed mathematical surfaces like a torus (Figure 8.18) via parameterized equations. The constructor that takes a parameterized surface as a first parameter requires a second parameter that tells the program whether the surface consists of planar quadrangles or not (a surface of revolution does!). When this is the case, you can save a lot of computation time.

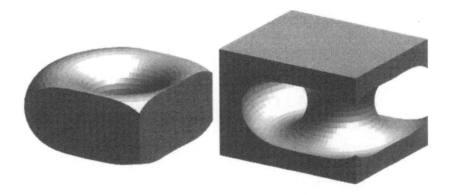

FIGURE 8.18. Boolean operations with closed mathematical surfaces like a torus (left: intersection, right: difference).

Listing of program `torus_x_cube.cpp` (Figure 8.18):

```
#include "opengeom.h"
#include "defaults3d.h"

class TubeSurf: public ParamSurface
{
public:
    virtual P3d SurfacePoint( Real u, Real v )
    {
        // This is the parameterized equation of a torus:
        const Real a = 5, b = 2.5;
        Real r = a + b * cos( v );
        return P3d( r * cos( u ), r * sin( u ), b * sin ( v ) );
    }
};

BoolResult Intersection;

void Scene::Init( )
{
    // Define a first solid by means of a closed param. surface
    TubeSurf ClosedSurf;
    ClosedSurf.Def( Gray, 51, 25, 0, 2 * PI, 0, 2 * PI );
    Solid Torus( ClosedSurf, true );
    // Define a second solid by means of a box
    Box box( Gray, 10, 12, 8 );
    box.Translate( -5, 4.5 - 12, -4 );
    Solid Block( box );
    // Now define the intersection
    Intersection = Torus * Block; // Image to the left
}

void Scene::Draw( )
{
    Intersection->Shade( );
}
```

Just in order to show that the surface can be rather complicated, we manipulated the formula of the torus a little bit in order to get a "funny solid" (Figure 8.19):

FIGURE 8.19. Boolean operations with more complicated closed mathematical surfaces. By definition, the surface is closed in the interval $0 \leq u$, $v \leq 2\pi$. We cut off the sector $[x > 0, y > 0]$ and the upper part of the surface $(z > 0)$.

Listing of program X/Boole/wildbool.cpp (Figure 8.19):

```
#include "opengeom.h"
#include "defaults3d.h"


Real b = 4, c = 0.3;


class FunnySurf: public ParamSurface
{
public:
    virtual P3d SurfacePoint( Real u, Real v )
    {
        const Real a = 8;
        Real bv = b * ( 1 − c * sin( 2.5 * u ) );
        Real r = a + bv * cos( v );
        return P3d( r * cos( u), r * sin( u ), bv * sin ( v ) );
    }
};


BoolResult Result;


void Scene::Init( )
{
    FunnySurf ClosedSurf;
    int order = 50, n = 24;
```

```
                    // Do not increase these numbers too much:
                    // calculation time increases quadratically!
                ClosedSurf.Def( Gray, order, n, 0, 2 * PI, 0, 2 * PI );
                Solid Exterior( ClosedSurf, false );
                b = 3; c = 0.5; // This defines a smaller "interior"
                ClosedSurf.Def( Gray, order, n, 0, 2 * PI, 0, 2 * PI );
                Solid Interior( ClosedSurf, false );
                BoolResult HollowObject = Exterior − Interior;
                // Cut off the sector x > 0, y > 0
                Box box;
                box.Def( Gray, 20, 20, 20 );
                box.Translate( 0, 0, −10 );
                BoolResult R = *HollowObject − Solid( box );
                // Cut off the upper half
                box.Def( Gray, 40, 40, 40 );
                box.Translate( −20, −20, 0 );
                Result = *R − Solid( box );
            }

            void Scene::Draw( )
            {
                Result−>Shade( );
            }
```

As a final example, we want to illustrate how the planar intersection of a solid
can be achieved. The intersecting plane has a normal vector that points to the
outside of the Boolean result.

Listing of program `torus_x_plane.cpp` (Figure 8.20):

```
#include "opengeom.h"
#include "defaults3d.h"

const Real a = 5, b = 2.5;

class TubeSurf: public ParamSurface
{
public:
    virtual P3d SurfacePoint( Real u, Real v )
    {
        Real r = a + b * cos( v );
        return P3d( r * cos( u ), r * sin( u ), b * sin ( v ) );
    }
};
```

FIGURE 8.20. Planar sections of a torus. The intersection curve in the middle is a "lemniscate."

```
BoolResult Result [ 3 ];

void Scene::Init( )
{
    Plane plane;
    TubeSurf ClosedSurf;
    ClosedSurf.Def( Gray, 51, 15, 0, 2 * PI, 0, 2 * PI );
    Real z0 =  6.5;
    ClosedSurf.Translate( 0, 0, z0 );
    for ( int i = 0; i < 3; i++ )
    {
        Real y = a − b + ( i − 1 ) * 0.15;  // i = 1...Lemniscate
        plane.Def( P3d( 0, y, 0 ), V3d ( 0, 1, 0 ) );
        Result [i] = Solid( ClosedSurf, true ) * plane;
        ClosedSurf.Translate( 0, 0, −z0 );
    }
}
void Scene::Draw( )
{
    for ( int i = 0; i < 3; i++ )
        Result [i]−>Shade( );
}
```

9

Kinematics—Geometry of Motion

In this chapter, we will introduce programming of 2D Kinematics by means of OPEN GEOMETRY. Kinematics means—roughly speaking—geometry of motion. It investigates point paths, envelopes, velocities, and accelerations, etc., during constrained motions.

Before we deal with programming examples, we will give a short introduction into planar Kinematics. We will line out the basic concepts and give a number of samples of constrained motions—like the elliptic motion, the planetary motion, and the coupler motion.

Second, we will explain how to write an OPEN GEOMETRY program that deals with 2D graphics and 2D animation. We will list the classes available and briefly explain their member functions.

Finally, we will give listings of relevant sample programs, including explanations. The samples fit to the theoretical part of this chapter. Thus, it is advisable to at least browse through these pages—even if you are already an expert in Kinematics.

9.1 Basic Concepts of Planar Kinematics

Kinematics studies the point paths, envelopes, velocities, and accelerations, etc., of moving objects. Thus, it is the basis for the analysis and synthesis of all mechanisms. In the following sections, we will discuss mainly the geometrical aspects.

There are two systems: the fixed system Σ, and the moving system Σ'.

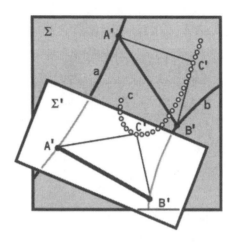

FIGURE 9.1. Two-point guidance of the system Σ'.

All systems are rigid: the distance of any two points remains constant within each system during the motion. Thus, positions of the moving system Σ' are congruent. Each point $C' \in \Sigma'$ of the moving system traces a path c in Σ, when it undergoes a *constrained motion* Σ'/Σ.

The motion Σ'/Σ can be a planar motion or a more complicated spatial motion. We call the motion planar when a plane $\varepsilon' \subset \Sigma'$ slides on another plane $\varepsilon \subset \Sigma$. Apart from pure translations, rotations are trivial examples for planar motions: all point paths are circles centered on the rotation axis. Points in the same plane ε move on concentric circles.

For planar motions, it is sufficient to study the motion of a single plane $\varepsilon = \varepsilon'$, i.e., both Σ and Σ' can be considered as planes.

To determine the position of Σ' at a certain time, we only need to mark the instantaneous positions A and B of two points $A' \in \Sigma'$ and $B' \in \Sigma'$. Thus, the motion Σ'/Σ is geometrically well-defined when the paths $a, b \subset \Sigma$ of two points A', $B' \in \Sigma'$ are given. Σ'/Σ is "geared" (constrained) by a and b; we speak of a "two-point guidance" (Figure 9.1).

The rod $A'B'$ represents Σ' . Then each point $C' \in \Sigma'$ follows a point path $c \subset \Sigma$. Points of c can be found by fitting $A'B'$ in a, b at an arbitrary position, and then mark the corresponding position C of C'. [1]

---

[1]When we do that by hand, we will use a transparent sheet and proceed in a natural manner. When we do it on the computer, however, we have to say more precisely what to do: first choose a point $A \in a$. It is the center of a circle with radius $\overline{AB}$. Then we intersect this circle with the line b. If there are several intersection points, we choose "the right one" (which can be tricky) as point B. Finally, we have to reconstruct the triangle $A'B'C'$ above the base side AB (orientation!).

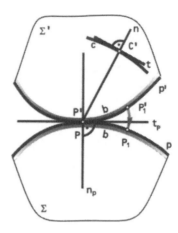

FIGURE 9.2. Guidance of the system Σ' by means of rolling curves.

The motion Σ'/Σ can also be constrained through the specification of "rolling" curves p and p'. The curve p' rolls on the curve p without sliding. This means that the points of p and p' are related to each other by the same arc lengths (Figure 9.2).

We now come to a **main theorem of planar Kinematics**:

> At every moment, any constrained nontranslatory planar motion can be approximated (up to the first derivative[2]) by an *instantaneous rotation*. The center of this rotation is called the *instantaneous pole* $P = P'$. Thus, for each position of Σ', we generally have exactly one point with velocity zero (as a result of that, P is also called *velocity center*).

Let c be the path of an arbitrary point $C' \in \Sigma'$, and n_C be the normal to this curve at a position C. From the main theorem, it follows that n_C passes through the pole $P = P'$ (Figure 9.3).

The set of all velocity centers (poles) in Σ' is the *moving polode* $p' \subset \Sigma'$. It corresponds to the *fixed polode* $p \subset \Sigma$. During the constrained motion, these polodes *roll* on each other without sliding. The instantaneous rolling point is the pole P.

Another consequence of the main theorem is, at every planar motion Σ'/Σ (except translatory motions), *exactly* two curves $p' \subset \Sigma'$ and $p \subset \Sigma$ roll on each other. Thus, every planar motion can be defined by the polodes p' and p.

---

[2]The first derivative determines the velocity of a point. For the calculation of its acceleration, we need the second derivative. Accelerations do not follow the rules of the approximating rotation.

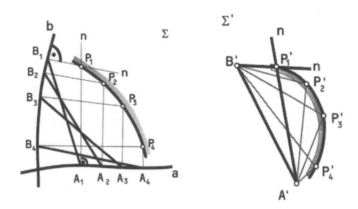

FIGURE 9.3. All path normals coincide with the instantaneous pole P.

To define a constrained motion differently from what we have seen so far, we can optionally combine two guidances from the following possibilities (Figure 9.4):

- Points A' can glide along fixed curves a.

- Fixed curves $c \subset \Sigma$ can force moved curves in Σ' to glide along them. Since points on one curve correspond to points on the other curve, we have a so-called *enveloping pair* $\{c,\ c'\}$.

- A moving curve a' glides through a fixed point $A \in \Sigma$, called the *slot point* of a'.

Let us also define the **inverse motion** Σ/Σ'. So far we have assumed Σ to be fixed. As soon as the observer takes position in Σ', the moving system becomes subjectively fixed and the fixed system Σ becomes the moving system. The polodes change their roles. Also, point guidance and line guidance change their roles. A sliding guidance, however, still remains a sliding guidance.

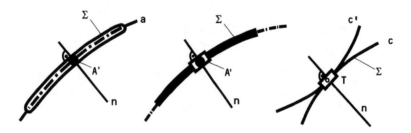

FIGURE 9.4. Different ways of guidances: point guidance, line guidance, enveloping pairs of curves.

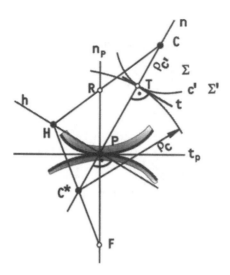

FIGURE 9.5. Osculating circles for path curves and for envelopes.

9.2 Theory of Curvature

The theory of curvature is important for the computation of accelerations and for the development of special approximation mechanisms.

We distinguish osculating circles for path curves and for envelopes (Figure 9.5).

The points C of a curve c and the corresponding osculation centers c^* are two point-fields that are related by the so-called *curvature transformation*. This transformation $\mathbf{C}\colon C \to C^*$ is nonlinear (quadratic) and reversible.

If two pairs $A \mapsto A^*$ and $B \mapsto B^*$ of $\mathbf{C}$ on different pole normals are given, the transformation $C \mapsto C^*$ can be completed (in both directions). Geometrically, this is done by the construction of BOBILLIER (Figure 9.6a).

A special case: If $A =: R$ and $A^* = R^* =: F$ lie on the pole normal, we do not need a second pair B, B^* (EULER-SAVARY, Figure 9.6b) to complete $\mathbf{C}$ (Figure 9.6b).[3]

Let $r = \overline{PR}$, $r^* = \overline{PR^*}$, $c = \overline{PC}$, $c^* = \overline{PC^*}$, and let θ be the angle between PC and PR. Then we have the implicit condition

$$\cos\theta \left(\frac{1}{c} - \frac{1}{c^*} \right) = \frac{1}{r} - \frac{1}{r^*} =: \varrho = \text{const,} \tag{1}$$

---

[3]The construction of EULER-SAVARY is a special case of the construction of BOBILLIER.

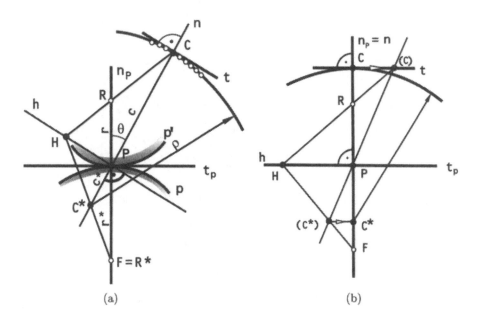

(a)   (b)

FIGURE 9.6. The geometrical completion of the quadratic curvature transformation

or, evaluated explicitly for c and c^*:

$$c^* = 1 \Big/ \left(\frac{1}{c} - \frac{\varrho}{\cos\theta} \right) \quad \text{and} \quad c = 1 \Big/ \left(\frac{1}{c^*} + \frac{\varrho}{\cos\theta} \right) \qquad (2)$$

If two pairs $A \mapsto A^*$ and $B \mapsto B^*$ of $\mathbf{C}$ are given that do not lie on the same pole normal, we have the equation system

$$\cos\theta_A \left(\frac{1}{a} - \frac{1}{a^*} \right) = \cos\theta_B \left(\frac{1}{b} - \frac{1}{b^*} \right) = \varrho. \qquad (3)$$

Let the vectors $\vec{a}$ and $\vec{b}$ be the normalized direction vectors from the pole to A and B, and $\vec{n}$ be the normalized direction vector of the pole normal. Then we have

$$\frac{\cos\theta_B}{\cos\theta_A} = \frac{\vec{n}\vec{b}}{\vec{n}\vec{a}} = \left(\frac{1}{a} - \frac{1}{a^*} \right) \Big/ \left(\frac{1}{b} - \frac{1}{b^*} \right) =: \gamma \quad \Rightarrow \quad \vec{n}(\vec{b} - \gamma\vec{a}) = 0. \qquad (4)$$

This means the vector $\vec{n}$ is perpendicular to the vector $\vec{b} - \gamma\vec{a}$. Geometrically speaking, the vector $\vec{b} - \gamma\vec{a}$ is the direction vector of the common tangent t_P of the polodes. Now, by (3), we can determine ϱ explicitly:

$$\varrho = \vec{n}\vec{a} \left(\frac{1}{a} - \frac{1}{a^*} \right) \quad \text{or} \quad \varrho = \vec{n}\vec{b} \left(\frac{1}{b} - \frac{1}{b^*} \right). \qquad (5)$$

Now that we have finished this short theoretical introduction, we will give some practical applications.

9.3 The Elliptic Motion

When two points A' and B' slide along two straight lines $a \subset \Sigma$ and $b \subset \Sigma$ that must not be parallel (two-point guidance), the motion is called elliptic motion.

According to the well-known theorem of DE LA HIRE, each point C' on the line $A'B' \subset \Sigma'$ moves on an *ellipse* (circles and straight lines included). However, we will soon see that any point of Σ' has an elliptic path curve.

For the time being, let a and b be perpendicular and $O = a \cap b$ (Figure 9.7). Due to the fact that the normals of the path curves coincide with the velocity pole P, we can find P, and thus the tangents of any path curve (ellipse) of points $C' \in \Sigma'$.

Due to $\overline{OP} = \overline{AB} = const.$, the fixed polode $p \subset \Sigma$ is a circle (with the center O and the radius $r := \overline{OP}$). According to THALES' theorem, the moving polode $p' \subset \Sigma'$ is a circle as well, with its center in the midpoint M' of $A'B'$ and the radius $r' = r/2$. The *pole curves of an elliptic motion are two circles* with the radius-ratio $r : r' = 2 : 1$, called a pair of CARDAN circles.

Now let the CARDAN circles p and p' be given and roll on each other. We link an arbitrary point $C' \in \Sigma'$ rigidly to p' by means of a diameter rod $A'B'$. Then we compare Figure 9.8 with Figure 9.7 and see: the antipodal points A' and B' have straight path curves through O. Thus, the path curve c of C' is an ellipse.

We note: *Each point on the small* CARDAN *circle p' has a diameter line of the big* CARDAN *circle as its path* (Figure 9.8).

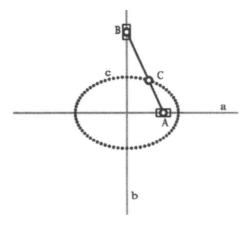

FIGURE 9.7. Elliptic motion: $A' \in \Sigma'$ moves on the straight line a and $B' \in \Sigma'$ moves on the straight line b.

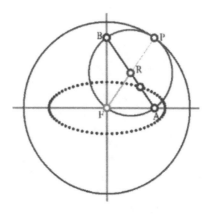

FIGURE 9.8. The pair of CARDAN circles.

Finally, we investigate the general case: the guiding lines a and b are not perpendicular (and not parallel). If such a two-point guidance is given, we first reconstruct the pole and draw the CARDAN circles. Again due to THALES' theorem, the four points R, A', B', and P lie on the small circle. Then we switch to a two-point guidance on orthogonal sliding lines by choosing points on the corresponding diameter of p' (Figure 9.9). Thus, the general case is again interpreted as the special case with perpendicular guiding lines.

An elliptic motion can also be forced by two circles that glide along two fixed straight lines (Figure 9.10). This follows from the fact that the centers of the circles follow parallels to the given straight lines. As an example, specific *arc-biangles* (*arc-triangles*) can be revolved inside a regular triangle (square). For a

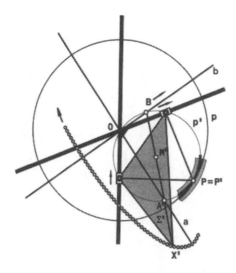

FIGURE 9.9. The guiding lines a and b need not be perpendicular.

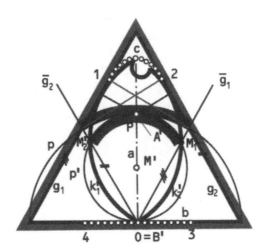

FIGURE 9.10. Elliptic motions are defined by circles gliding along straight lines. The arc-biangle (arc-triangle) can be completely revolved in a regular triangle (square). Its vertices will not reach the vertices of the triangle (square). Their path consists of straight lines and parts of ellipses.

complete revolution, three (four) elliptic motions are required. As an application, triangular (square) holes with rounded corners can be drilled.

Elliptic motions can also be generated by a *slider crank*: starting up from the perpendicular two-point guidance, we substitute one of the points of the thread guidance by guiding the center M' of p' on a circle around O by means of a crank, provided $\overline{O'M'} = \overline{M'A'}$.

Each point $C \in MA$ on the connecting rod describes an ellipse with the axes a and b. Only A and B follow the axes. This is the exact straight guidance for B by a slider crank. In practice, it can be useful that it is unnecessary to materialize the tracing path of B by a rod or slits (Figure 9.11).

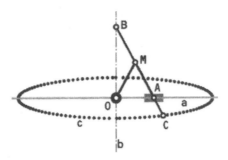

FIGURE 9.11. The elliptic motion can also be achieved by a slider crank. This is useful if the path of B cannot be materialized.

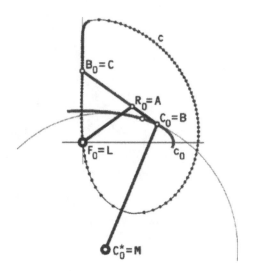

FIGURE 9.12. A slider crank for an approximated straight guidance, derived from an elliptic motion.

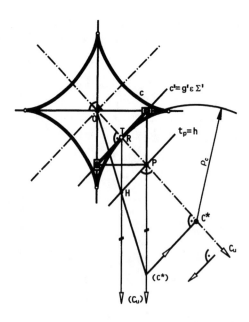

FIGURE 9.13. The curve enveloped by a diameter of the small CARDAN circle is an astroid.

This example shows the essential applications of kinematics: mechanisms for exact or approximate constructions of predefined paths can be developed. This is applied in industry in the production of artificial links, hydraulic ramps, levers, etc.

The unfavorable force proportions at the cross-shaped slider drive of the aforementioned slider crank, however, lead to force loss and material wear. Thus, it is advisable to add a second point $C' \in \Sigma'$ running on a circle (crank). As M' is the only point in Σ' following a circle, we substitute the elliptic trace c of $C \in \Sigma'$ by one of its osculating circles (Figure 9.12). This leads to an *approximate straight guidance* derived from an elliptic motion.

M follows a circle around O, and C follows an osculating circle of the elliptic path. MC is called the *coupler* of a *four-bar linkage* (in this case, the linkage is a so-called *double rocker*).

As a last example for the elliptic motion, we take a look at the enveloped curve c of a diameter line g' of the rolling CARDAN circle p'. It is a fourfold symmetric, cuspidal curve called *astroid* (Figure 9.13). The mechanism is frequently found on garage doors. At every moment, the pedal point of g' with respect to the pole is the point of contact with the enveloping curve c.

9.4 The Trochoid Motion

An elliptic motion can be defined by the two CARDAN circles p and p' ($r : r' = 2 : 1$). The smaller circle p' rolls inside p. We now generalize this special case.

We call the motion Σ'/Σ a trochoid motion (planetary motion), if both polodes $p \subset \Sigma$ and $p' \subset \Sigma'$ are circles. The paths are called trochoids.

If the moving polode p' is enclosed by the fixed polode p, we speak of *inside rolling*: $r > r' > 0$ (Figure 9.14a).

We can distinguish between two cases of *outside rolling*: $r\,r' > 0$ ($\Rightarrow r' > r > 0$, Figure 9.14b) and $r\,r' < 0$ (Figure 9.14c).

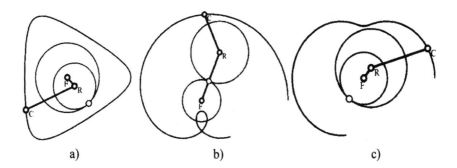

a)   b)   c)

FIGURE 9.14. Inside rolling and the two cases of outside rolling

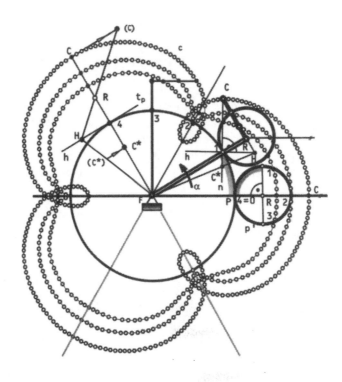

FIGURE 9.15. Trochoid with given ratio $r : r' = 3 : -1$.

Figure 9.15 shows an outside rolling (ratio $r : r' = 3 : -1$). The paths of three points $C' \in \Sigma'$ are marked. Depending on the respective distance from the center of the moving polode, the path is curtate, cuspidal, or prolate. Due to the ratio $3 : -1$, all paths are closed after the third rolling. Trochoids are closed curves, if the ratio $r : r'$ is rational.

A trochoid can be realized technically: the circles p and p' are usually fitted out with a gear cross, and their centers are linked by a crank FR. When the crank rotates with a constant angular velocity α around the bearing point $F \in \Sigma$, the system Σ' revolves with a proportional angular velocity α' around R. The ratio of the radii and the ratio of the angular velocities is connected by the formulas

$$\alpha : \alpha' = r : (r - r') \quad \text{and} \quad r : r' = (\alpha - \alpha') : \alpha. \tag{6}$$

Every trochoid can be generated in two ways (L. EULER): In Figure 9.16 the angular velocities $\alpha : \alpha' = 1 : 3$ ($\Rightarrow r : r' = 2 : -1$) and the rod lengths $\overline{FR} : \overline{RC} = 6 : 1$ are chosen. Because of $r\,r' < 0$, we have an outside rolling. Because of $\overline{RC} < r'$, the path trochoid c is prolate.

When the trochoid-creating rod pair FR, RC is extented to a joint parallelogram, the motion will not be disturbed. It is evident that the same trochoid can be

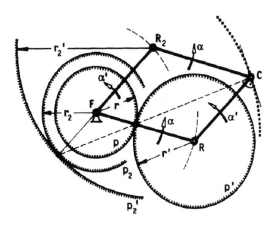

FIGURE 9.16. Two generations of one and the same trochoid by two different trochoid motions.

created by the second rod pair FR_2, R_2C that rotates with angular velocities $\alpha' : \alpha = 3 : 1$.

The second planetary motion can also be constrained by the rolling of two circles p_2 and p'_2. Their centers F and R_2 and their radii can be calculated by means of equation (6) ($r_2 : r'_2 = 2 : 3 > 0$). Note that due to the positive ratio, the circles p_2 and p'_2 are placed on the same side with respect to the pole tangent. The contact point P_2 placed on the rod FR_2 divides this rod externally in the ratio $2 : 3$. P_2 can also be found by intersecting the path normals FR_2 and PC.

For the second creation, the point can also be found in a different way, for example, the upper one by rotating FR_2 from the marked position by an angle of 180°.

In our example a complete rotation of FR_2 corresponds with a rotation of R_2C of only 120°. Thus, the three points C, C^+, and C^- on the curve create a regular triangle Δ. By connecting C' rigidly to p', C' follows the trochoid c. At the same time, we can connect C^+ and C^- rigidly with p'_2. These points also follow c, but they run "in front of" or "behind" the point C. This means that when the wheel p'_2 is driven by a crank, the vertices of the regular triangle Δ are running on the prolate and closed trochoid c. The triangle and the trochoid create the border of the chamber space of the WANKEL engine. In practice, the borders of the triangular runner are not straight: the runner is constructed in such a way that it slides along the chamberspace. Thus, there are three chambers of different sizes.[4]

---

[4]The WANKEL engine is a four-stroke engine. The working stroke (ignition) happens at the moment of minimal chamberspace. During one whole cycle, there are three ignitions and three revolutions of the engine shaft in F.

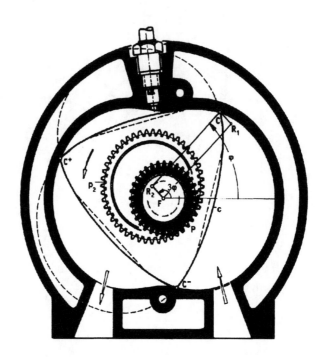

FIGURE 9.17. The WANKEL engine.

9.5   The Coupler Motion

If two points $A', B' \in \Sigma'$ are guided along two circles around two nonidentical fixed points $L, M \in \Sigma$ (the *bearing points*), we call the motion Σ'/Σ a coupler motion. We already had an example for this motion when we derived an approximated straight line guidance from an elliptic motion.

The mechanism corresponding to the coupler motion consists of four flexibly connected rods, hence a four-bar linkage $LA'B'M$. The fixed rod $LM \subset \Sigma$ is called *frame*, the moving rod $A'B' \subset \Sigma'$ is called *coupler*, the arms LA' and MB' are called *crank* or *rocker*, depending on whether a full revolution is possible or not.

We get the form of the linkage, when the four lengths $\overline{LA'}$, $\overline{MB'}$, $\overline{A'B'}$, and $\overline{LM}$ are given. The stretched positions of crank arm and coupler show the borders of the oscillation area of the rocker. Concerning the drive, the mechanism should have at least one crank, which is not always easy to achieve. In some cases, the joint quadrilateral must be expanded to a seven-bar or even eight-bar linkage.

An arbitrary point $C' \in \Sigma'$ can be rigidly connected to the coupler $A'B' \subset \Sigma'$ (coupler triangle Δ). Its path curve c can feature up to three double points, positioned on a circle, containing L and M with the peripheral angle of the coupler triangle.

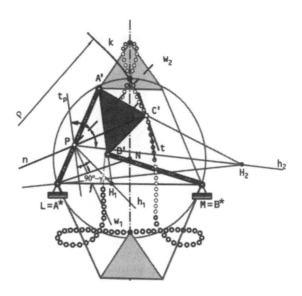

FIGURE 9.18. Four-bar linkage (double rocker: $\overline{LM} = 8$, $\overline{LA} = \overline{MB} = 5.5$, $\overline{AB} = 3.5$, $\overline{AC} = \overline{BC} = 3$).

Example: coupler curve. The shape of a coupler curve can vary considerably. Figure 9.18 shows a double rocker.[5]

Now let a coupler curve c be given by a four-bar linkage. For technical reasons, it is often necessary to substitute the original four-bar linkage by another linkage that creates exactly the same curve. This can be achieved by ROBERTS' theorem. It says that there are three ways of designing a given coupler curve. The following example shows how mechanisms with a crank can be found if we start from a coupler curve c created by the four-bar linkage $LABM$.

Next, the defined four-bar linkage, including the coupler triangle, is lifted out of the bearings L and M and stretched into a separate construction (Figure 9.19a). In stretching it into a parallel scheme, it shows the measures of the replaced mechanism. In this nine-link system, the parallelograms do not disturb each other in the motion of $LABM$. The point $N \in \Sigma$ is fixed and forms an extra bearing, as shown in ROBERTS' theorem. In fact, the triangles LMN and ABC are directly similar. The curve c can be generated by the three four-bar linkages $LABM$, $LDEN$, and $MFGN$ (Figure 9.19b). In case there is no crank in the

---

[5]The lower part of Figure 9.18 shows the path of c in an approximately straight line. This was the inspiration for CHEBYCHEV in developing practical and useful coupler motions.

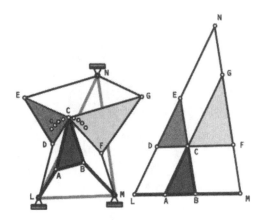

FIGURE 9.19. One and the same coupler curve c can be generated by three different four-bar-linkages (ROBERTS' theorem).

system of the arms,[6] there is still the possibility to add flexibly connected rods to a crank-drive mechanism (Figure 9.20).

As an example, we will develop an approximate straight guidance from the rolling of a circle on a straight line (Figure 9.21, 9.22). The center C' of p' moves along a straight line. The points $A', B' \in \Sigma'$ describe ordinary trochoids. In a symmetric position, we now replace these curves by the corresponding osculating circles in A and B (we get the osculating centers A^* and B^* by means of the curvature transformation) and guide A and B along these circles by means of two arms fixed at $A^* =: L$ and $B^* =: M$. The result is a moving symmetric four-bar linkage. In the initial position, the path c is now almost straight.

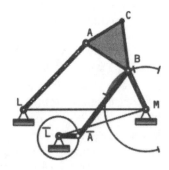

FIGURE 9.20. An additional crank rocker may drive a four-bar linkage.

[6]The condition for a crank rocker is that $\overline{LA'}$ is the minimum of $\overline{LA'}$, $\overline{MB'}$, $\overline{AB}$, and $\overline{LM}$, and $\overline{MB'} > |\overline{AB} - \overline{LM'} \pm \overline{LA'}|$.

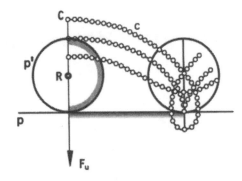

FIGURE 9.21. A circle rolling on a straight line.

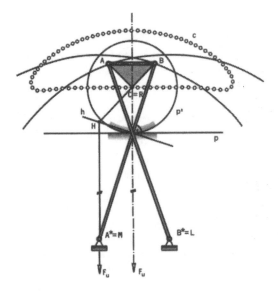

FIGURE 9.22. Approximate straight guidance developed from the rolling of a circle on a straight line.

9.6 Special Four-Bar Linkages

Among the variety of four-bar linkages, there are some remarkable special cases.

- **Parallelogram linkage:** $\overline{LA} = \overline{MB}$, $\overline{LM} = \overline{AB}$, $LM \parallel AB$, $LA \parallel MB$.

  The path curves of all points $C' \in \Sigma'$ are circles c congruent to the paths of A and B (Figure 9.23). C can also be directed by an additional crank. Technical applications are electrical locomotives and drawing machines.

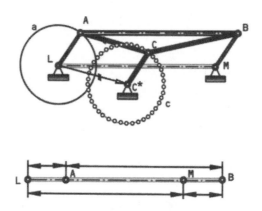

FIGURE 9.23. Parallelogram linkage.

The parallelogram linkage belongs to the group of the so-called folding four-bar linkages. In such a folded position, we have a straight joint row with four bearings. From here we can confine the parallelogram motion or change to a motion of the so-called

- **Antiparallelogram linkage:** $\overline{LA} = \overline{MB}, \overline{LM} = \overline{AB}, LM \nparallel AB, LA \nparallel MB$.

This special case is one of a few among the four-bar linkages where the polodes are of technical interest: for the instantaneous pole $P = MA \cap NB$, we have (due to symmetry) $|\overline{LP} \pm \overline{PM}| = |\overline{LP} \pm \overline{PA}| = \overline{MA} = \overline{LA} = const$ (Figure 9.24). Thus, the fixed polode p is an ellipse (hyperbola) with L and

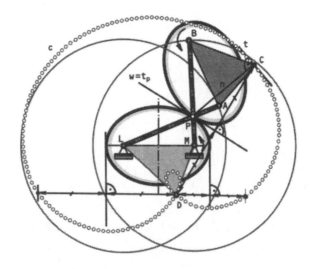

FIGURE 9.24. Antiparallelogram.

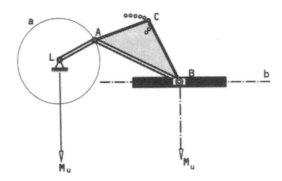

FIGURE 9.25. Slider crank.

M as focal points. When Σ and Σ' switch their position, the moving polode takes the place of the fixed polode. Again due to symmetry, we see that the moving polode is an ellipse (hyperbola) congruent to the fixed polode (focal points in A' and B').

For an observer on a crank (for example on MB), the joints M and B seem to be fixed. The ellipses rotate around their focal points and roll on each other. Since this happens without sliding, both pole curves can be supplied with gears or a rough surface. There are elliptic gear wheels, if they have a variable pulsing transmission ratio of $i = \overline{MP}/\overline{BP}$. (Round gears have a constant transmission ratio of $i = r'/r$). When p' is driven with constant speed, p spins rhythmically faster and slower.

- **Slider crank** (pleuel-motion): One of the two bearing points—e.g., M— is a point of infinity. Then B follows a straight line b (case-guidance or slit-guidance, Figure 9.25).

The path curves are so-called pleuel-curves. Note that we already had an example for such a mechanism when we substituted the elliptic motion (Figure 9.11).

9.7 Sample Kinematics Programs

In this section, we will give some samples for applied kinematics, introduce some new classes like *Trochoid*, *CurvatureTransformation*, *ForBarLinkage* and *Slider-Crank*.

The first example shows how an elliptic motion can be simulated. Note the use of the class *PathCurve2d*, as it is convenient for kinematic motions. Please also take a look at the animation part in Scene::Animate( ).

Elliptic Motion

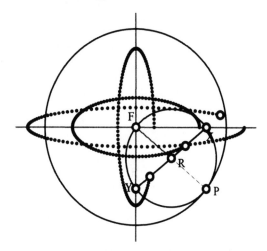

FIGURE 9.26. Output of the program `X/2D/ellipse.cpp`.

Begin listing of `X/2D/ellipse.cpp` (Figure 9.26)

```cpp
#include "opengeom.h"

// Elliptic motion

Circ2d FixedCircle, RotatingCircle; // The CARDAN circles
P2d Pole, FixedCenter, RotatingCenter;
Rod2d SingleRotatingRod, DoubleRotatingRod;
PathCurve2d Path[3]; // The elliptic path curves

void Scene::Init( )
{
    // Initialize CARDAN circles
    const Real LargeRadius = 6, SmallRadius = LargeRadius / 2;
    FixedCenter( 0, 0 );
    RotatingCenter( LargeRadius − SmallRadius, 0 );
    FixedCircle.Def( PureRed, FixedCenter, LargeRadius );
    RotatingCircle.Def( PureGreen, RotatingCenter, SmallRadius );
    // Initialize the rods
    SingleRotatingRod.Def( LightGray, FixedCenter, RotatingCenter );
    Pole( LargeRadius, 0 );
    DoubleRotatingRod.Def( Black, RotatingCenter, Pole );
}
```

```
void Scene::Draw( )
{
   WriteNice( Black, "Elliptic Motion", −4.5, 8, 0, 2 );

   // Draw the axes, the CARDAN circles, and the rods.
   Xaxis.Draw( LightGray, −7, 7, THICK );
   Yaxis.Draw( LightGray, −7, 7, THICK );
   FixedCircle.Draw( THICK );
   RotatingCircle.Draw( THICK );
   SingleRotatingRod.Draw( THICK );
   DoubleRotatingRod.Draw( THICK );

   // Show rod XY,
   P2d X = DoubleRotatingRod [2];
   X.Mark( Black, 0.3, 0.15 );
   V2d v = X − RotatingCenter;
   P2d Y = RotatingCenter − v;
   StraightLine2d( Black, RotatingCenter, Y, THICK );
   StraightLine2d( Gray, RotatingCenter, Pole, THIN );

   // Mark points and attach names to them.
   FixedCenter.Mark( Gray, 0.3, 0.15);
   RotatingCenter.Mark( PureGreen, 0.3, 0.15 );
   Pole.Mark( PureRed, 0.3, 0.15 );
   Y.Mark( Black, 0.3, 0.15, 2 );
   Pole.AttachString( PureRed, 0.4, −0.2, "P" );
   FixedCenter.AttachString( PureRed, −0.5, −0.7, "F" );
   RotatingCenter.AttachString( PureGreen, 0.4, −0.5, "R" );
   X.AttachString( Black, −0.1, −0.8, "X" );
   Y.AttachString( Black, −0.7, −0.1, "Y" );

   // Add new points to the elliptic paths, corresponding
   // to three parameters on the line XY.
   static Real parameter [3] = { −0.2, 0.3, 0.8 };
   P2d P [3];
   for ( int i = 0; i < 3; i++ )
   {
      P [i] = X.InBetweenPoint( Y,  parameter [i] );
      if ( FrameNum( ) < 120 )
         Path [i].AddPoint( P [i] );
      Path [i].MarkPoints( Blue, 0.1, 0 );
      P [i].Mark( Blue, 0.3, 0.15);
   }
}
```

```
void Scene::Animate( )
{
   // Rotate the center RotatingCenter of the smaller CARDAN circle.
   Real angle = 3; // 3 degrees for each frame
   Rotation2d.Def( FixedCenter, angle );
   SingleRotatingRod.Rotate( );
   RotatingCircle.Rotate( );
   Pole.Rotate( );
   DoubleRotatingRod.Rotate( );
   RotatingCenter = RotatingCircle.Mid( );
   DoubleRotatingRod.Rotate( RotatingCenter, −2 ∗ angle );
}
void Scene::CleanUp( )
{
}
void Projection::Def( )
{
  if ( FrameNum( ) == 1 )
  {
     xyCoordinates( −10.0, 10.0, −7.0, 7.0 );
  }
}
```

End listing `X/2D/ellipse.cpp` (Figure 9.26)

The next example (Figure 9.27) illustrates the general case of an elliptic motion. The code can be found at the location `X/2D/ellipse2.cpp`. The program uses simple analytic geometry (intersection of lines and with lines and circles). The third vertex of the triangle, e.g., is calculated in function ThirdPointOfTriangle( ) by intersecting two circles with radius.

The third example (Figure 9.28) shows how envelopes of straight lines can be calculated (in the case of an elliptic motion, it is an astroid or a parallel curve to it, a "parastroid"). The envelope of the normal of the elliptic path curve is also a parastroid. This curve is the location of all osculating centers.

The program `X/2D/astroid.cpp` that creates Figure 9.28 uses an OPEN GE-OMETRY class named *CurvatureTransformation*. Its constructor and its member functions are defined in `kinemat.h`:

```
CurvatureTransformation( const P2d &F0, const P2d &R0, Real rad1 );
   // EULER−SAVARY
P2d CenterOfOsculatingCircle( const P2d &C );
P2d GetPole( );
```

Elliptic Motion

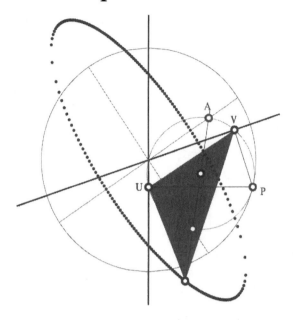

FIGURE 9.27. Output of the program X/2D/ellipse2.cpp.

The next application (X/2D/troch2d.cpp) works with the OPEN GEOMETRY class *Trochoid* (defined in kinemat.h).

```
void Def( Color c, Real FR, Real RC,
        Real deg1, Real deg2, Real delta_deg );
    // deg1 and deg2 are the inclinations of
    // FR and RC to the x-axis,
    // delta_deg is the angle for the animation.
void Def( Color c, Real rad1, Real rad2, Real RC,
        Real deg1, Real deg2, Real delta_deg );
    // alternative: The radii of the CARDAN circles are given
void ShowPoleCurves( Real deg, ThinOrThick linestyle );
    // CARDAN circles
void ShowBars( Real deg, ThinOrThick linestyle, Real r = 0 );
P2d GetF( );
P2d GetR( Real deg );
P2d GetC( Real deg );
P2d GetPole( Real deg );
P2d CenterOfOsculatingCircle( const P2d &C, Real deg );
```

Elliptic Motion

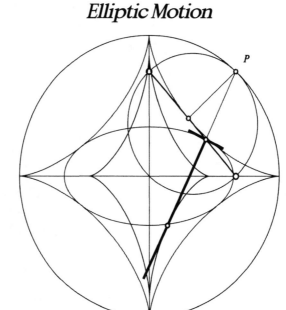

Envelope... Astroid
Osc. centers... Parastroid
Polodes... CARDAN circles

FIGURE 9.28. Output of the program X/2D/`astroid.cpp`.

In order to learn how to use the class, please compare the output (Figure 9.29) with the corresponding code.

Begin listing of X/2D/`troch2d.cpp` (Figure 9.29)

```
#include "opengeom.h"
#include "kinemat.h"


Trochoid Curve;
const Real Radius1 = 5, Radius2 = 2, DistFromR = 5;
Real Angle = 0;
void Scene::Init( )
{
   Curve.Def( Black, Radius1, Radius2, DistFromR, 0, 720, 4 );
   HiQuality( );
}
void Scene::Draw( )
{
   Curve.Draw( THICK );
```

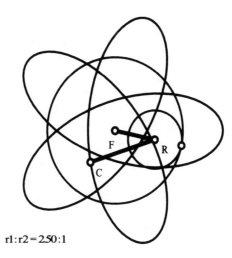

rl:r2 = 2.50 : 1

FIGURE 9.29. Output of the program `X/2D/troch2d.cpp`.

```
      Curve.ShowPoleCurves( Angle, THICK );
      Curve.ShowBars( Angle, VERY_THICK, 0.3 );
      Curve.GetPole( Angle ).Mark( Red, 0.3, 0.2 );
      PrintString( Black, −12, −10, "r1:r2 =%.2f:1\n", Radius1/Radius2 );
}
void Scene::Animate( )
{
    Angle += 4;
}
void Scene::CleanUp( )
{
}
void Projection::Def( )
{
  if ( FrameNum( ) == 1 ) // Initialization of the drawing window
  {
      xyCoordinates( −15.0, 15.0, −15.0, 15.0 );
  }
}
```

End listing `X/2D/troch2d.cpp` (Figure 9.29)

Another class defined in `kinemat.h` is *FourBarLinkage*. The member functions of this class are:

```
void Def( Real LA, Real AB, Real MB, Real LM,
          Real start_alpha_in_deg, Real delta_alpha );
void Def( const P2d &L, const P2d &A, const P2d &B, const P2d &M,
          Real delta_alpha = 1 );
void Draw( Color c, ThinOrThick thick,
           Real r1, Real r2, Boolean with_names,
           Boolean show_circles );
P2d CalcPoint( Real AC, Real BC, int side = 1, Boolean calc_N = false );
void DrawTriangle( Color c, Real r1, Real r2 );
void Move( );
void PutAtPosition( Real x, Real y, Real rot_angle_in_deg );
P2d Joint( int i );
void CalcAlternateMechanisms( FourBarLinkage &Alt1,
    FourBarLinkage &Alt2 );
P2d GetL( ) { return Lt; }
P2d GetM( ) { return Mt; }
P2d GetA( ) { return At; }
P2d GetB( ) { return Bt; }
Real GetLM( ) { return d; }
Real GetAB( ) { return c; }
Real GetLA( ) { return a; }
Real GetLB( ) { return b; }
P2d GetPole( );
StrL2d GetPolodeTangent( );
P2d CenterOfOsculatingCircle( const P2d &C );
Boolean PathClosed( ) { return (Boolean) Closed; }
```

The use of these functions can best be learned by means of a practical application (Figure 9.30):

Another application shows how we can easily calculate the alternate mechanism (ROBERTS).

Begin listing of X/2D/foubar.cpp (Figure 9.30)

```
#include "opengeom.h"
#include "kinemat.h"

FourBarLinkage Mechanism;
PathCurve2d PathC( PureRed );

void Scene::Init( )
{
    Mechanism.Def( 7, 10.5, 12, 15.7, 0, -1 );
```

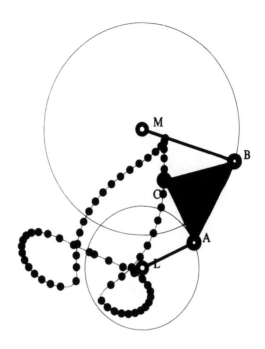

FIGURE 9.30. Output of the program X/2D/foubar.cpp.

```
//    Mechanism.Def( 7, 10.5, 12, 10,  0, −1 );
//    Mechanism.Def( 10, 10.5, 12, 10, 30, 0.5 );
      Real rot_angle = 90;
      V2d trans_vector( 0, 0 );
      Mechanism.PutAtPosition( trans_vector.x, trans_vector.y,  rot_angle );
      ScaleLetters( 2 );
}
void Scene::Draw( )
{
      const Real r1 = 0.2, r2 = r1 / 2;
      P2d C = Mechanism.CalcPoint( 8, 9 );
      if ( !Mechanism.PathClosed( ) )
         PathC.AddPoint( C );
      Mechanism.DrawTriangle( Green, 2 * r1, r1 );
      Mechanism.Draw( Black, VERY_THICK, r1, r2, true, true );
      PathC.Draw( THIN );
      PathC.MarkPoints( Pink, 0.2, 0, 10 );
      C.AttachString( Black, −3 * r1, − 5 *r1, "C" );
}
void Scene::Animate( )
{
      Mechanism.Move( );
```

```
}
void Scene::CleanUp( )
{
}
void Projection::Def( )
{
  if ( FrameNum( ) == 1 )
  {
    xyCoordinates( −20, 25, −25, 30 );
  }
}
```

End listing X/2D/foubar.cpp (Figure 9.30)

Begin listing of X/2D/roberts.cpp (Figure 9.31)

```
#include "opengeom.h"
#include "kinemat.h"
```

// ROBERTS theorem

FourBarLinkage Mechanism, Alt1, Alt2;
PathCurve2d PathC(*Red*);
Real AC = 9, BC = 6;

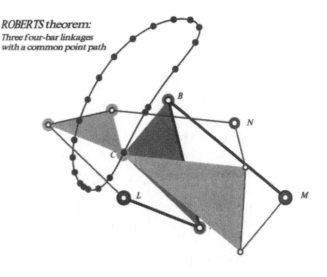

FIGURE 9.31. Output of the program X/2D/roberts.cpp.

```
void Scene::Init( )
{
    Real LA = 7, AB = 11, MB = 13, LM = 14;
    Mechanism.Def( LA, AB, MB, LM, 0, 1 );
    Mechanism.PutAtPosition( 0, −2, 0 );
    InclineLetters( 75 );
    HiQuality( );
}

void Scene::Draw( )
{
    Real r1 = 0.2, r2 = r1 / 2;
    P2d C = Mechanism.CalcPoint( AC, BC, 1, true );
    P2d N = Mechanism.Joint( 3 );
    N.Mark( Blue, r1, r2 );
    if ( !Mechanism.PathClosed( ) )
        PathC.AddPoint( C );
    Mechanism.CalcAlternateMechanisms( Alt1, Alt2 );
    Alt1.DrawTriangle( LightBlue, 0.4, 0.2 );
    Alt1.Draw( DarkBlue, THICK, 0.25, 0.15, false, false );
    Alt2.DrawTriangle( LightGreen, 0.25, 0.15 );
    Alt2.Draw( DarkGreen, THICK, 0.25, 0.15, false, false );
    Alt1.Joint( 2 ).AttachString( Black, 3 * r1, −r1, "N" );
    Mechanism.DrawTriangle( Yellow, 0.5, 0.25 );
    Mechanism.Draw( Black, VERY_THICK, 0.25, 0.15, true, false );
    PathC.Draw( THICK );
    PathC.MarkPoints( Red, 0.25, 0, 18 );
    C.AttachString( Red, −4 * r1, −r1, "C" );
    Real x0 = −10.5;
    ScaleLetters( 1.3 );
    PrintString( Black, x0, 12, "ROBERTS' theorem:" );
    ScaleLetters( 1 / 1.3 );
    PrintString( Black, x0, 11, "Three four-bar linkages" );
    PrintString( Black, x0, 10.2, "with a common point path" );
}
void Scene::Animate( )
{
    Mechanism.Move( );
}
void Scene::CleanUp( )
{
}
void Projection::Def( )
{
    if ( FrameNum( ) == 1 )
```

```
{
    xyCoordinates( −10.5, 17, −12, 22 );
}
}
```

End listing X/2D/roberts.cpp (Figure 9.31)

Once more back to the elliptic motion. A class *SliderCrank* is used. It is derived from *FourbarLinkage* and described in kinemat.h.

void Def(*Real* LA, *Real* AB, *Real* Lb, *Real* start_alpha_in_deg, *Real* delta_alpha);
    // B runs on straight line b (distance Lb from L)
    // delta_alpha is the step in the animation.
void Def(**const** *P2d* &L, **const** *P2d* &A, **const** *P2d* &B);
void Draw(*Color* c, *ThinOrThick* style, *Real* r1, *Real* r2, *Boolean* with_names);
    // r1 and r2 are the radii of the circles around the points
void Move( );
    // Rotate A about L through delta_alpha.

Begin listing of X/2D/ell_slider_crank.cpp (Figure 9.32)

```
#include "opengeom.h"
#include "kinemat.h"
```

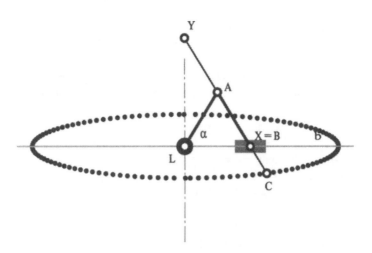

FIGURE 9.32. Output of the program X/2D/ell_slider_crank.cpp

```
SliderCrank SCrank;
PathCurve2d c( Blue, 200, 0.3 );

void Scene::Init( )
{
    const Real LA = 4, AB = 4, Dist = 0;

    SCrank.Def( LA, AB, Dist, 55, 3 );
    SCrank.PutAtPosition( 0, 0, 0 );
    P2d L = SCrank.GetL( );
    HiQuality( );
}
void Scene::Draw( )
{
    P2d M = SCrank.GetA( );
    P2d X = SCrank.GetB( );
    Rect2d r;
    r.Def( Gray, 2, 0.8, FILLED );
    r.Translate( X.x - 1, X.y - 0.4 );
    r.Shade( );
    V2d AM = M - X;
    P2d Y = M + AM;
    P2d C = X - 0.5 * AM;
    StraightLine2d( Black, C, Y, THICK );
    c.AddPoint( C );
    c.MarkPoints( Blue, 0.15, 0 );
    Circ2d c;
    P2d L = SCrank.GetL();
    c.Def( Gray, L, SCrank.GetLA() );
    c.MarkPoints( Blue, 0.1 );
    Xaxis.Draw( LightGray, -11, 11, THICK );
    Yaxis.LineDotted( Black, -6, 6, 12, THIN );
    SCrank.Draw( Black, VERY_THICK, 0.3, 0.15, false );
    Y.Mark( Blue, 0.3, 0.15 );
    C.Mark( Blue, 0.3, 0.15 );
    SCrank.GetL( ).AttachString( Black, -1, -1, "L" );
    SCrank.GetL( ).AttachString( Black, 1, 0.5, "$alpha$" );
    X.AttachString( Black, 0.2, 0.4, "X =B b" );
    Y.AttachString( Black, 0.2, 0.4, "Y" );
    C.AttachString( Black, -0.2, -1, "C" );
    SCrank.GetA( ).AttachString( Black, 0.4, 0, "A" );
}

void Scene::Animate( )
```

OTTO-engine (slider crank)

FIGURE 9.33. Output of the program `X/2D/otto_engine.cpp` (background image: Markus Strahlhofer).

```
{
    SCrank.Move( );
}
void Scene::CleanUp( )
{
}
void Projection::Def( )
{
    if ( FrameNum( ) == 1 )
    {
        xyCoordinates( −10.0, 10.0, −7.0, 7.0 );
    }
}
```

End listing `X/2D/ell_slider_crank.cpp` (Figure 9.32)

Another application of *SliderCrank* can be found in `X/2D/otto_engine.cpp`. (Figure 9.33).

9.8   Geometry of Gearing

As an application of the theory of Kinematics, we we will now learn about the principles of gearing. We start with the following.

The Fundamental Law of Gearing

The idea behind gearing is very simple: we would like to transmit a rotation of a system Σ_1' around a fixed center A_1 with constant angular velocity ω_1 to the rotation of another system Σ_2' around another fixed point A_2 with some constant angular velocity ω_2. According to the so-called theorem of ARONHOLD-KENNEDY, the velocity pole P of the relative motion Σ_1'/Σ_2' has to be situated on the pole line A_1A_2 and, by our claim above, fixed in Σ. Therefore, Σ_1'/Σ_2' is a trochoid motion with the ratio of radii $r_1' : r_2' = \omega_1 : \omega_2$ and, of course, $|r_1' - r_2'| = \overline{A_1A_2}$.

If the polodes $p_1' \subset \Sigma_1'$, $p_2' \subset \Sigma_2'$ of Σ_1'/Σ_2' are represented by contacting wheels, one can transmit rotations by virtue of friction developed at their interface. Since the available frictional force is limited by nature, it is inevitable to form teeth.

During a certain interval I of time, each tooth profile $c_1' \subset \Sigma_1'$ has to contact its mating profile $c_2' \subset \Sigma_2'$. In other words, the pair (c_1', c_2') of conjugate tooth profiles is a pair of enveloping curves of Σ_1'/Σ_2'. Thus, at every fixed instant $t_j \in I$, the common normal to both profiles at the instantaneous point E_j of contact, the so-called meshing point, has to pass through the relative pole P, the so-called pitch point.[7] The locus of all meshing points in the fixed system Σ is called the meshing line (corresponding to the pair (c_1', c_2')) (Figure 9.34).

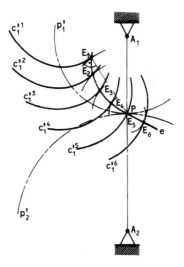

FIGURE 9.34. The construction of the meshing line e for a given tooth profile c_1'.

---

[7]In the following, we will use indices that indicate the respective position of elements of the moving systems. For instance, $c_1'^j$ marks the position of c_1' at the moment t_j. Contrary to that, if we just want to emphasize that some element corresponds (in some sense) to position j, we write the index j down. As an example, take the instantaneous meshing point E_j from above which is, of course, not the position j of some point E.

Now let us summarize the previous considerations in the following *fundamental law of gearing: the transmission ratio* $\omega_1 : \omega_2$ *of mating gears will be constant, if and only if in each position j the common normal to the tooth profiles* $c_1^{\prime j}, c_2^{\prime j}$ *at the instantaneous meshing point E_j intersects the line $A_1 A_2$ in the pitch point P that is fixed in Σ.*

The Construction of the Meshing Line and of Conjugate Tooth Profiles

As an immediate consequence of the fundamental law of gearing, we detect easily how to construct points of the meshing line corresponding to a pair (c_1', c_2') of conjugate tooth profiles: the meshing line is just the locus of feet E_j of those perpendiculars that can be drawn from the fixed pitch point P to all positions $c_1^{\prime j}$ of c_1' (or, equivalently, $c_2^{\prime j}$ of c_2') (Figure 9.34).

Now let us think about the determination of appropriate tooth profiles. Let us take, for example, $c_1' \subset \Sigma_1'$ (and p_1', p_2') be given. To construct the corresponding profile $c_2' \subset \Sigma_2'$, we have two major possibilities:

1. Recall that (c_1', c_2') is a pair of enveloping curves with respect to the trochoid motion Σ_1'/Σ_2'. Therefore, we can determine points, tangents and, applying the curvature transformation, curvature centers of c_2' very easily.

2. The second method due to REULEAUX is a direct application of the fundamental law of gearing. This construction provides two big advantages: First, one does not have to draw a lot of positions of c_1'. Second, this method yields the meshing line simultaneously. The procedure is the following (Figure 9.35): Let $c_1^{\prime j}$ be the given j-th position of c_1' and choose $C_1' \in c_1'$ arbitrarily. This point will become a meshing point, when one point $P_1' \in p_1'$ of intersection between p_1' and the normal to c_1' at C_1' coincides with the pitch point P. Thus, we rotate both wheels to obtain these positions $\Sigma_1^{\prime k}, \Sigma_2^{\prime k}$. At this moment, C_1' merges with its corresponding point $C_2' \in c_2'$ and the meshing point E_k of $c_1^{\prime k}$ and $c_2^{\prime k}$, i.e., $C_1^{\prime k} = C_2^{\prime k} = E_k$; P_1' and $P_2' \in p_2'$ merge with the pitch point. Afterwards, we transfer the common line element of $c_1^{\prime k}$ and $c_2^{\prime k}$ back into the initial position j to get $C_2^{\prime j} \in c_2^{\prime j}$. Now vary C_1' on c_1'.

The angle α measured between PE_k and the pole tangent is called the (instantaneous) pressure angle.

How to Get the Whole Shape of the Gears

In practice, not the whole part of the geometrically correctly constructed mating profile c_2' might be useful. For instance, some point C_2' might be a cusp of c_2', or c_1' might intersect c_2' at some point E_k (three-point contact between $c_1^{\prime k}$ and $c_2^{\prime k}$ at E_k). One question that arises is the following: Can we reduce the whole curve c_2' to just a part of it and therefore avoid undesired occurrences? In other

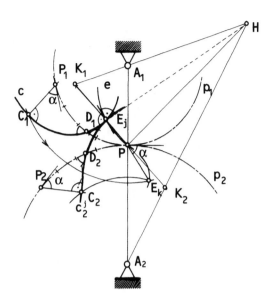

FIGURE 9.35. The construction of the corresponding mating profile c_2' for a given tooth profile c_1' using REULEAUX'S method.

words; where should we choose the limiting points of c_1'? However, we will not go into detail here. The reader is encouraged to experience with the construction of tooth profiles to get a better feeling for the problems that might occur.

We get a whole gear in Σ_1' by using a certain number of congruent profiles c_1'. We also reflect these curves at certain diameter lines of p_1' to make rotations of the opposite direction possible.

Finally, in 3-space the surfaces of teeth can be either cylindrical at straight spur gears or helical at helical gears. The latter guarantee a smoother transmission but they produce axial forces that have to be absorbed by suitable thrust bearings or by combining two opposite helical gears (double-helical gears).

Some Important Special Cases

1. *Involute gearing*: If we require a constant pressure angle α (usually specified as $\alpha = 20°$), the meshing line e must be a straight line through the pitch point P, and both profiles have to be (parts of) involutes of the so-called base circles g_1', g_2', respectively; these circles are concentric with the pitch circles and touch e. Now we speak of involute gears (Figure 9.36, Figure 9.37).

   Some advantages of involute teeth are the following:

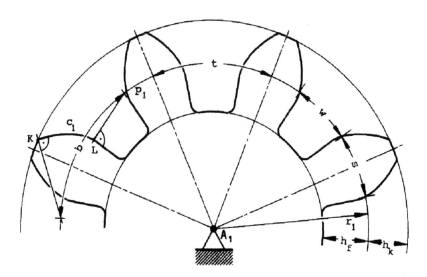

FIGURE 9.36. This picture shows the typical shape of an involute gear. The rolling of p_1 on p_2 implies that distances t (circular pitch) between two adjacent tooth-centers, measured along the pitch circles p_1, p_2, respectively, have to be equal. The teeth are limited by addendum circle and root circle. One has to pay attention to the contact ratio λ: before two conjugate tooth profiles (c_1, c_2) end meshing, two new curves have to begin their contact. In the definition $\lambda = b/t$, b is the length of the circular arc that is traced by the pitch point as long as one tooth profile is meshing. This arc is shown in the figure under the assumption that K, L are the limiting points of contact on c_1. If z_1, z_2 denote the number of teeth for both wheels and r_1, r_2 the radii of the pitch circles, the circular pitch t is given by $t = 2r_1\pi/z_1 = 2r_2\pi/z_2$, where $m := 2r_1/z_1 = 2r_2/z_2$ is the module. All other principal terms to describe gear tooth profiles are standardized multiples of the module, e.g., the addendum $h_k = m$ and the dedendum $h_f = 1.2 \cdot m$. The circular width s of any tooth has to be less than the space width w, both measured along the pitch circles.

- The meshing line coincides with the line of action of the transmitting force. Therefore, a constant input torque implies a constant transmitting force.

- The tooth surfaces $\gamma_1' \subset \Sigma_1'$, $\gamma_2' \subset \Sigma_2'$ of helical gears based on involute profiles are torses. At every moment t_k, each two mating surfaces contact one another along a straight line e_k (instantaneous meshing line), and the common tangent plane is constant along e_k. The union of all meshing lines in the fixed system is called the meshing surface (with respect to (γ_1', γ_2')) and, in this case, is a ruled surface.

- The conjugate action of involute teeth is not influenced by adjustments of the distance $\overline{A_1 A_2}$ of the centers. The main (geometric) effect of altering this distance is to change the pressure angle and the pitch radii. (The base circles and the transmission ration $\omega_1 : \omega_2$ are independent.)

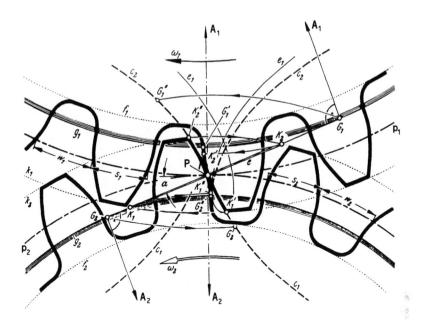

FIGURE 9.37. This figure shows a corresponding pair of involute gears. In particular, g_1, g_2 denote the base circles, f_1, f_2 the root circles, and k_1, k_2 the addendum circles, respectively. e_1 is the path of the limiting point $K_1' \in \Sigma_1'$ under the relative motion Σ_1'/Σ_2'.

2. In particular, if one of the pitch circles, say p_1', degenerates into a straight line, the corresponding gear becomes a rack. The condition $\alpha = const$ implies that the profile c_1' is straight and perpendicular to the meshing line. As an application, most of the manufacturing methods of involute gears are based on rackshaped cutters (Figure 9.38).

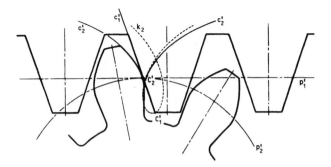

FIGURE 9.38. If p_1' is a straight line, the gear in Σ_1' becomes a rack. Again, the relative path of $C_1' \in \Sigma_1'$ under the motion Σ_1'/Σ_2' is of interest.

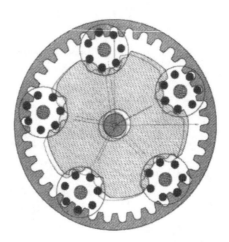

FIGURE 9.39. J. BROSOWITSCH'S variant of the CYCLO-mechanism: the displayed mechanism provides uniform transmission with a high transmission ratio. It works as follows: excenters on the input shaft (which is a circle in Σ_0 with center M_0) are used for the drive of two or more disks (our figure shows two: in Σ_2 and $\bar{\Sigma}_2$, respectively), each of them meshing with three or more pin-geared planetary wheels in $\Sigma_1, \bar{\Sigma}_1, \bar{\bar{\Sigma}}_1, \ldots$ (the figure shows five exemplares). At the same time, these wheels perform a trochoid motion inside the geared frame Σ_0. (The pitch circle in Σ_0 is concentric with the input shaft.) Then the rotation of the centers of the planetary wheels around the center M_0 of the frame is the desired output motion. More precisely, let z_0 denote the number of teeth at the frame wheel in Σ_0 (in the figure: $z_0 = 37$). Then the transmission ratio equals $(z_0 + 1) : 1$. This means when the centers of the disks $\Sigma_2, \bar{\Sigma}_2, \ldots$ rotate with the angular velocity $z_0 + 1$ around M_0, the centers of the planetary wheels $\Sigma_1, \bar{\Sigma}_1, \bar{\bar{\Sigma}}_1, \ldots$ rotate with the angular velocity 1 around M_0.

3. *Pin gearing*: In this case, one tooth profile, say c_1', is assumed to be (part of) a circle (Figure 9.39, [20]). Therefore, the conjugate profile c_2' is a parallel curve to the path traced by the center of c_1' under the relative motion Σ_1'/Σ_2'. Pin gearing is the geometrical basis of ROOT'S blowers.

4. *Cycloid gearing* is an important application of the so-called *Principle of CAMUS*: *If an auxiliary curve h' rolls on the pitch circles p_1', p_2', then any point C' attached to h' traces conjugate tooth profiles c_1', c_2'. Analogously, any curve m' attached to h' envelopes conjugate tooth profiles.*

A proof of this theorem can be given by using REULEAUX'S method. We speak of cycloid gearing, iff h' is a circle (Figure 9.40, Figure 9.41).

Conversely, let any pair (c_1', c_2') of conjugate tooth profiles and the corresponding pitch circles p_1', p_2' be given. It can be shown that this pair can also be generated by applying the principle of CAMUS to p_1', p_2' and some appropriate auxiliary curve h'. Moreover, one can choose whether to generate c_i' as a path (of an auxiliary point C') or as an enveloping curve (using an auxiliary curve m').

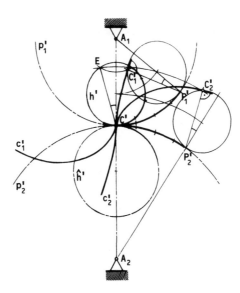

FIGURE 9.40. Here we see the construction of conjugate tooth profiles according to the principle of CAMUS. To get the whole profiles, two auxiliary circles $h', \hat{h}'$ are used. Note that the curvature radius of c_1' and c_2' at the marked point C' is zero.

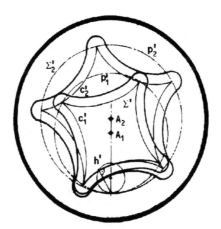

FIGURE 9.41. This figure shows a gear-based pump, consisting of the runner Σ_1' (which rotates around $A_1 \in \Sigma$) and the box Σ_2', rotating around A_2. The used profiles in Σ_1', Σ_2' are parts of parallel curves of cuspidal trochoids c_1', c_2' that were generated using the ratio of radii 4 : 1 (astroid) and 5 : 1, respectively. According to CAMUS (auxiliary circle h'), (c_1', c_2') is a pair of corresponding tooth profiles. Note that, at the same time, c_2' is path of all cusps of c_1' under the relative motion Σ_1'/Σ_2'.

Interesting Classes of Surfaces

In this chapter, we will introduce some classes of surfaces that are probably not very well described in the literature. Among them are the spiral and the so-called "helispiral" surfaces that are common in nature. We will present some approximations to horns of antelopes and shells.

10.1 Spiral Surfaces

Screwing Motion

To get more familiar with the idea of spiral surfaces, we will first recall the notion of a screwing motion. Let a be an axis in euclidean 3-space. A screwing motion (helical motion) is the combination of a continuous rotation around a with constant angular velocity and a continuous translation along a, also with constant velocity. Therefore, the angle t of rotation and the length l of translation are proportional, i.e., there exists a real constant $p \neq 0$ such that $l = p \cdot t$ where p is called the *parameter*. (The case $p = 0$ leads to the special case of rotation, which is of no interest here.) The path of any point is called a helix. By definition, such a curve lies on a cylinder of revolution with axis a.

Screwing motions have been studied in detail since they play an important role in mechanical engineering, for instance.

The Concept of Spiral Motion—Spiral Lines

Now we will develop the principles of spiral motions which are, in some sense, a generalization of screwing motions. Let us take an axis a again and, additionally, a fixed point O on a, which we will call the asymptotic point. Then, a spiral motion is just a continuous family of stretch rotations, each of them the (commutative) product of a rotation around a and a homothety with center O; for any pair of angle t of rotation and stretch-factor s, the relation $s = e^{pt}$ holds where the real nonzero constant p is called the spiral parameter. Thus, a spiral motion is determined if a, O, and p are given.

The path of any point X (different from the asymptotic point, which remains fixed) is called a spiral line. By reasons of continuity, O is considered to belong to any such curve. (That is why we call O the asymptotic point.) If X is on a, then a is its path. If X is contained in the plane π through O and perpendicular to a, then it moves just on a logarithmic spiral in π, i.e., a plane curve that intersects all straight lines through O under a constant angle α; α is called the direction angle and satisfies $p = \cot\alpha$. Further, by definition, any other ("general") spiral line is contained in a cone of revolution with axis a and vertex O, with the normal projection in π being just a logarithmic spiral. Additionally, a spiral line intersects all generator lines of the cone under a constant angle γ, since stretch rotations preserve angles. γ can be calculated from the formula $\tan\gamma = \tan\alpha \cdot \sin\theta$, where θ denotes half of the apex angle of the cone mentioned before. Therefore, if we develop this cone, the spiral line on it will be mapped to a logarithmic spiral with γ as its direction angle.

Spiral Surfaces

We get a spiral surface if we apply a given spiral motion (a, O, p) to a curve k; k, of course, must not be a spiral line. It is clear that a given spiral surface can be generated by infinitely many curves to which the spiral motion is applied. By an appropriate choice of the generator curve k, one can create surfaces that look like shells, the houses of snails, or the horns of goats. And this is a good reason to investigate this class of surfaces. They are of no great importance in technical sciences. But at least the natural law of exponential growth, which, for instance, can be realized from the blossoms of sunflowers should encourage the reader to further considerations on that topic.

Ruled Spiral Surfaces

Among the spiral surfaces, one can find such surfaces that also belong to another class of surfaces. For instance, if we apply a spiral motion to a straight line g, we achieve a ruled spiral surface (Figure 10.1, Figure 10.2). Here we do not treat the trivial cases where g coincides with the asymptotic point O (here we get a cone of revolution) or belongs to the plane π. According to the four types of

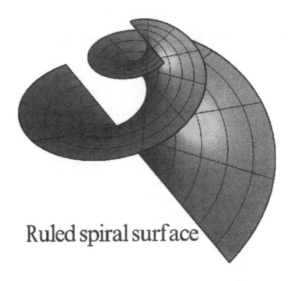

FIGURE 10.1. A ruled spiral surface, generated by a straight line that intersects the axis perpendicularly.

ruled screwing surfaces, one has to distinguish whether the angle between a and g equals $\pi/2$ or not, and whether a and g have a common point or not. The case where the generator line g intersects the spiral axis perpendicularly is very closely related to the well-known right helicoid (Figure 10.1). Note that if we intersect a right helicoid with a cone of revolution with the same axis, we do not get a ruled spiral surface.

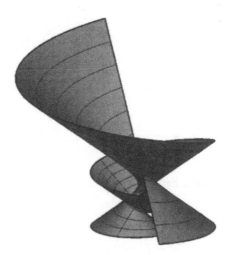

FIGURE 10.2. Another ruled spiral surface.

Listing of program BOOK/ruled_spiral.cpp (Figure 10.1):

```cpp
#include "opengeom.h"
#include "defaults3d.h"

class RuledSpiralSurf: public ParamSurface
{
    Real t;
    P3d SurfacePoint( Real u, Real t )
    {
        P3d P( u, 0, 4 );
        const Real p = 0.4;
        P.Rotate( Zaxis, Deg( t ) );
        P *= exp( p * t );
        return −5 * P;
    }
};
RuledSpiralSurf Surf;
void Scene::Init( )
{
    Silent( );
    Surf.Def( Red, 20, 50, −3 , 3 , − 2 * PI , 0 );
    Surf.Translate( 0, 0, 10 );
    Surf.PrepareContour( );
}
void Scene::Draw( )
{
    Surf.Shade( SMOOTH, REFLECTING );
    Surf.Contour( Black, MEDIUM );
    Surf.WireFrame( Black, 10, 10, THIN );
    Surf.WireFrame( Black, 2, 2, MEDIUM );
    Surf.ULines( Black, 2, MEDIUM );
    PrintString( Black, −5, −10, "Ruled spiral surface");
}
```

Developable Spiral Surfaces

Among the ruled spiral surfaces, there are (since $O \notin g$) two types of developable surfaces. One of them is the spiral cylinder, which is a cylinder with a logarithmic spiral in π as its basis and its generator lines parallel to the spiral axis a. Thus, a spiral cylinder is generated by applying the underlying spiral motion to one of its generator lines. This shows that any nonplanar spiral curve is a curve of

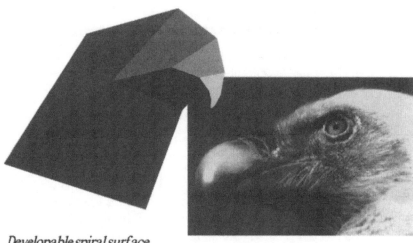

Developable spiral surface,
consisting of seven similar frustums of pyramids

FIGURE 10.3. Spiral surfaces are common in nature. The beak or the claws of a vulture or an eagle look very much like them (Photo: Zoo Hellabrunn, Salzburg). In this case, the beak is approximated by seven similar frustums of pyramids (Idea: W. FUHS; see program X/FUHS/2.cpp).

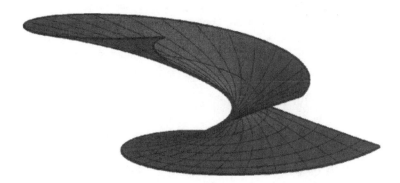

FIGURE 10.4. The shown surface is called MUELLER's spiral surface and is very special: suppose a plane to be given. It can be shown that all straight lines lying in the plane and being tangent to some spiral line envelope a parabola. By applying the underlying spiral motion to this curve, we get the surface shown above. Moreover, each position of the parabola is a fall line (line of steepest slope) of the surface with respect to the invariant plane π.

constant slope with respect to the plane π; the corresponding angle is $\pi/2 - \beta$, where $\cot\beta = \cos\alpha\cot\theta$ or $\sin\alpha\sin\beta = \sin\gamma$.

Now let us take a nonplanar spiral line. From differential geometry, it is well-known that its tangents form a developable surface. By definition of the spiral motion, this surface can be generated by applying the given spiral motion to any tangent of the spiral line.

Special Spiral Surfaces

What result will we get if we take a plane η and apply a spiral motion? By our basic definition of spiral motions, we get an invariant one-parameter family of planes which, in general, envelope the tangent surface of some spiral line. From differential geometry we know that the osculating planes of this curve are just the enveloping planes. (The reader is encouraged to discuss the "special" cases which are: (a) η contains the spiral axis a; (b) O is the only common point of η and a; (c) η is parallel to the axis, and; (d) η is perpendicular to the axis.)

A canal surface is, by definition, the enveloped surface of a one-parameter family of spheres. Thus, to get a spiral canal surface, one just has to apply a spiral motion to an arbitrary sphere (Figure 10.5). Note that if we proceed in this way, the generated canal surface might not be real. With some calculation, we can show that our procedure leads to a real canal surface if, and only if, the radius R of the given sphere satisfies $R \cdot \cos\alpha \cdot \sin\beta < 1$, where β corresponds to the path of the center.

From the theory of enveloping surfaces, it is known that each inscribed sphere contacts the generated spiral canal surface along a circle. It is clear, again from our very first definition, that such a surface can also be defined by applying the basic spiral motion to such a *characteristic circle*. This means that, by definition, a spiral canal surface is a (special) circular spiral surface.

An Analytic Approach

We are going to describe spiral lines and surfaces in an appropriate Cartesian coordinate system. Let the asymptotic point be the origin and the spiral axis the z-axis (and therefore x- and y-axis in our plane π).

The path of a point $P = (x_0, y_0, z_0)$, i.e., the spiral line through P, can be parameterized by

$$x(t) = e^{pt}(x_0\cos t - y_0\sin t)$$
$$y(t) = e^{pt}(x_0\sin t + y_0\cos t)$$
$$z(t) = z_0 e^{pt}$$

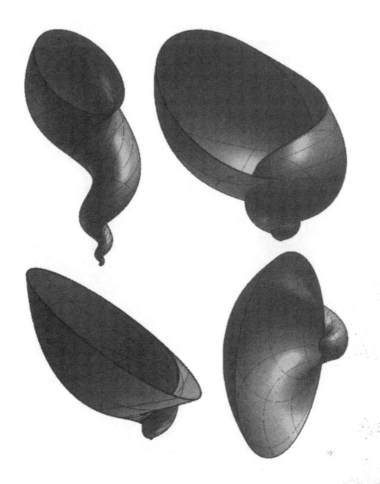

FIGURE 10.5. Various spiral surfaces (three of them are canal surfaces). Depending on the chosen generating sphere Σ_0, the surface can have self-intersections that are, of course, spiral lines. The third surface (first column) in the picture above is a very special spiral canal surface: its characteristic circles are exactly the osculating circles of some nonplanar spiral line.

where t varies in the real numbers. Therefore, if $(x(u), y(u), z(u))$ is the parameterization of a generator curve of a spiral surface, the surface can be written in the form

$$x(u, t) = e^{pt}(x(u)\cos t - y(u)\sin t)$$
$$y(u, t) = e^{pt}(x(u)\sin t + y(u)\cos t)$$
$$z(u, t) = z(u)e^{pt}.$$

In particular, if the generator is a straight line g

$$x(u) = d,\ y(u) = u,\ z(u) = ku + 1,$$

where d and k are real constants and u runs in an interval of the reals, the generated ruled spiral surface has the parameterization

$$x(u, t) = e^{pt}(d \cos t - u \sin t)$$
$$y(u, t) = e^{pt}(d \sin t + u \cos t)$$
$$z(u, t) = e^{pt}(ku + 1).$$

The meaning of the constants is immediately clear.

The parameterization of a spiral cylinder or the tangent surface of a spiral line is very easily done and therefore left as an exercise.

Now let us calculate a spiral canal surface. Without loss of generality, the given sphere Σ_0 has the center $M_0 = (1, 0, z_0)$ and the radius r_0. Then, after a longer calculation, the characteristic circle k of Σ_0 has the form

$$x(u) = 1 - p^2 r_0^2 \sin^2 \gamma + R_0 \sin \alpha \cos u - R_0 z_0 \sin \beta \cos^2 \alpha \sin u$$
$$y(u) = -r_0^2 p \sin^2 \gamma - R_0 \cos \alpha \cos u - R_0 z_0 \cos \alpha \sin \gamma \sin u$$
$$z(u) = z_0 - z_0 p^2 r_0^2 \sin^2 \gamma + R_0 \sin \beta \sin u$$

where the radius R_0 of k satisfies $R_0^2 = r_0^2 - (p r_0^2 \sin \gamma)^2$, and β and γ are the angles corresponding to the path of M_0.

Shells and Snails

To get a shell-shaped spiral surface, one can use an ellipse k as generator curve: let the asymptotic point O be a minor vertex of k with tangent a. If r and s denote half of the major and minor axes, respectively, we can parameterize k as follows:

$$x(u) = s + s \cos u, \quad y(u) = 0, \quad z(u) = r \sin u, \quad u \in [0, 2\pi].$$

We recommend the values $r = 35mm$, $s = 25mm$, and $p = 0.4$.

Listing of program BOOK/snail.cpp (Figure 10.6):

```
#include "opengeom.h"
#include "defaults3d.h"

class SpirSurf: public ParamSurface
```

FIGURE 10.6. Shells of snails are almost perfect spiral surfaces.

```
{
    virtual P3d SurfacePoint( Real u, Real v )
    {
        const Real param = 0.1;
        const Real tilt = −Deg( atan( 1 / param ) );
        P3d P( 4.2 − 3 * sin( u ), −3 * cos( u ), 0 );
        P.Rotate( Xaxis, tilt );
        P.z += 5;
        P.Rotate( Zaxis, Deg( v ) − 90 );
        P *= exp( param * v );
        return  −1 * P;
    }
};
SpirSurf Surface;
void Scene::Init( )
```

```
{
    Surface.Def( Orange, 30, 120, −2, 1.75, −2 * PI, 1.5 * PI );
    Surface.PrepareContour( );
    SetBackgroundTexture( "BMP/snail.bmp" );
    ScaleBackgroundTexture( 0.7, 0.7 );
}
void Scene::Draw( )
{
    Surface.Shade( SMOOTH, REFLECTING );
    Surface.WireFrame( Black, 2, 2, MEDIUM );
    Surface.Contour( Black, MEDIUM );
}
```

Appropriate circular spiral surfaces are good approximations of houses of snails (Figure 10.6). Apply, for instance, a spiral motion to a circle k in the xz-plane. One should use small parameters such as $p = 0.1$, which means that the circle does not grow "too quickly."

The reader is encouraged to create further "nice" examples.

It gets more interesting when the generating line can be chosen "by hand" and not by means of mathematical equations. The idea is to just give the coordinates of a few points on the generating line and then to calculate a spline curve through those points. When it comes to smooth shading, the exact surface normal cannot be calculated. The surface is therefore triangulated into a polyhedron T. For a vertex P of T, the "average normal" of the normals of all triangles through P is determined. The result is very satisfying, even for a comparatively small number of points on the surface (Figure 10.7).

FIGURE 10.7. This shell was generated by means of a spline curve. (We chose only five points on the spline.)

When you look at the corresponding listing, you can see that the defining function Def( ) of the surface is overwritten. The same is true for the shading function Shade( ).

Listing of program BOOK/snail2.cpp (Figure 10.7):

```
#include "opengeom.h"
#include "defaults3d.h"

class SpirSurf: public ParamSurface
{
public:
    virtual P3d SurfacePoint( Real u, Real v )
    {
        // 0 <= u <= 1 is mapped to an index n0
        // of the spline: 1 <= n0 <= spline.Size( )
      int n0 = 1 + Round( ( spline.Size( ) - 1 ) * u );
        P3d P = spline [n0];
        P.z -= 10;
        P *= exp( -0.1 * v ); // Scaling exponential v
        P.Rotate( Zaxis, Deg( v ) ); // rotation about z-axis prop. v
        P.z += 5;
        return P;
    }
    void Def( int n, Coord3dArray points )
    {
        spline.Def( Gray, n, points, 50 );
        Silent( ); // This is to avoid annoying messages
        // the u-parameter must be in the interval [0, 1]
        AllowSmoothApproximation( ); // BEFORE Def( )!
        ParamSurface::Def( Brown, 50, 140, 0, 1, 0, 8.5 * PI );
        PrepareContour( );
    }
    void Shade( Boolean smooth ) // Overwrite the shading function
    {
        T.Smooth( smooth );
        // We display the triangulated polyhedron T
        // instead of the surface itself. Normals are interpolated.
        T.Shade( col );
    }
private:
    CubicSpline3d spline;
};
```

```
SpirSurf Surface;
void Scene::Init( )
{
    Coord3dArray points = // some points on the generating line
    {
        { 0, 1, 0 },{ −4, 2, −2 },{ −3, 8, −1 },{ 2.5, 4.5, 2.7 },{ 0, 1, 0 }
    };
    Surface.Def( 5, points);
}
void Scene::Draw( )
{
    Surface.Shade( SMOOTH );
    Surface.ULines( Black, 2, MEDIUM );
    Surface.Contour( Black, MEDIUM );
}
```

Here are three more nice examples, created by means of a few points on a spline curve: the approximations to various shells and a nautilus (Figure 10.8, 10.9, 10.10).

10.2 Helispiral Surfaces

In this section, we will introduce a class of surfaces that has not been investigated much so far. We call them the helispiral surfaces, since they have some properties that have both helical surfaces and classical spiral surfaces. For some reason, we

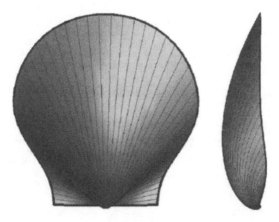

FIGURE 10.8. The emblem of a big company. (Nine points on the spline.)

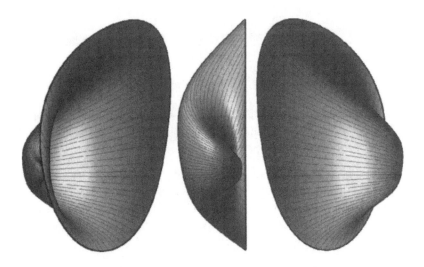

FIGURE 10.9. Another shell, found on the beach.

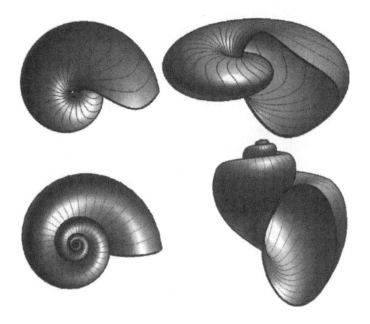

FIGURE 10.10. The nautilus is still one of the best examples for spiral surfaces. The other example is the shell of a water snail, directly from the aquarium.

dismissed the name conical helical surfaces—which would be a consequence of the name "conical helix" which is used, for example, in [3].

Some Words About the Helical Motion

The ordinary *helical motion* is a combination of a rotation about a fixed axis a (angle t) and a proportional translation along a (length pt). The proportionality factor p is called the parameter.

The path curves of a helical motion are helices. A helix runs on a cylinder of revolution with the axis a. When the carrier cylinder ζ is developed, the helix appears as a straight line. (The helix is a loxodrome on its carrier cylinder.) In a projection orthogonal to a, it appears as a sine curve (Figure 10.11).

More About the Classical Spiral Motion

The aforementioned *spiral motion* is a combination of a rotation about a fixed axis a (angle t) and a proportional exponential distortion from a fixed point $O \in a$ (the spiral center, factor e^{pt}). The proportionality factor p is called the spiral parameter.

The path curves are cylindroconic spirals. Projected in the direction of a, such a spiral appears as a logarithmic spiral. The curve will develop into a straight line when the logarithmic carrier cylinder ζ is developed. The spiral also runs on a cone of revolution Γ with axis a and apex O (Figure 10.12). Since the spiral is a loxodrome on this carrier cone, it will develop into a logarithmic spiral when the cone is developed.

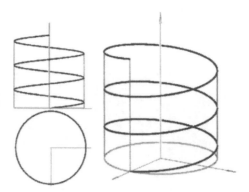

FIGURE 10.11. The ordinary helical motion is the composition of two transformations. It is characterized by one parameter.

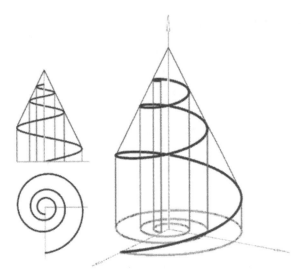

FIGURE 10.12. The previously mentioned spiral motion is also the composition of two transformations, being characterized by one parameter.

Definition of the Helispiral Motion

The *helispiral motion* shall now be defined as a combination of rotation about an axis a (angle t) and a proportional (and not exponential) scaling transformation from a fixed point $O \in a$ (factor pt). The proportionality factor p is again a characteristic parameter.

The path curves are called helispirals, or—in other context ([3])— conical helices.[1] The reason for this name is that their cylindrical projections from the axis a are helices in the common sense.

With $O(0,0,s)$ and the helispiral parameter p, the path curve of a point with the cylindrical coordinates $r = r_0, \varphi = \varphi_0, z = z_0$ is described by the time parameter t

$$r = p\,t\,r_0, \quad \varphi = \varphi_0 - \frac{1}{p} + t, \quad z = s + p\,t\,(z_0 - s) \tag{1}$$

---

[1]The definition of a conical helix, though, is different from our approach. Such a curve is defined as the intersection of a right helicoid with a cone. For the generation of a helispiral surface in such a context, one needs the section line of the surface with a plane perpendicular to the axis a.

For $t = 0$, we get the helispiral center O; thus, each path curve contains O. This point is no singular point on the curve, i.e., there is a well-defined tangent in O.[2] For $t = \frac{1}{p}$, we get the point itself. Branches of the path curve corresponding to the intervals $[0, t]$ and $[0, -t]$ are congruent. Rotated about the axis a through the angle $\frac{1}{p} - \varphi_0$, the parameterized equation of a helispiral is

$$x = p\,t\,r_0 \cos t, \quad y = p\,t\,r_0 \sin t, \quad z = s + p\,t\,(z_0 - s). \tag{2}$$

Since t is the time parameter, the tangent vector can be interpreted as a velocity vector:

$$\dot{x} = p\,r_0\,(\cos t - t \sin t), \quad \dot{y} = p\,r_0\,(\sin t + t \cos t), \quad \dot{z} = p\,(z_0 - s). \tag{3}$$

The length of the velocity vector is

$$v = \sqrt{\dot{x}^2 + \dot{y}^2 + \dot{z}^2} = p\sqrt{r_0^2(1 + t^2) + (z_0 - s)^2}. \tag{4}$$

Points on the axis a ($r_0 = 0$) move along the axis with constant velocity. On the radial ray through O, the point also moves with constant velocity

$$v_r = p\sqrt{r_0^2 + z_0^2}. \tag{5}$$

Therefore, a helispiral appears as an archimedic spiral when it is projected in the direction of a. It also runs on a cone of revolution Γ with axis a and apex O (Figure 10.13). When Γ is developed, the curve is developed into an archimedic spiral. When the archimedic carrier cylinder ζ is developed, the curve does *not* develop into a straight line, as one might have expected.

According to Equation 1, a helispiral motion can be composed with an additional proportional translation along the axis. The path curves are still helispirals—corresponding to the same parameter p and a translated center $\tilde{O}(0, 0, \tilde{s})$:

$$z = s + p\,t\,(z_0 - s) + d\,t = \tilde{s} + p\,t\,(z_0 - \tilde{s}) - \frac{d}{p} \quad \text{with } \tilde{s} = s + \frac{d}{p}. \tag{6}$$

Here is the OPEN GEOMETRY program that produced the images in Figure 10.11–Figure 10.13.

---

[2]Probably one of the first images of a conical helix was drawn by A. DÜRER ([3], p. 369).

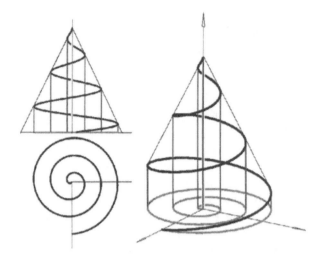

FIGURE 10.13. The helispiral motion is a composition of a rotation **and a proportional** scaling transformation.

Listing of program X/HELISPIRALS/helispiral_motion.cpp (Figure 10.13):

```cpp
#include "opengeom.h"
#include "defaults3d.h"

Real Fi0 = 6 * PI; // 3 Rotations
const Real Height = 10;

P3d sweep( Real t, P3d P )
{
    int curveType = 3;
    switch ( curveType )
    {
    case 1: // helix
        P.Rotate( Zaxis, Deg( t ) ); // rotation about z-axis
        P.z += ( Height / Fi0 ) * t; // translation along z-axis
        break;
    case 2: // classic spiral
        P *= exp( -t / Fi0 );
        P.Rotate( Zaxis, Deg( t ) ); // rotation about z-axis
        break;
    case 3: // helispiral
        P *= t / Fi0;
        P.Rotate( Zaxis, Deg( -t ) ); // rotation about z-axis
        break;
```

```
      }
      return P;
   }

   L3d Curve;

   void Scene::Init( )
   {
      int i, n = 200;
      Real t = 0, dt = Fi0 / ( n − 1 );
      P3d M( 5, 0, −Height );
      Curve.Def( Black, n );
      for ( i = 1, t = 0 ; i <= n; i++, t += dt )
         Curve[i] = sweep( t, M );
      Curve.Translate( 0, 0, Height );
   }

   void Scene::Draw( )
   {
      ShowAxes( Green, 7, 7, 12 );
      Curve.Draw( THICK );
      Curve.DrawUprightProjCylinder( 0, Gray, THIN, NoColor, false );
   }
```

Some Examples for Helispiral Surfaces

The following examples were the result of a joint cooperation with our colleagues Franz Lesák, Anita Aigner, and Peter Auer from the Vienna University of Technology, Institute of Art and Design.

The corresponding source code is not documented, but you can find the files in the directory X/HELISPIRALS. These or similar images were published in [15].

Natural Growth

In the literature, the classical spiral motion is frequently quoted when it comes to the mathematical description of natural growth ([3], [23]). This is true for exponential growth. To give you an example for exponential growth, say, a tiny creature with diameter d_0 is able to increase its actual diameter by one percent every day. Then, after n days, its diameter will be $d = 1.01^n d_0$. In this way, it will have doubled its diameter (and increased mass with factor $2^3 = 8$!) within ≈ 70 days (and not in 100 days), and it will have diameter $4d_0$ (the mass is now $4^3 = 64$ times larger) after ≈ 140 days, etc. When this growth is at the

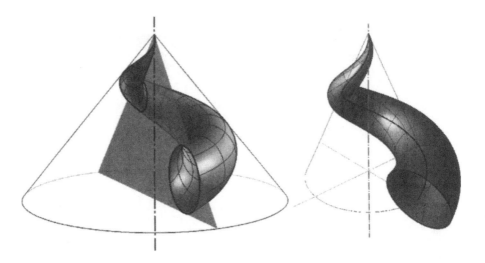

FIGURE 10.14. A circle is undergoing a helispiral motion. Left: the circle lies in a plane through the spiral axis (**X/HELISPIRALS/fig1.cpp**). Right: the tangent of the mid-helispiral is the axis of the corresponding generating circle (**X/HELISPIRALS/fig2.cpp**).

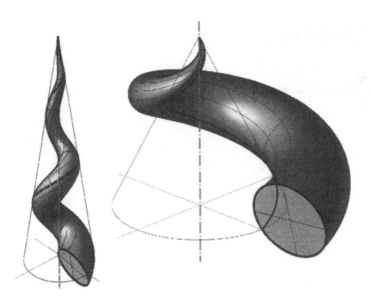

FIGURE 10.15. One can circumscribe or inscribe cones of revolution to helispiral surfaces. The lines of tangency are also helispirals (**X/HELISPIRALS/fig3.cpp** and **fig4.cpp**).

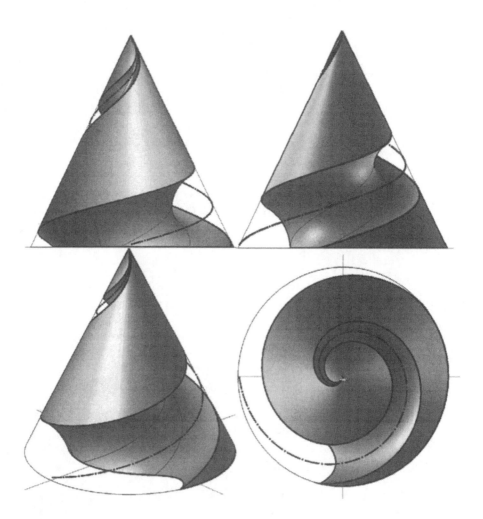

FIGURE 10.16. A circular helispiral surface intersects a cone of revolution (X/HELISPIRALS/fig7.cpp).

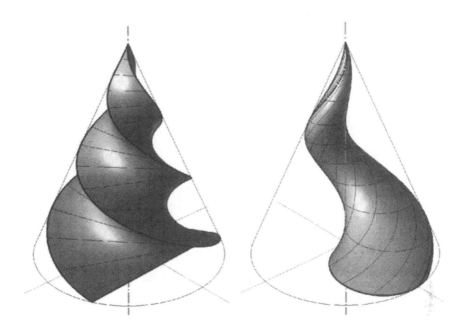

FIGURE 10.17. Left: a horizontal regular triangle is undergoing a helispiral motion with an upright axis through its center (`X/HELISPIRALS/fig5.cpp`). Right: the generating line is a horizontal circle (`X/HELISPIRALS/fig6.cpp`).

same time composed with a rotation about an axis (like in the case of shells and snails), the result can be described as a spiral motion.

Exponential growth is of course not the only way of natural growth. Sometimes rapid growth at the beginning is necessary in order to reach a reasonable size. Then relative size increase slows down (Figure 10.18), e.g., trees grow in such a way that their trunk diameter increases more or less by the same amount each year (though differently in summer and winter). The annual rings can be approximated by archimedic spirals. When this kind of growth is composed with a rotation, helispiral transformation is the appropriate approximation.

Figure 10.19 shows the horns of an antelope (blackbuck). They have both grown exactly "helispirally," especially at the sharp ends as the horn looks essentially different from an ordinary spiral surface. Below is the code to create the corresponding image:

Listing of program `X/HELISPIRALS/blackbuck.cpp` (Figure 10.19):

```
#include "opengeom.h"

// The horn of an antilope...
```

FIGURE 10.18. The shell of this worm (*Mimachlamys gloriosa*) shows different strategies of natural growth. In the first stage, the shell grows exponential (and is a spiral surface). Later on, size increase becomes linear (and the surface is helispiral). Finally, the worm is big enough to increase the parameter of the helispiral motion in order to gain better access to food. The shell stems from the Museum of Natural History in Vienna.

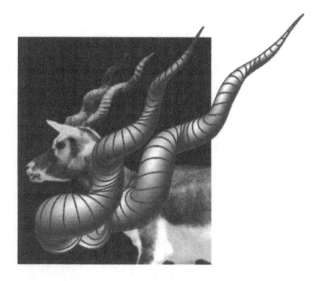

FIGURE 10.19. This image illustrates how the horn of the antelope (blackbuck) has grown "helispirally."

```
class HeliSpiralSurf: public ParamSurface
{
public:
    HeliSpiralSurf( char plus_minus ) // constructor
    {
        v2 = 6 * PI;
        a = 0.4; b = 0.5;
        height = 6.5;
        c = 1 / v2;
        Def( Brown, 35, 120, 0, 2 * PI, 0.1, v2 );
        Rotate( Yaxis, -18 );
        Translate( -3, 0, 0 );
        if ( plus_minus == '-' )
            Reflect( YZplane );
        PrepareContour( );
    }
    virtual P3d SurfacePoint( Real u, Real v )
    {
        // Point on tiny circle
        P3d P( a + b * cos( u ), b * sin( u ), 0 );
        P.Rotate( Xaxis, -40 );
        P.Rotate( Yaxis, -40 );
        P.z -= height;

        // Point undergoes helispiral motion
        P *= c * v; // Scaling proportional v
        P.Rotate( Zaxis, 40 - Deg( v ) ); // rotation about z-axis prop. v
        return P;
    }
private:
    Real a, b, height, c, inclination, cos_t, sin_t;
};


HeliSpiralSurf Horn1( '+' ), Horn2( '-' );
```

```
void Scene::Init( )
{
   SetBackgroundTexture( "BMP/blackbuck.bmp" );
   ScaleBackgroundTexture( 0.7, 0.7 );
}

void Scene::Draw( )
{
   Horn1.Shade( SMOOTH, MATTE );
   Horn1.Contour( DarkBrown, MEDIUM );
   Horn1.ULines( DarkBrown, 40, MEDIUM );
   Horn2.Shade( SMOOTH, MATTE );
   Horn2.Contour( DarkBrown, MEDIUM );
   Horn2.ULines( DarkBrown, 40, MEDIUM );
}
void Projection::Def( )
{
   if ( FrameNum( ) == 1 ) // Get close to the background image
   {
      DefaultCamera( -55, 7, 12 );
      ChangePosition( -53.1656, -12.893, 12.0174);
      ChangeTarget( 0.601435, 1.56899, -3.44929);
      ChangeFocus( 198.452 );
      ChangeTwist( -40 );
      if ( !TheCamera.IsOrthoProj( ) )
         TheCamera.SwitchProjection( );
      ParallelLight( -0.8098, 0.347056, 0.47305);
   }
}
void Scene::CleanUp( )
{
}
void Scene::Animate( )
{
}
```

We give some more explicit examples ("proofs") that the horns of antelopes, etc., are helispiral surfaces (Figure 10.20, 10.21–10.24. Other nice examples are given in [3]).

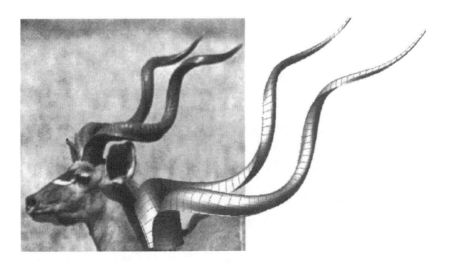

FIGURE 10.20. The horns of the greater kudu are very impressive—and helispiral surfaces (X/HELISPIRALS/kudu.cpp).

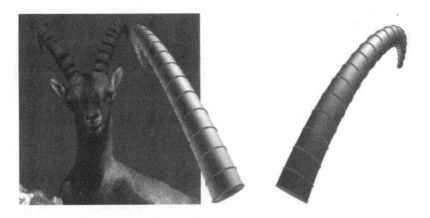

FIGURE 10.21. An ibex (National Park "Hohe Tauern", Austria) and the corresponding helispiral surfaces (X/HELISPIRALS/ibex.cpp).

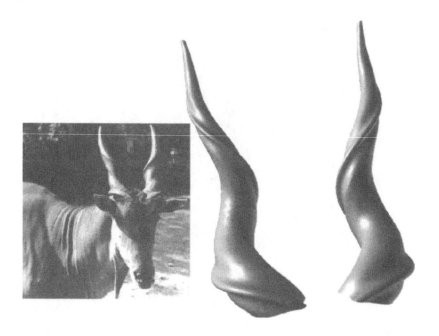

FIGURE 10.22. The horns of the giant eland (X/HELISPIRALS/eland.cpp).

FIGURE 10.23. The impressive horns of a markhor (X/HELISPIRALS/markhor.cpp).

FIGURE 10.24. Water buffalos (`X/HELISPIRALS/buffalo.cpp`).

10.3 DUPIN-Cyclides

Introduction and Definition

Every mathematician is familiar with the problem of APOLLONIUS. Let three arbitrary circles in the Euclidean plane be given. One has to find all circles in this plane that contact the given circles simultaneously. The solution is well-known: in general, there exist four such circles.

What will happen if we substitute the plane above by the Euclidean 3-space, the three given circles by three arbitrary spheres, and now look for all spheres that touch the given ones simultaneously? It is easy to show, by use of appropriate inversions, for instance, that in general there exist four one-parameter families of spheres, each of them with the desired property. By definition, the envelope of such a family of spheres is called a DUPIN-cyclide.[3] Therefore, this means that, in general, three arbitrary spheres determine four DUPIN-cyclides in the sense above (Figure 10.28).

Problems with circles and spheres, as mentioned before, are typical in two- or three-dimensional Moebius geometry. Roughly speaking, three-dimensional Moebius geometry deals with two kinds of basic objects: points on the one hand, and spheres and planes on the other hand. This means, in particular, that Moebius geometry does not distinguish between spheres and planes, and therefore DUPIN-cyclides are invariant under inversions.

Special Cases

From the Euclidean point of view, one can, for instance, substitute "three spheres" by "three planes" in the definition of a DUPIN-cyclide. We have two

---

[3]Pierre Charles François baron de Dupin (1784–1873) found these surfaces in 1822.

FIGURE 10.25. A day in the zoo (Schönbrunn, Vienna): Himalaya Dhar, Nyala, elephant, young markhor, water buffalo, barbary sheep. The reader is encouraged to approximate the corresponding surfaces.

cases. If these planes are parallel to a straight line (and do not belong to a pencil of planes), we get four cylinders of revolution. In the second case, where the given planes have exactly one point in common, we get four cones of revolution. (This is actually the problem to construct cones or cylinders of revolution where three tangent planes are given.) Other specifications lead to the three types of tori of revolution: we only need to take three spheres with collinear centers.

The Two Enveloping Families of Spheres

By definition, a DUPIN-cyclide is the enveloping surface of a one-parameter family of spheres (or planes) and, therefore, a canal surface. We will now show that, for a given DUPIN-cyclide Φ, there exist two one-parameter families of spheres (planes) that envelope the surface, i.e., each DUPIN-cyclide is a canal surface in two different ways. Let us first check this for the special cases. If Φ is a cylinder or cone of revolution, the first family contains all spheres that contact Φ along circles ("parallel circles" of Φ). The second family is the set of tangent planes of Φ. Let Φ now be a torus of revolution. Then one family consists of all spheres ("meridian spheres" of Φ) that contact Φ along meridian circles; the spheres of the second family have their centers on the axis of Φ. Finally, the stated property is valid for all DUPIN-cyclides since each can be transformed by an appropriate inversion into a torus of revolution.

The Three Types of Tori

Now we consider the three types of tori Φ of revolution. Let R and r denote the radius of the center circle and meridian circles of Φ, respectively. There are three cases: If $R > r$, Φ has no (real) singularities and is therefore called "Ring torus." If $R = r$, then we get the "Dorn torus," which has one (real) singularity, a so-called cuspidal point. Then, if we take $R < r$, we get a "Spindel torus," which has two (real) conical singularities.

The Types of DUPIN-Cyclides

If we apply arbitrary inversions to the different forms of the torus, the types of singularities will not change. Therefore, the DUPIN-cyclides can be classified as follows: cyclides with no (real) singularity ("Ring cyclides"), cyclides with exactly one cuspidal point ("Dorn cyclides" and "onehorns"), and those with two different (real) conical singularities ("Spindel cyclides" and "twohorns"). Among the twohorns, there is a metric special case, the so-called symmetric twohorn: it is the only DUPIN-cyclide with exactly three planes of symmetry; all other forms (if they are not a cylinder, cone, or torus) have exactly two planes of symmetry. To become more familiar with the different types, the reader is encouraged to create some pictures on the screen, using the appropriate parameterization given at the end of this section.

The Focal Curves

Now let us use some differential geometry. Take an arbitrary surface Φ. From differential geometry it is well-known that the two-parameter family of all normals of Φ envelopes another surface, called the focal surface of Φ, which consists of two parts. If at least one of these parts degenerates into a space curve, then Φ must be a canal surface. A DUPIN-cyclide can then be characterized as the only surface for which both parts of the focal surface degenerate into a space curve. These curves are called focal curves and form a pair of focal conics, described as follows: each curve is a conic, the plane of one conic is a symmetry plane of the other and vice versa, and the vertices of one conic are the focal points of the other. The length of the minor axis of both conics is equal. Two cases appear: the pair can consist of an ellipse and a hyperbola, or of two parabolas. In the first case, the corresponding DUPIN-cyclide must be of order four, otherwise of order three.

By the definition of the focal surface, each normal of a DUPIN-cyclide intersects the focal curves. These two conics are also the locus of the centers of the spheres enveloping the cyclide.

A One-Parameter Family of Dupin-Cyclides

On the other hand, if a pair of focal conics is given, the corresponding Dupin-cyclide is not unique: there exists a one-parameter family of Dupin-cyclides for which the given conics are the focal curves. By construction, all surfaces have the same normals and are of the same order. Each two surfaces in the family are parallel surfaces of each other.

Circles that Intersect Perpendicularly Four Times

Now consider a fixed Dupin-cyclide that is not a cone or cylinder. It is possible to find circles that intersect the surface perpendicularly four times; if there is a cuspidal point, two points of intersection coincide with it. By means of Moebius geometry, one can show that there exists a two-parameter family of such circles. The cross-ratio of the four intersecting points does not depend on the choice of the circle; it is only dependent on the chosen cyclide.

Another One-Parameter Family of Dupin-Cyclides

A Dupin-cyclide cannot be reconstructed from the set of circles that intersect perpendicularly four times. Appropriate inversions lead to the following: there exists a one-parameter family of Dupin-cyclides, each of which inherits the same set of circles with the desired property. This family contains exactly one Dupin-cyclide of order three, which contains the centers of all those circles. This is rather surprising since the center of a circle is not invariant under inversions.

Dupin-Cyclides with a Special Relation to a Ring-Torus

If one looks for circles that intersect a given torus Φ twice perpendicularly and also contact it at another point, one can find "a lot" of them. The circles of appropriate subsets of all those circles form, as can be shown by stereographic projection, a Dupin-cyclide Ψ. By construction, Ψ intersects Φ perpendicularly along two meridian circles and touches it along another one (Figure 10.26).

If the radii of the center circle and meridian circles of Φ satisfy a certain condition, it is possible to construct a "chain" of Dupin-cyclides Ψ with the properties mentioned above in such a way that no space is left between two neighboring cyclides. Figure 10.27 shows the part of this "chain" that is inside the torus.

Parameterization of Dupin-Cyclides

The special cases of Dupin-cyclides, namely cylinders and cones of revolution and torus, are surfaces of revolution. Therefore, it is easy to calculate a parameterization, which is left as an exercise for the reader. The determination of

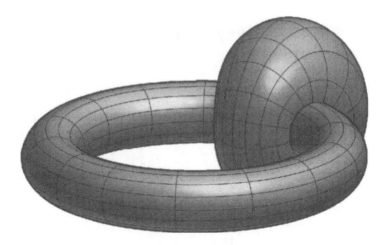

FIGURE 10.26. A Spindel cyclide Ψ that intersects a Ring torus Φ along two meridian circles perpendicularly and touches it along another one.

an appropriate parameterization for the general case is not trivial since inversion is not very helpful here. Here we present one for DUPIN-cyclides of order four. (Those of order three cause some problems because they contain points at infinity.)

Let a and b denote the half length of the major and minor axes of the focal ellipse, respectively. Let $c^2 := a^2 - b^2$ and $0 < b, c < a$. Then the following parameterization holds:

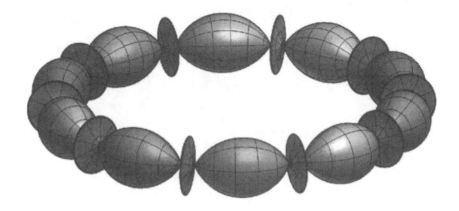

FIGURE 10.27. A "chain" of parts of Spindel cyclides.

$$x(\varphi, \psi) = \frac{d(c - a \sin \varphi \sin \psi) - b^2 \sin \varphi}{c \sin \varphi \sin \psi - a},$$

$$y(\varphi, \psi) = \frac{a + d \sin \psi}{c \sin \varphi \sin \psi - a} \cdot b \cos \varphi, \qquad \varphi, \psi \in [0, 2\pi], \ d \geq 0 \qquad (7)$$

$$z(\varphi, \psi) = \frac{d + c \sin \varphi}{c \sin \varphi \sin \psi - a} \cdot b \cos \psi;$$

The real $d \geq 0$ comes from integration and manages the type of the DUPIN-cyclide (Figure 10.28):

$$d = 0 \quad \text{symmetric twohorn,}$$
$$0 < d < c \quad \text{nonsymmetric twohorn,}$$
$$d = c \quad \text{onehorn,}$$
$$c < d < a \quad \text{Ring cyclide,}$$
$$d = a \quad \text{Dorn cyclide,}$$
$$a < d \quad \text{Spindel cyclide.}$$

A Family of Ring-Tori and a Special Orthogonal Trajectory

Let Φ be a Ring torus and v a fixed loxodrome circle of Φ. (Each such circle that lies in a double tangent plane of Φ is called a Villarceau circle of Φ, here "V circle"

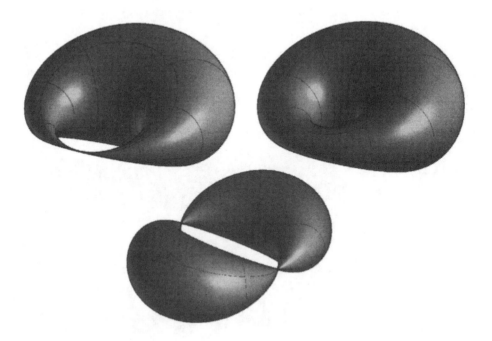

FIGURE 10.28. Three types of DUPIN cyclides: onehorn, Ring cyclide, symmetric twohorn.

for short.) Now let us take all of the circles that intersect Φ perpendicularly at a point of v and three other points, respectively. One can show that these circles belong to one family of V circles of a DUPIN-cyclide Ψ of third order. Thus, Ψ intersects the given torus perpendicularly along v and another V circle, respectively. Moreover, there exists a one-parameter family $F = \{\Phi_j\}, \Phi \in F$, of tori such that Ψ intersects all surfaces of the family perpendicularly, i.e., Ψ is a so-called orthogonal trajectory of F; the real part of the corresponding intersections $\Psi \cap \Phi_j$ consists exactly of two V circles of Φ_j, and all these circles together belong to the second family of V circles of Ψ (Figure 10.29).

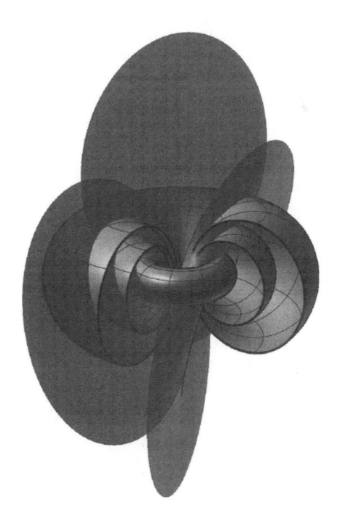

FIGURE 10.29. A DUPIN-cyclide, parameterized by its V circles, which intersects three tori of the family F perpendicularly.

10.4 Rotoid Surfaces

As a final example for special surfaces, we introduce the so-called rotoid surfaces. They have been investigated carefully in [5] and [6].

The Rotoid Motion

The "rotoid motion" is a generalization of the helical motion: points of 3-space rotate about an axis a_2 (angular velocity ω_2). Additionally, they undergo a proportional rotation (angular velocity ω_1) about a fixed axis a_1 ($a_1 \perp a_2$, $a = \overline{a_1 a_2} \neq 0$) (Figure 10.30).

Let us now apply such a motion to a point $P(a - b, c, 0)$. Then $b = \overline{P a_2}$ is the constant distance from the rotating axis a_2, and $c = \overline{P \xi}$ is the distance of P from the rotating auxiliary plane ξ ($\xi \perp a_2, \xi \supset a_1$). Let $p = \frac{\omega_1}{\omega_1}$ be the ratio (proportionality factor) of the angular velocities. Then

$$x(t) = (a - b\cos pt)\cos t - c\sin t$$

$$y(t) = (a - b\cos pt)\sin t + c\cos t$$

$$z(t) = b\sin pt$$

describes the path curve of P. All path curves of points with the same distances b and c are congruent. Path curves with $c = 0$ ($P \in \xi$) are called "torus rotoids," since they lie on a torus.

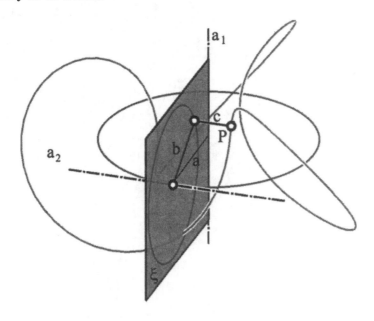

FIGURE 10.30. The rotoid motion is a composition of two proportional rotations about nonintersecting perpendicular axes. (Output of X/3D/ROTOIDS/rotoid _motion.cpp).

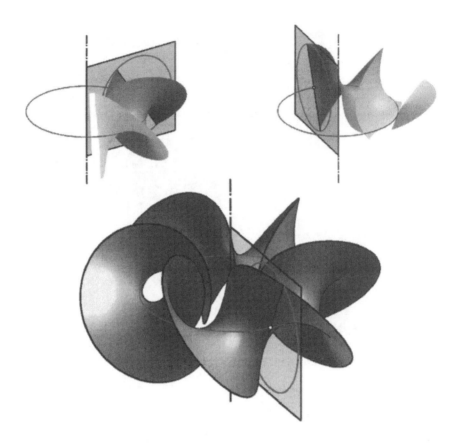

FIGURE 10.31. A right rotoid helicoid, generated by a straight line g which intersects the axis a_2 perpendicularly ($p = 3$) (`X/3D/ROTOIDS/rotoid_surf.cpp`).

Right Rotoid-Helicoids

We now investigate rotoid surfaces that are generated by straight lines g. Similar to the four types of ruled helical surfaces, we distinguish whether the angle between a and g equals $\pi/2$ or not, and whether a_2 and g have a common point or not. The case where the generator line g intersects the rotating axis a_2 perpendicularly is related to the right helicoid (Figure 10.31).

Right helicoids have a remarkable property: they not only carry ∞^1 ordinary path curves (i.e., helices), but also ∞^2 nontrivial helices that are contour lines for parallel projections. (They correspond to parameter $\bar{p} = 2p$ and are the intersection lines with cylinders of revolution that contain the helical axis.) An analogous property can be proved for right rotoid helicoids: besides the ∞^1 trivial rotoid curves, they carry ∞^2 nontrivial rotoids (parameter $\bar{p} = 2p$) (Figure 10.32). These lines are the intersection lines with tori that carry the midcircle.

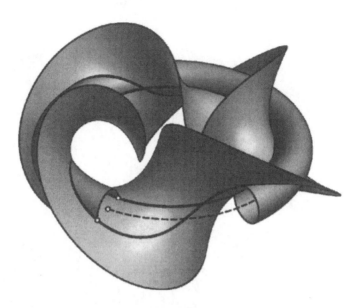

FIGURE 10.32. Nontrivial rotoid on a right rotoid helicoid ($p = 2$). The corresponding program is `X/3D/ROTOIDS/non_trivial_rotoids.cpp`.

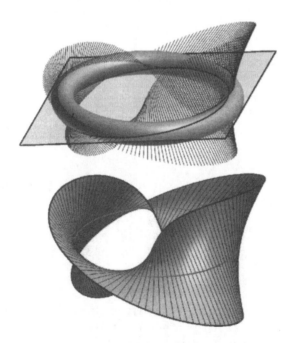

FIGURE 10.33. Right rotoid helicoid ($p = 1$) as a limiting case of a "normal surface" of a torus (`X/3D/ROTOIDS/torus_normals.cpp`).

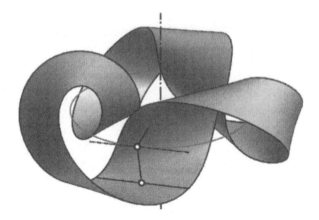

FIGURE 10.34. Conoidal rotoid surfaces $(p = 3)$ (`X/3D/ROTOIDS/con_rotoid _surf.cpp`).

Right rotoid helicoids belonging to parameter $p = 1$ are of degree 4 and can be interpreted as the limiting case of the ruled surface that consists of the normals of a torus along a Villarceau circle ([14], Figure 10.33).

Conoidal Rotoid Surfaces

As a second special case, the generating straight line can be parallel to the rotating axis a_2. In this case, g stays parallel to the base plane $\pi \perp a_1$. For $p = \frac{1}{2}$, the surface turns out to be of degree 4. Its self-intersection is a hyperbola (Figure 10.35), its "striction line" an ellipse.

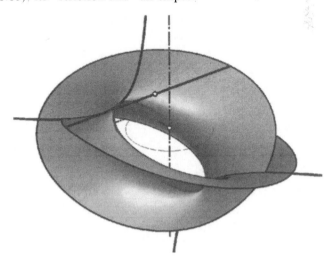

FIGURE 10.35. Conoidal rotoid $p = \frac{1}{2}$ with double hyperbola and elliptic striction line (`X/3D/ROTOIDS/con_rotoid_surf2.cpp`).

11

Data Exchange, Printouts

An important criterion for successful program systems is the compatability with other programs on the market. When a system can import from and export to a standardized data format, it is "connected to the world."

OPEN GEOMETRY can import 3D data from commercial CAD programs like 3D STUDIO MAX, and it can export 3D data via DXF (*D*rawing e*X*change *F*ormat) files. OPEN GEOMETRY is also fully compatible with the CAD3D-System that was originally developed for the DOS environment. Furthermore, OPEN GEOMETRY allows you to save the drawn images as bitmap files. This enables the user to convert the output into any image format.

In the WINDOWS NT environment, OPEN GEOMETRY allows you to create printed images with a near incredible resolution (namely, printer resolution).

11.1 DXF File Output

Exporting DXF files is very easy in OPEN GEOMETRY, and nearly every CAD program can load such files. You can store your 3D data as a DXF file by simply selecting "`Export as DXF-file`" from the `Image` menu.

There are a few things to keep in mind, however, when working with DXF files.

- DXF files that contain many polygons need a lot of disk space.

- You cannot store mapping coordinates or material properties in DXF files.

- DXF files are text files that cannot be loaded very quickly.

- OPEN GEOMETRY will only store polygons. It will not export lines!

If you are going to load DXF files with 3D STUDIO MAX, activate the "force two sided" option and keep in mind that OPEN GEOMETRY stores the whole scene as a single object.

If you want to create several objects, you can proceed as follows:

- Let OPEN GEOMETRY only draw the part you want to store as one object (by commenting-out the other command lines).

- Save the scene under a distinct name.

- Repeat the process for the other parts of the scene. Since the storage is done in 3D, you need not worry about viewport or camera.

11.2 How to Import 3D Objects from 3D STUDIO

In order to import 3D objects from the commercial Graphics-Software 3D STU-DIO, proceed as follows:

- Create your object(s) in 3D STUDIO (3D STUDIO MAX, respectively).

- Save your scene as an ASCII file (suffix **asc**). If you are using 3D STUDIO MAX, you can only save a single object as an ASCII file. Take care that there are no lights or cameras in your scene to avoid errors during the loading process. OPEN GEOMETRY will ignore every kind of light source and background image you define. (If you want to attach a background image to your scene, use the OPEN GEOMETRY routine *SetBackground-Texture*( ).)

- Derive an instance variable of the OPEN GEOMETRY class *Polyhedron*.

- Now you can define the polyhedron via the member function Read3DS( ). This function takes two parameters: The first is the name of the ASCII file. The other parameter is Boolean, and tells the program whether the normals of the triangles have to be turned or not. (This is important when objects are solid.) The member function FitIntoSphere( ) is sometimes quite useful in order to scale the object in a way that it can be proceeded optimally by OPEN GEOMETRY.

- Draw your object using the member function Shade( ) (or ShadeWithTex-ture( ), respectively).

The following sample program shows how to import a "house" including textures (Figure 11.1):

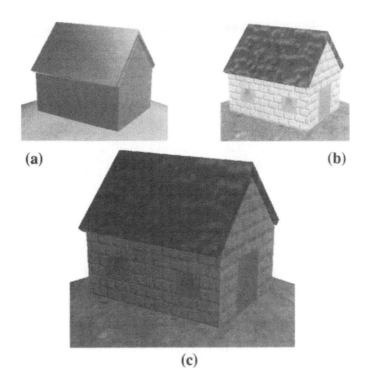

(a)   (b)

(c)

FIGURE 11.1. Smooth-shaded house, imported as ASCII file from 3D STUDIO MAX: (a) with color "white," (b) with "no color" (just textures), (c) both shaded and textured.

Listing of program X/3D/IMPORT/house.cpp (Figure 11.1):

```
#include "opengeom.h"
#include "defaults3d.h"

Polyhedron House;
TextureMap Map( "BMP/house2.bmp" );

void Scene::Init( )
{
   House.Read3DS( "DATA/house.asc", false );
   House.FitIntoSphere( 15 );
}

void Scene::Draw( )
```

```
{
    House.ShadeWithTexture( White, REFLECTING, ALL_FACES, Map );
}
```

Another example shows how to import a "drill" without any textures (Figure 11.2):

Listing of program `X/3D/IMPORT/drill.cpp` (Figure 11.2):

```
#include "opengeom.h"
#include "defaults3d.h"

Polyhedron Drill;

void Scene::Init( )
{
    Drill.Read3DS( "DATA/drill.asc", false );
    Drill.FitIntoSphere( 15 );
}

void Scene::Draw( )
{
    Drill.Shade( Gray, REFLECTING, ONLY_FRONTFACES );
}
```

A third example shows how to import two completely different data files and combine them (Figures 11.3, 11.4). Additionally, background textures can be included.

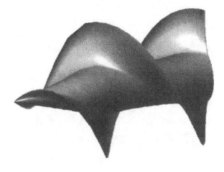

FIGURE 11.2. A data file without textures (drill).

Listing of program X/3D/IMPORT/pot_and_skeleton.cpp (Figure 11.3):

```
#include "opengeom.h"
#include "defaults3d.h"

Polyhedron Skeleton, Teapot;

void Scene::Init( )
{
    Skeleton.Read3DS( "DATA/skeleton_kneeing.asc", false );
    Skeleton.FitIntoSphere( 15 );
    Skeleton.Rotate( Xaxis, 90 );
    Teapot.Read3DS( "DATA/teapot.asc", false );
    Teapot.FitIntoSphere( 3 );
    Teapot.Translate( -2, -13, -7.5 );
    SetBackgroundTexture( "BMP/stego.bmp" );
}

void Scene::Draw( )
{
    Skeleton.Shade( Gray, REFLECTING, ALL_FACES );
    Teapot.Shade( Gray, REFLECTING, ONLY_FRONTFACES );
}
```

On the enclosed CD (in the directory **DATA**), you can find some ASCII data and source code for the reading and processing of this data. The data files partly come from public **ftp**-sources (Thanks to the authors!). Figures 11.5 and 11.6 show some more samples.

The source code for the flying aircraft is:

Listing of program X/3D/IMPORT/b737.cpp (Figure 11.5):

```
#include "opengeom.h"
#include "defaults3d.h"

Polyhedron Aircraft;

void Scene::Init( )
{
    Aircraft.Read3DS( "DATA/B737.asc", false );
    Aircraft.FitIntoSphere( 10 );
    Aircraft.Rotate( Zaxis, 80 );
    SetBackgroundTexture( "BMP/alps.bmp" );
```

FIGURE 11.3. A combination of different data and background texture.

FIGURE 11.4. Another variation of the skeleton.

FIGURE 11.5. A Boing 737 is flying over the alps (and—later on—toward the sun). The data file was downloaded from a public site on the Internet, the background textures are scanned photographs, partly from the authors.

```
}

void Scene::Draw( )
{
    Aircraft.Shade( Gray, REFLECTING, ONLY_FRONTFACES );
}
```

The source code for the two dinos (actually, it is only one...) is the following:

Listing of program X/3D/IMPORT/dinohead.cpp (Figure 11.6):

```
#include "opengeom.h"
#include "defaults3d.h"
```

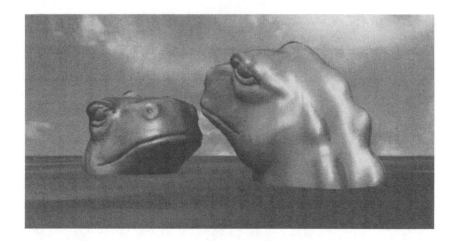

FIGURE 11.6. Two dinos in love (who knows?). The data file (a **3ds** file) comes from `http://www.grafix3d.dyn.ml.org/web/`. The background texture is a scanned photograph.

```
O3dGroup Dino( 2 );
Polyhedron Head, Eyes;

void Scene::Init( )
{
   SetBackgroundTexture( "BMP/sky.bmp" );
   Head.Read3DS( "DATA/dinohead.asc", false );
   Eyes.Read3DS( "DATA/dinoeyes.asc", false );
   Dino.AddMember( 1, Head );
   Dino.AddMember( 2, Eyes );
   Dino.Scale( 25 );
   Silent( ); // Some triangles are bad, and we don't
           // want to hear the complaints...
   Dino.Translate( 0, −4, 0 );
   Dino.Rotate(Zaxis, 180 );
}
TextureMap WaterSurface( "BMP/sky.bmp" );
void paint_water( )
{
   Rect3d water;
   water.Def( LightGray, 100, 100, FILLED );
   water.Translate( −50, −50, −2.5 );
   water.ShadeWithTexture( WaterSurface, 1, 1, 0, 0,  0, true );
}
void Scene::Draw( )
```

```
{
    paint_water( );
    V3d t( 2, −4, −2 );
    Head.Shade( Gray, REFLECTING, ALL_FACES );
    Eyes.Shade( Red, REFLECTING, ALL_FACES );
    Dino.Rotate( Zaxis, 180 );
    Dino.Translate( t );
    Head.Shade( Gray, REFLECTING, ALL_FACES );
    Eyes.Shade( Red, REFLECTING, ALL_FACES );
    Dino.Translate( −t ); // undo translation
    Dino.Rotate( Zaxis, −180 ); // undo rotation
}
```

Speaking of dinos, we also have the data for a stegosaurus (remember "Lost World"?):

Listing of program X/3D/IMPORT/stego_family.cpp (Figure 11.7):

```
#include "opengeom.h"
#include "defaults3d.h"

Polyhedron BigOne, Baby;
TextureMap Skin( "BMP/dino_skin.bmp" );

void Scene::Init( )
```

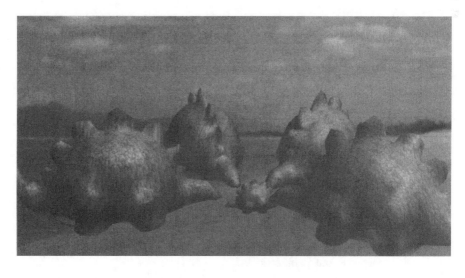

FIGURE 11.7. The Stegosaurus family.

```
{
    BigOne.Read3DS( "DATA/dino2.asc", false );
    BigOne.FitIntoSphere( 10 );
    Baby.Def( BigOne );
    BigOne.Smoothen( );
    Baby.Scale( 0.3 );
    Baby.Translate( 0, 0, −8 );
    Baby.Rotate( Zaxis, 30 );
    BigOne.Translate( 0, 8, −6 );
    SetBackgroundTexture( "BMP/stego.bmp" );
}

void Scene::Draw( )
{
    for ( int i = 0; i < 4; i++ )
    {
        BigOne.ShadeWithTexture( Gray,REFLECTING,ALL_FACES,Skin );
        BigOne.Rotate( Zaxis, 72 );
    }
    BigOne.Rotate( Zaxis, 72 );
    Baby.ShadeWithTexture( Gray, REFLECTING, ALL_FACES, Skin );
}
```

11.3 How to Add Textures to Your Objects

Create your texture maps and save them as **bmp** files. Store these files in a subdirectory of 3D STUDIO called **maps**, so that 3D STUDIO has access to them. Keep in mind that the width and height of your texture map image have to be a power of 2 (good values are 128, 256, or 512). Of course you can set them to any size you want, but OPEN GEOMETRY will chop your texture. (This is due to the OPENGL convention.)

Enter 3D STUDIO and switch to the material editor to create some kind of a pseudomaterial(use your own texture map image) which is only used for modelling and designing purposes.

After that, attach the new material to your object and apply the appropriate texture mapping coordinates. Do not use more than one material per object and try to avoid box mapping.

Render the scene. Check if everything is okay and that the texture maps fit correctly onto the objects.

Save your scene as an ASCII file.

FIGURE 11.8. St. Stephen's cathedral in Vienna. The roof is textured.

Before you can draw your objects with OPEN GEOMETRY, you have to create the texture maps by means of the member function *LoadFromBitmapFile*( ). (The class *TextureMap* is defined in **texture.h**.) Therefore, use lines like:

TextureMap Wall_Map("wall.bmp"), Floor_Map("floor.bmp");

Now load the ASCII file and draw your scene (see above).

Some more hints:

- If you are using more than one texture per scene, unite the objects that have the same texture map.

- In many cases, it is useful to copy more texture maps into a single bmp file if you do not want to repeat these texture maps on your polygon. If you want to repeat a texture on a polygon (e.g., if you map the bricks of a wall), you have to store this texture map as a single BMP file.

- When attaching the texture maps to your objects, it can be quite useful to set the texture-mapping image as a background image (enable the "See background" option). Then adjust the mapping plane with "region fit" so that it fits exactly to the background image. This is extremely helpful because you now know the position of your texture map. All you have to do now is to move, scale, and rotate the object until the texture map is where you want it to be.

11.4 Export as BMP File, Animated GIF Files

Bitmap files (BMP files) are a common standard in 2D graphics. You can easily export your file as a BMP file. Just select "Save as BMP-file (24 bit)" or "Save as BMP-file (8 bit)" from the **Image** menu (shortcuts CTRL + B and CTRIL + 8). For example, if you want to print the drawing, and direct printing does not work (in fact, it only works when you work with WINDOWS NT), create a bitmap file and process it with other programs like PAINT, PAINTBRUSH, or CORELDRAW (more about printing in the following section).

The quality of the image highly depends on the screen resolution. If the program produces writings, it may be better to use the command

    HiQuality(false);

Sometimes, you may want to store several frames (e.g., in order to create an animated GIF file). In this case, you can use the OPEN GEOMETRY class *BitMap* (defined in `bitmap.h`):

```
BitMap Image;
Image.CopyViewport( );
Image.SafeAsFile( "BMP/some_name.bmp", 24 );
```

This will save your image as a 24-bit bitmap file.

If you want to create a series of bitmap files—e.g., in order to create a GIF animation—you can do that very conveniently by means of the method **SaveAsBitmapAnimation( )** of the class *Scene*. You should call this method in the implementation of **Scene::Animation( )** as follows:

```
void Scene::Animate( )
{
  const int start_frame = 1, // save first frame
        increase = 3, // save every third frame
        max_files = 20, // create 20 files
        bit_depth = 24; // 24-bit images
  const char *directory = "ANIM"; // write into this directory
  SaveAsBitmapAnimation( directory, start_frame,
                increase, max_files, bit_depth );

  // Do the actual
  // animation here...
}
```

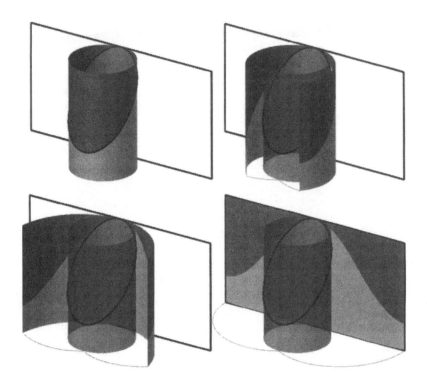

FIGURE 11.9. The development of a cylinder. You can find the GIF animation on the CD-ROM in the **ANIM**-directory: `cyl_develop`.

As you can see, you can start at any frame, skip frames, or set a limit to the number of files (otherwise your hard disk will be full very soon). Shaded 3D images should be saved as 24-bit bitmap files, although such files are three times as large as 8-bit bitmap files. (Also, some GIF-animators require 24-bit bitmap files.)

As we have mentioned before, the directory name should not contain backslashes. A more complicated name might be

```
"This/is_a_more_complicated/path_than/the_previous1"
```

The reason why you should use the method in the animation part is quite simple: if your scene is animated, the image is stored. Thus, you can resize your window or change some parameters like light direction first, until you decide to let the animation start.

The images are now stored in the desired directory. Their names are `001.bmp`, `002.bmp`, `003.bmp`, etc. (up to `max_files.bmp`.). Please be aware that they may consume large amounts of disk space. If you store an image with a resolution of $n \times m$ pixels, this requires $3nm$ bytes for each frame. For f frames, you need $3fmn$

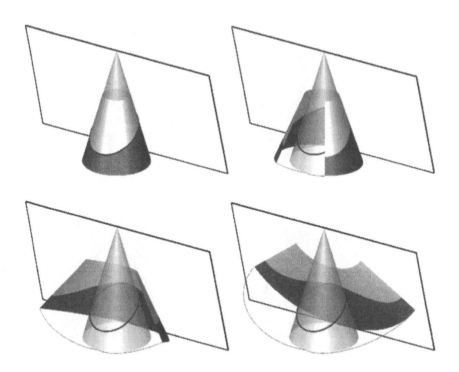

FIGURE 11.10. The development of a cone. You can find the GIF animation in the ANIM-directory: cone_develop.

bytes. To give you an example: if you want to store 50 frames with a window size of 400 × 300 pixels, this requires ≈ 18 MB, with a size of 800 × 600 pixels you will need 72 MB, etc. And 50 frames is just 2 seconds of real-time-animation! So, reduce window size in order to stay within reasonable boundaries.

Some shareware programs (like GIFCON32, see e. g. http://www.golden.net/~durettep/sharewar.htm or http://www.mindworkshop.com) allow you to create animated GIF files. On the enclosed CD (directory ANIM), you can find some GIF animations created by OPEN GEOMETRY. They can be viewed with all Internet browsers like NETSCAPE or INTERNET EXPLORER. The directory also contains the source code of the corresponding files.

11.5 How to Make Proper Printouts

For any user of graphics program systems, it is extremely important to be able to print the graphics result in high quality.

When you are working on a graphics workstation, you will most probably know the best way to save parts of the contents of the screen as an RGB file or similar (on SILICON GRAPHICS workstations, e.g., you can use the **snapshot** program to do so). This file can then be imported and printed by existing graphics programs.

In the WINDOWS environment, you have several choices:

1. Click into the image and use the **print** option on the keyboard (key combination ALT + PRINT). This copies the contents of the OPEN GEOMETRY window into temporary memory. You can then paste these contents (CTRL + V) into other programs like CORELDRAW or PAINT. There you can make printouts and/or conversions. You can also chop the borders (Figure 11.11) of the image before you proceed.

   Always be aware that the quality of the printout depends heavily on the screen resolution. In practice, a screen resolution of 1280 × 1024 turns out to be sufficient for printouts at the size of the images in this book. (In fact, the majority of the images in this book were created like this.)

2. Save the image as a **bmp** file via menu or with the shortcuts CTRL + B (24-bit) or CTRL + 8 (8-bit) (this will chop the image borders automatically), and then proceed with the image by means of other programs (as described above).

3. The following only works in WINDOWS NT: Make a direct printout by means of the menu item **Image → Print image**. With high resolution printers (600 DPI and more), this produces perfect images. The image will fit optimally into the given paper size (e.g., A4 or B4).

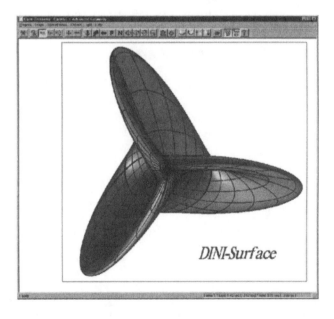

FIGURE 11.11. The result of the key combinations ALT + PRINT and CTRL + V.

In this way, you can produce images with a quality that is really satisfying. While printing, OPENGL works with the actual printer resolution. When the z-buffering is done, this requires enormous amounts of memory. Thus, the computer will be extremely busy for a longer period of time—until the image is printed.

On our EPSON STYLUS COLOR 600, the printouts come out perfect, with a tiny bug in the 720 dpi mode. For whatever reason, the paper has to be chosen as "landscape." When the image is rather a portrait than a landscape, one can twist it 90 degrees via the menu option Image → Landscape.

Again: Note that the print option does *not* work in the WINDOWS 95 environment!

An alternative to the pixel-oriented methods of saving drawings is to use the POSTSCRIPT format. It is vector-orientated, and accuracy is not limited. Especially when only straight lines, curves, or 2D polygons are drawn, the image can be stored very efficiently and, what is more important, accurately. You can proceed with POSTSCRIPT files by the public domain software GHOSTSCRIPT (which is available at many academic ftp servers in the Internet). When you proceed with the image with CORELDRAW, import the file as PostScript Interpreted (PS, PRN, EPS) and, on request, choose the button Import as curves. You can then make your changes and export the drawing to nearly any format (CORELDRAW manages to save files extremely efficiently in its own format *.cdr).

You can save your image as an eps file (encapsulated POSTSCRIPT) by means of the menu item Image → Save image as EPS file, or, more quickly, with the key combination CTRL + E. But please keep in mind that POSTSCRIPT does not support such sophisticated features like z-buffering or transparency.

Summing up, it is a good idea to store 2D scenes very economically in POSTSCRIPT format. When you draw in 3-space and hidden surface removal is of importance, POSTSCRIPT will normally produce drawings that do not correspond to what you see on the screen.[1]

---

[1]In [9], it has been shown that even complex scenes can be displayed with POSTSCRIPT when you draw the polygons in the correct order, i.e., from back to front. Since this method is restricting, we did not implement such a feature in OPEN GEOMETRY.

More Classes and Examples

In this chapter, we will give some more examples for typical OPEN GEOMETRY programs. They partly deal with OPEN GEOMETRY classes that have not been explained so far.

12.1 Sample 2D Programs

In this section, we will give some more examples for 2D applications, e.g., program X/2D/simpson.cpp illustrates how to solve an integral.

Begin listing of X/2D/simpson.cpp (Figure 12.1)

```
#include "opengeom.h"
#include "defaults2d.h"

// As a test function, we take the derivation of the arc tangent.
// The integral from 0 to 1 is then PI / 4.

Real TestFunction( Real t )
{
    return 1 / ( 1 + t * t );
}
void Scene::Init( )
{
    ScaleLetters( 2.5, 3);
    InclineLetters( 75 );
```

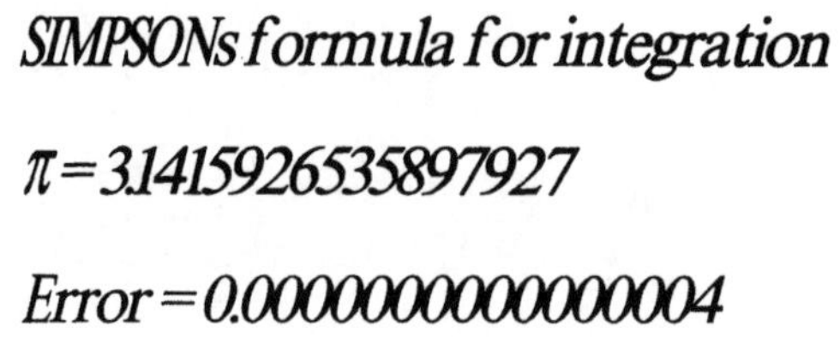

SIMPSONs formula for integration

$\pi = 3.1415926535897927$

Error = 0.0000000000000004

FIGURE 12.1. Output of the program X/2D/`simpson.cpp`.

```
}
void Scene::Draw( )
{
    int number_of_nodes = 200;
    Real t1 = 0, t2 = 1;
    Real pi = 4 * Integral( TestFunction, t1, t2, number_of_nodes );
    PrintString( Black, −12, 4, "SIMPSONs formula for integration" );
    PrintString( Black, −12, 0, "$pi$=%.16f", pi );
    PrintString( Red, −12, −4, "Error =%.16f", 4 * atan( 1 ) − pi );
}
```

End listing X/2D/`simpson.cpp` (Figure 12.1)

As a practical application, we will now show how to draw a curve that is given by integrals (the clothoid is a 2D curve that is used for road constructions as its curvature increases linearly).

Begin listing of X/2D/`clothoid.cpp` (Figure 12.2)

```
#include "opengeom.h"
#include "defaults2d.h"
```

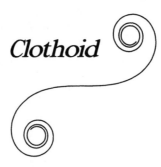

Clothoid

FIGURE 12.2. Output of the program X/2D/`clothoid.cpp`.

// This program calculates a "clothoid:" this is a planar curve with
// the following property: the curvature changes proportionally to the
// arclength. Clothoids are used in road construction:
// When a car moves along such a curve, the steering wheel has to be
// turned constantly.
// The curve has a rather complicated explicit parametric equation:
// $x = \int cos^2(t^2/2A)dt, y = \int sin^2(t^2/2A)dt.$

```
L2d Curve;
const Real A = 1;

Real Cos2( Real t )
{
   return cos( t * t / ( 2 * A * A ) );
}

Real Sin2( Real t )
{
   return sin( t * t / ( 2 * A * A ) );
}

void Scene::Init( )
{
   int n = 300;
   Curve.Def( Black, n );
      Real t = -2 * PI, dt = 4 * PI / ( n - 1 );
   for ( int i = 1; i <= n; i++, t += dt )
      Curve[i]( Integral( Cos2, 0, t ), Integral( Sin2, 0, t ) );
   Curve.Scale( 10, 10 );
   InclineLetters( 75 );
   ScaleLetters( 6 );
}
void Scene::Draw( )
{
   PrintString( Black, -14, 5, "Clothoid" );
   Curve.Draw( THICK );
}
```

End listing X/2D/clothoid.cpp (Figure 12.2)

Next we will show how to solve a differential equation. Please have a look at the listing of program X/2D/runge.cpp.

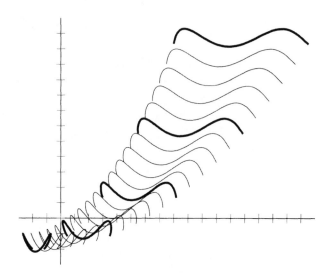

FIGURE 12.3. Output of the program X/2D/runge.cpp.

Begin listing of X/2D/runge.cpp (Figure 12.3)

```
// This example illustrates how the user can extend
// the given hierarchy in order to solve new problems.
// In this case: integration of tangent fields by means of RUNGE-KUTTA.
// After the work is done, one can transfer the relevant code
// into a module and henceforth treat the new class like
// any other class of OpenGEOM.

#include "opengeom.h"
#include "defaults2d.h"

// We derive a new class from a given one.
// The following declaration can later be put into
// the include file "diff_equation.h".

class DiffEquation: public L2d
{
public:
    DiffEquation( ) { }
    virtual void Solve( Real t1, Real t2, Real h, const P2d &StartPoint );
    virtual V2d TangentVector( Real t, const P2d &P) = 0;
    virtual V2d Delta( Real t, const P2d &P, Real h );
    virtual ~DiffEquation( ) { }
};
```

// The following two methods of the class DiffEquation
// can later be put into an additional module.

```
void DiffEquation::Solve( Real t1, Real t2, Real h, const P2d &StartPoint)
{
  int n = Round( ( t2 - t1 ) / h );
  h = ( t2 - t1 ) / n;
  O23d::Def( Red, n + 1 );
  pPoints[1] = StartPoint;
  Real t = t1:
  V2d d;
  for ( int i = 1; i <= n; i++, t += h ) {
      d = Delta( t, pPoints[i], h );
      pPoints[i+1] = pPoints[i] + d;
  }
}


V2d DiffEquation::Delta( Real t, const P2d &P, Real h )
{
    V2d k1, k2, k3, k4;
    P2d Q;
    V2d t0 = TangentVector( t, P );
    k1 = h * t0;
    Q = P + 0.5 * k1;
    t0 = TangentVector( t + h/2, Q );
    k2 = h * t0;
    Q = P + 0.5 * k2;
    t0 = TangentVector( t + h/2, Q );
    k3 = h * t0;
    Q = P + k3;
    t0 = TangentVector( t + h, Q );
    k4 = h * t0;
    return ( 1.0 / 6 ) * ( k1 + 2 * k2 + 2 * k3 + k4 );
}
```

// Now we derive applications from the new class

```
class Sample1: public DiffEquation { // The solution curves are circles
    virtual V2d TangentVector( Real t, const P2d &P)
    {
        return V2d( P.x / 10 + cos( 0.75 * t ), sin( 1.75 * t ) );
    }
};
class Sample2: public DiffEquation { // More complicated solutions.
    virtual V2d TangentVector( Real t, const P2d &P)
```

```
    {
        if ( &P ) ; // dummy
        return V2d( 1, sin( t ) );
    }
};
void Scene::Init( )
{
}
void Scene::Draw( )
{
    // Coordinate system ( Grid )
    Xaxis2d.Draw( Black, −3, 18, THIN );
    Yaxis2d.Draw( Black, −3, 13, THIN );
    P2d P, Q;
    P.x = Q.x = −2; P.y = 0.3; Q.y = −P.y;
    for ( ; P.x < 18; P.x += 1, Q.x += 1 )
        StraightLine2d( Gray, P, Q, THIN );
    P.y = Q.y = −2; P.x = 0.3; Q.x = −P.x;
    for ( ; P.y < 13; P.y += 1, Q.y += 1 )
        StraightLine2d( Gray, P, Q, THIN );
    // Now solve the diff. equations
    for ( int j = 0; j <= 20; j++ )
    {
        P2d StartPoint( −2 + j / 2.0, −2 + j * j / 30. );
        Sample1 Sample;
        Sample.Solve( −PI, PI, 0.03, StartPoint );
        if ( j % 5 == 0 )
            Sample.Draw( THICK );
        else
            Sample.Draw( THIN );
    }
}
```

End listing X/2D/runge.cpp (Figure 12.3)

Another application for the integration of a vector field is X/2D/runge.cpp. The above-mentioned clothoid is calculated as the solution curve of a differential equation. The implemtation of the class *DiffEquation* is now inserted into the header file diff_equation.h.

Begin listing of X/2D/clothoid2.cpp (Figure 12.4)

```
#include "opengeom.h"
#include "diff_equation.h"
#include "defaults2d.h"
```

Clothoids as integral curves of a vector field

FIGURE 12.4. Output of the program X/2D/clothoid2.cpp.

```
class Clothoid: public DiffEquation
{ // The solution curves are clothoids
    virtual V2d TangentVector( Real t, const P2d &P )
    {
        if ( P.x )
            NULL; // dummy line (otherwise compiler warning )
        V2d tg( cos( f( t ) ), sin( f( t ) ) );
        const Real size_factor = 3.5;
        return size_factor * tg;
    }
    Real f( Real t )
    {
        return 1.2 * t * t;
        // return 0.2 * t * t * t; Alternative
        // return t; ==> Circle
    }
};
void Scene::Init( )
{
    ScaleLetters( 1, 1.8 );
}
void Scene::Draw( )
{
    TheWindow.ShowRaster( Red, 1, 1, 0.25 );
    Clothoid Curve;
```

```
for ( Real x = −13.5; x < 13; x += 7.8 )
{
    for ( Real y = −13.5; y < 15; y += 7.8 )
    {
        Curve.Solve( −PI, PI, 0.03, P2d( x, y ) );
        Curve.ChangeColor( Blue );
        Curve.Draw( MEDIUM );
    }
}
PrintString( Black, −8, −0.3,
    "Clothoids as integral curves of a vector field" );
}
```

End listing X/2D/clothoid2.cpp (Figure 12.4)

The program X/2D/function.cpp contains an implementation of a 2D function graph that allows you to calculate zeros of arbitrary functions by means of Newton's iteration or the "regula falsi."

The next example shows how versatile the function WriteNice( ) is.

The following examples are student works. Their listings can be found at the given locations.

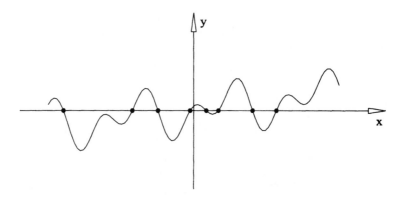

FIGURE 12.5. The output of the program X/2D/function.cpp. Given an arbitrary function, the zeros are calculated.

FIGURE 12.6. The output of the program X/2D/omega.cpp.

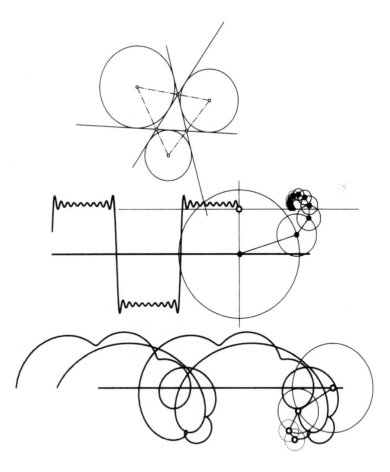

FIGURE 12.7. The output of the programs excircle.cpp, fourier.cpp, and cycloids.cpp (directory X/STUDENTS/ERIK).

12.2 Sample 3D Programs

Begin listing of X/3D/cones.cpp (Figure 12.8)

```
#include "opengeom.h"
// A cone of revolution rolls on another one.
// The path curves of space points are spherical trochoids.
RegFrustum Cone1, Cone2;
StrL3d AxisOfCone2;
P3d Point[3];
PathCurve3d Path[3];
void Scene::Init( )
```

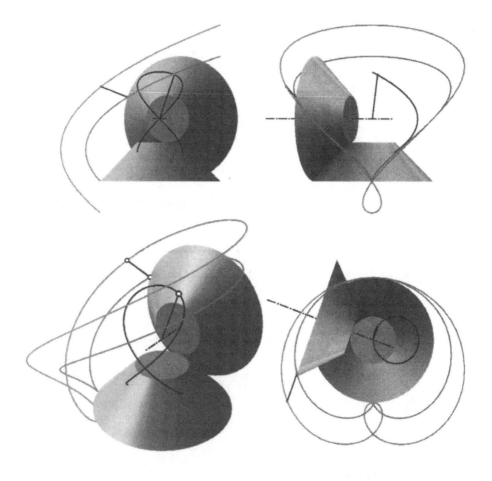

FIGURE 12.8. Output of the program X/3D/cones.cpp.

```
{
    int order = 60;
    Real height = 5;
    Cone1.Def( Red, 3 + height, 3, height, order, SOLID );
    Cone1.Translate( 0, 0, −3 − height);
    Cone2.Def( Red, 3 + height, 3, height, order, SOLID );
    Cone2.Translate( 0, 0, −3 − height);
    Cone2.Rotate(Xaxis, −90 );
    Cone2.col = Green;
    AxisOfCone2 = Yaxis;
    Point[0] = Cone2[1];
    Point[1] = Point[0];
    Point[1].Scale( 1.5, 1, 1.5 );
    Point[2]( 0, 0, 6 );
    Path[0].ChangeColor( Blue );
    Path[1].ChangeColor( Yellow );
    Path[2].ChangeColor( Black );
}
const int AnimAngleInDeg = 5;
void Scene::Draw( )
{
    Cone1.Shade( );
    Cone2.Shade( );
    AxisOfCone2.LineDotted( Black, −15, 3, 15, MEDIUM );
    StraightLine3d( Black, Point[0], Point[1], MEDIUM );
    StraightLine3d( Black, Point[2], AxisOfCone2.GetPoint( ), MEDIUM );
    for (int i = 0; i < 3; i++)
        Point[i].Mark(Black, 0.15, 0.08 );
    int f = FrameNum( );
    if ( f <= 360 / AnimAngleInDeg + 1 )
    {
        for ( i = 0; i < 3; i++)
            Path[i].AddPoint( Point[i] );
    }
    for ( i = 0; i < 3; i++)
        Path[i].Draw( MEDIUM );
}
void Scene::Animate( )
{
    Cone2.Rotate( Zaxis, −AnimAngleInDeg );
    AxisOfCone2.Rotate( Zaxis, −AnimAngleInDeg );
    for ( int i = 0; i < 3; i++)
    {
        Point[i].Rotate( Zaxis, −AnimAngleInDeg );
        Point[i].Rotate( AxisOfCone2, −AnimAngleInDeg );
```

```
      }
   }
   void Scene::CleanUp( )
   {
   }
   void Projection::Def( )
   {
      if ( FrameNum( ) == 1 )
      {
         DefaultCamera( 35, 30, 15 );
         ParallelLight( 2, 1, 2 );
      }
   }
```

End listing X/3D/cones.cpp (Figure 12.8)

Begin listing of X/3D/develop.cpp (Figure 12.9)

```
#include "opengeom.h"

RegPrism Cylinder;
Rect3d Rect;
const Real R = 3, H = 10;
const int Order = 100;
const Real Delta = 360.0 / ( Order − 1 );
StrL3d GenLine [Order + 1];
L3d Curve;
Plane Section;
PathCurve3d Path [2];

void Scene::Init( )
{
   Cylinder.Def( Cyan, R, H, Order, HOLLOW );
   Cylinder.Rotate( Zaxis, −Delta );
   Rect.Def( Gray, 2 * R * PI, H );
   Rect.Translate( −R * PI, 0, 0 );
   Rect.Rotate( Xaxis, 90 );
   Rect.Rotate( Zaxis, 90 );
   Rect.Translate( −R, 0, 0 );
   Curve.Def( DarkOrange, Order + 1);
   Section.Def( P3d( 5, 0, 0 ), P3d( −R, 1, H ), P3d( −R, −1, H ) );
   for ( int i = 1; i <= Order; i++ )
```

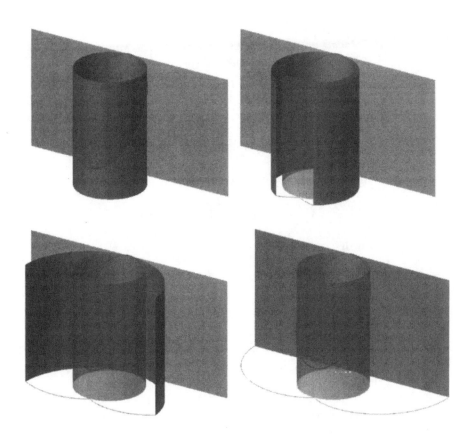

FIGURE 12.9. Output of the program X/3D/develop.cpp.

```
    {
        int j = ( i % Order ) + 1;
        GenLine [i].Def( Cylinder [j], Cylinder [j + Order] );
        Curve [i] = Section * GenLine [i];
    }
    Curve [i] = Curve [1];
    Cylinder.Scale( 0.99, 0.99, 1 );
}

void DevelopAndPlot( const Poly3d &p0, Color col, int i, int k )
{
    Poly3d p;
    p0.Copy( p );
    p.ChangeColor( col );
#define VERSION1
#ifdef VERSION1
    int f = FrameNum( ) − 1;
    Real angle = 0.1 * f;
```

```
      if ( angle > Delta )
         angle = 360. / ( Order − 2 );
      for ( int j = i; j < Order / 2; j++ )
      {
         p.Rotate( GenLine [j + 1], angle  );
      }
#else
      int f = FrameNum( Order ) − 1;
      int fmax = Minimum( f, Order / 2 );
      for ( int j = i; j < fmax; j++ )
      {
         p.Rotate( GenLine [j + 1], 1.01 ∗ Delta );
      }
#endif
      if ( k != 0 )
         p.Reflect( XZplane );
      p.Shade( );
      if ( i == 1 && p [1].z == 0 )
         Path [k].AddPoint( p [1] );
   }

   void Scene::Draw( )
   {
      Rect.Shade( );
      Poly3d p( Orange, 4 );
      for ( int k = 0; k < 2; k++ )
      {
         for ( int i = 1; i <= Order / 2; i++ )
         {
            p [1] = GenLine [i].InBetweenPoint( 0 );
            p [2] = GenLine [i + 1].InBetweenPoint( 0 );
            p [3] = Curve [i + 1];
            p [4] = Curve [i];
            DevelopAndPlot( p, Orange, i, k );
            p [1] = GenLine [i].InBetweenPoint( H );
            p [2] = GenLine [i + 1].InBetweenPoint( H );
            DevelopAndPlot( p, Cyan, i, k );
         }
      }
      Curve.Draw( MEDIUM );
      Path [0].Draw( THIN );
      Path [1].Draw( THIN );
      SetOpacity( 0.5 );
      Cylinder.Shade( SMOOTH, REFLECTING );
      SetOpacity( 1 );
```

```
}

void Scene::Animate( )
{
   const int start_frame = 1, // save first frame
           increase = 2, // save every other frame
           max_files = 25, // create 25 files
           bit_depth = 24; // 24-bit images
   const char *directory = "ANIM";
   SaveAsBitmapAnimation( directory, start_frame,
                    increase, max_files, bit_depth ) ;
}

void Scene::CleanUp( )
{
}

void Projection::Def( )
{
   if ( FrameNum( ) == 1 )
   {
      DefaultCamera( 28, 18, 20 ) ;
      ParallelLight( 2, 0.2, 2 ) ;
      Target( 0, 0, 5 ) ;
      ChangeFocus( 60 ) ;
   }
   if (!IsOrthoProj( ) )
      SwitchProjection( ) ;
}
```

End listing X/3D/`develop.cpp` (Figure 12.9)

Begin listing of X/3D/`texture3d.cpp` (Figure 12.10)

```
#include "opengeom.h"
#include "defaults3d.h"

TextureMap Map( "BMP/ibex2.bmp" );
const int N = 32;
Poly3d Poly;

void Scene::Init( )
{
   Real z = 0;
```

FIGURE 12.10. Output of the program X/3D/texture3d.cpp.

```
    Real h = 12, a = 2 * h / N;
    Poly.Def( PureWhite, 4 );
    Poly[1]( a, 0, 0 ); Poly[2]( −a, 0, 0 );
    Poly[3]( −a, 0, h ); Poly[4]( a, 0, h );
    Poly.Translate( 0, a / tan ( Arc( 180. / N ) ), −h/2 );
    Poly.Rotate( Zaxis, 25 );
}
void Scene::Draw( )
{
    //V2d translate( 0, 0 ), scale( 8.0 / N, 2 );  upper left
    V2d translate( 0, 0 ), scale( 4.0 / N, 1 );  // upper right
    //V2d translate( 0, 0 ), scale( 4.0 / N, 3 );  lower left
    //V2d translate( 0, 0 ), scale( 8.0 / N, 1 );  lower right
```

```
    Real angle = 0;
    Boolean repeat = true;
    for ( int i = 0; i < N; i++ )
    {
        Poly.ShadeWithTexture( Map, scale.x, scale.y, angle,
                        translate.x, translate.y, repeat );
        translate.x += scale.x;
        if ( translate.x >= 0.99 ) translate.x = 0;
        Poly.Rotate( Zaxis, 360. / N );
    }
}
```

End listing `X/3D/texture3d.cpp` (Figure 12.10)

Appendix A

OPENGL Function Reference

This book is not an OPENGL book. Nevertheless, OPEN GEOMETRY is based on OPENGL. In this appendix, we give a very short description of the most important OPENGL functions. Some of them—but by far, not all—were important for the development of the OPEN GEOMETRY library.

If you need more information, please refer to the books listed in the bibliography.

We have sorted the routines according to the following groups:

1. Coordinate Transformations
   glFrustum, glLoadIdentity, glLoadMatrix, glMatrixMode, glMultMatrix, glPopMatrix, glPushMatrix, glRotate, glScale, glTranslate

2. Primitives (Lines, Polygons, Points...)
   glBegin, glCullFace, glEdgeFlag, glEnd, glFrontFace, glGetPolygonStripple, glLineStripple, glLineWidth, glPointSize, glPolygonMode, glPolygonStripple, glVertex

3. Color
   glClearColor, glClearIndex, glColor, glColorv, glColorMask, glIndex, glIndexMask, glLogicOp, glShadeModel

4. Lighting
   glColorMaterial, glGetMaterial, glGetLight, glLight, glLightModel, glMaterial, glNormal3

5. Texture Mapping
   glTexCoord, glTexEnv, glTexGen, glTexImage2D, glTexImage1D, glTexParameter, glEnable

6. Raster Graphics
   glCopyPixels, glDrawPixels, glPixelMap, glPixelStore, glPixelTransfer, glPixelZoom, glReadPixels, glRasterPos

Now some words about the listed routine.

A.1 Coordinate Transformations

Whenever you write OPENGL code, it is important to have an understanding of how coordinate transformations in OPENGL work. In particular, you have to think about the order of the transformations if you apply several in a row. Always keep in mind that OPENGL transformations will not change the coordinates of your objects, whereas many OPEN GEOMETRY transformations will actually change them.

---

void *glFrustum*(*GLdouble* left, *GLdouble* right,
                    GLdouble bottom, *GLdouble* top,
                    GLdouble near, *GLdouble* far);
  ◇ Multiplies the current matrix by a matrix
  ◇ for a perspective-view frustum.

left, right   define left and right clipping planes
bottom, top   define bottom and top clipping planes
near, far   distance to the near and far clipping planes

---

void *glLoadIdentity*(**void**);
  ◇ Sets the current matrix to Identity.

void *glLoadMatrix*<d,f>(**const** TYPE* m);
  ◇ Sets the current matrix to the one specified.
  m   4 × 4 matrix

---

void *glMatrixMode*(*GLenum* mode);
  ⋄ Specifies the current matrix mode.
mode   can be *GL_MODELVIEW*, GL_PROJECION, GL_TEXTURE

---

void *glMultMatrix*<d,f>(TYPE *m);
  ⋄ Multiplies the current matrix by the one specified.
m   4 × 4 matrix

---

void *glPopMatrix*(**void**);
  ⋄ Pops the current matrix off the matrix stack.

---

void *glPushMatrix*(**void**);
  ⋄ Pushes the current matrix onto the matrix stack.

---

void *glRotate*<d,f>(TYPE angle, TYPE x, TYPE y, TYPE z);
  ⋄ Rotates the current matrix by a rotation matrix.

angle   specifies the angle of rotation in degrees
x,y,z   vector from the origin that is used as the
          axis of rotation.

---

void *glScale*<d,f>(TYPE x, TYPE y, TYPE z);
  ⋄ Multiplies the current matrix by a matrix that
  ⋄ scales an object along the x,y,z axes.
x,y,z   Scale factors along the x, y, and z axes

---

void *glTranslate*<d,f>(TYPE x, TYPE y, TYPE z);
  ⋄ Multiplies the current matrix by a matrix that
  ⋄ translates an object along the axes.
x,y,z   translation vector

A.2 Primitives

OPENGL only offers few geometrical primitives to be drawn: lines, polygons, and points. The auxiliary libraries provide the programmer with some other "primitives" like spheres or teapots.

---

void *glBegin*(*GLenum* mode);
  ⋄ Sets the beginning of a group of vertices
  ⋄ that build one or more primitives.

mode	type of primitive operation
GL_POINTS	individual points
GL_LINES	simple lines
GL_LINE_STRIP	series of connected lines
GL_LINE_LOOP	same as above with first and last vertex connected
GL_TRIANGLES	simple triangle
GL_TRIANGLES_FAN	linked fan of triangles
GL_TRIANGLES_STRIP	linked strip of triangles
GL_POLYGON	convex polygon
GL_QUADS	four-sided polygon
GL_QUAD_STRIP	linked strip of four-sided polygons

---

void *glCullFace*(*GLenum* mode);
mode   *GL_FRONT, GL_BACK, GL_FRONT_AND_BACK*;

---

void *glEdgeFlag*<v>(*GLboolean*<**const** *GLboolean* *>flag);
  ⋄ Indicates whether a vertex should be considered
  ⋄ as initializing a boundary edge of a polygon.
flag   Sets the edge flag to this value.
        GL_TRUE (default) or GL_FALSE

---

void *glEnd*( );
  ⋄ Terminates a group of vertices specified by *glBegin*( ).

void *glFrontFace*(*GLenum* mode) ;
  ⋄ Defines the front and back side of a polygon.
mode   *GL_CCW* faces with counterclockwise orientation
              are considered front-facing. (default)
          GL_CW faces with clockwise orientation
              are considered front-facing.

void *glGetPolygonStripple*(*GLubyte* ∗mask) ;
  ⋄ Returns the stripple pattern of a polygon.
∗mask   Pointer to the polygon stripple pattern.

void *glLineStripple*(*GLint* factor, *GLushort* pattern) ;
  ⋄ Specifies the stripple pattern for *GL_LINE...*
  ⋄ primitive operations. First enable strippling
  ⋄ by calling *glEnable*(*GL_LINE_STRIPPLE*).

factor   The pattern is stretched out by this factor.
pattern   Sets the 16-bit long strippling pattern.

void *glLineWidth*(*GLfloat* width) ;
  ⋄ Sets the current line width.
width   width of line in pixels (default is 1.0)

void *glPointSize*(*GLfloat* size) ;
  ⋄ Sets the current point size.
size   size of point (default is 1.0)

void *glPolygonMode*(*GLenum* face, *GLenum* mode) ;
  ⋄ Sets the drawing mode for the front faces and back faces of a polygon.

face   Specifies which faces are affected by
           the mode change.
           GL_FRONT, GL_BACK, GL_FRONT_AND_BACK
mode   can be *GL_POINT, GL_LINE, GL_FILL*

void *glPolygonStripple*(**const** *GLubyte∗* mask)
⋄ Specifies the stripple pattern used to fill polygons.
∗mask   pointer to a 32 ∗ 32-bit array that
             contains the stripple pattern.

void glVertex<2,3,4><s,i,f,d><v>(TYPE coords)
⋄ Specifies the 3D coordinates of a vertex.
⋄ Example: glVertex3f(1.0 , 1.5 , 4.0);

coords   can be 1–4 dimensional (x,y,z,w)
w   coordinate for scaling purposes
             (default is 1.0)

void *glClearColor*(*GLclampf* red, *GLclampf* green,
                      GLclampf blue, *GLclampf* alpha)
⋄ Specifies the current clear color for glClear.

void *glClearIndex*(*GLfloat* index);
⋄ Specifies the clearing value for the color index buffer.
index   clear color value

void *glColor*<3,4><b,i,s,u,d,f>(TYPE red, TYPE green,
                                     TYPE blue, TYPE alpha);
⋄ Sets the current drawing color.

void *glColor*<3,4><b,i,s,u,d,f>v(**const** TYPE ∗v);
⋄ Sets the current drawing color.
v   points to an array with four elements

> **void** *glColorMask*(*GLboolean* red, *GLboolean* green,
>   *GLboolean* blue, *GLboolean* alpha);
>   ⋄ Defines the current mask used to control
>   ⋄ writing in RGBA mode.

> **void** *glIndex*<i,s,d,f><v>(TYPE index);
>   ⋄ Sets the current drawing index color.
> index   color index;

> **void** *glIndexMask*(*GLuint* mask);
>   ⋄ Sets the mask used to control writing into the color
>   ⋄ index buffer by protecting individual bits from being set.
> mask   bit mask;

> **void** *glLogicOp*(*GLenum* opcode);
>   ⋄ Defines the current logical pixel operation for color
>   ⋄ index mode.
> opcode   can be *GL_CLEAR*, *GL_COPY* (**default**), *GL_NOOP*,
>   *GL_SET*, *GL_COPY_INVERTED*, *GL_INVERT*, *GL_AND*,
>   *GL_OR*, *GL_NOR*, *GL_XOR*, *GL_EQUIV*,
>   *GL_AND_INVERTED*, *GL_OR_INVERTED*;

> **void** *glShadeModel*(*GLenum* mode);
>   ⋄ Specifies the current shade model
> mode   *GL_FLAT* or *GL_SMOOTH* (**default**);

A.3 Color

OPENGL allows you to set RGB colors. Furthermore, it enables the programmer to set α-values for transparency.

void *glClearColor*(*GLclampf* red, *GLclampf* green,
                    GLclampf blue, *GLclampf* alpha)
◇ Specifies the current clear color for glClear.

---

void *glClearIndex*(*GLfloat* index);
◇ Specifies the clearing value for the color index buffer.
index   clear color value

---

void *glColor*<3,4><b,i,s,u,d,f>(TYPE red, TYPE green,
                    TYPE blue, TYPE alpha);
◇ Sets the current drawing color.

---

void *glColor*<3,4><b,i,s,u,d,f>v(**const** TYPE *v);
◇ Sets the current drawing color.
v   points to an array with four elements

---

void *glColorMask*(*GLboolean* red, *GLboolean* green,
                    GLboolean blue, *GLboolean* alpha);
◇ Defines the current mask used to control
◇ writing in RGBA mode.

---

void *glIndex*<i,s,d,f><v>(TYPE index);
◇ Sets the current drawing index color.
index   color index

---

void *glIndexMask*(*GLuint* mask);
◇ Sets the mask used to control writing into the color
◇ index buffer by protecting individual bits from being set.
mask   bit mask

void *glLogicOp*(*GLenum* opcode);
  ◇ Defines the current logical pixel operation for color
  ◇ index mode.
opcode   can be *GL_CLEAR*, *GL_COPY* (**default**), *GL_NOOP*,
             GL_SET, *GL_COPY_INVERTED*, *GL_INVERT*, *GL_AND*,
             GL_OR, *GL_NOR*, *GL_XOR*, *GL_EQUIV*,
             GL_AND_INVERTED, *GL_OR_INVERTED*;

void *glShadeModel*(*GLenum* mode);
  ◇ Specifies the current shade model
mode   *GL_FLAT* or *GL_SMOOTH* (**default**);

A.4 Lighting

When it comes to lighting, OPENGL offers a palette of functions that allow you to use a number of light sources and to provide the objects with physical properties like shininess, etc. Remember that OPEN GEOMETRY does not use those functions by default, and that it is up to the programmer to introduce the corresponding code.

void *glColorMaterial*(*GLenum* face, *GLenum* mode)
  ◇ Allows material colors to track the color set by glColor.

face   *GL_FRONT*, *GL_BACK* or *GL_FRONT_AND_BACK*
mode   *GL_EMISSION*, *GL_AMBIENT*, *GL_DIFFUSE*,
             GL_SPECULAR or *GL_AMBIENT_AND_DIFFUSE*

void *glGctMaterial*<i,f>v(*GLenum* face, *GLenum* pname,
                    TYPE param)
  ◇ Returns the current material property settings.

face   *GL_FRONT*, *GL_BACK* or *GL_FRONT_AND_BACK*

pname:	param:
GL_EMISSION	RGBA values
GL_AMBIENT	RGBA values
GL_DIFFUSE	RGBA values
GL_SPECULAR	RGBA values
GL_SHININESS	specular exponent
GL_COLOR_INDEXES	3 values (ambient, diffuse, specular components)

void *glGetLight*<i,f>v(*GLenum* light, *GLenum* pname,
                    TYPE *params)
  ◇ Returns information about the current light source settings.

light	light-source GL_LIGHT0 to GL_LIGHT7
pname	specifies which information about the light source is being queried
params	array of integer or floating point where the return values are stored

pname:	params:	
GL_AMBIENT	RGBA values	
GL_DIFFUSE	RGBA values	
GL_SPECULAR	RGBA values	
GL_POSITION	x,y,z coordinates of light source plus one element (usually 1.0)	
GL_SPOT_DIRECTION	direction vector for spotlight	
GL_SPOT_EXPONENT	spot exponent	
GL_SPOT_CUTOFF	cutoff angle of the spot source	
GL_SPOT_CONSTANT_ATTENUATION		constant attenuation
GL_SPOT_LINEAR_ATTENUATION		linear attenuation
GL_SPOT_QUADRATIC_ATTENUATION		quadratic attenuation

void *glLight*<i,f><v>(*GLenum* light, *GLenum* pname,
                    TYPE param))
  ◇ Sets the parameters of a light source.

light   light source *GL_LIGHT0* to *GL_LIGHT7*
pname   defines which lighting parameter is
             to be set (see glGetlight-pname)
param   one or more values that are required
             to set the lighting parameter

---

void *glLightModel*<i,f><v>(*GLenum* pname, TYPE param)
  ◇ Sets the lighting model parameters.

pname: params:
model parameter   value(s) for model parameter
GL_LIGHT_MODEL_AMBIENT   array that points to
                                          four RGBA components

GL_LIGHT_MODEL_LOCAL_VIEWER
GL_LIGHT_MODEL_TWO_SIDED   0.0 indicates that only fronts
                                          of polygons are illuminated

---

void *glMaterial*<i,f><v>(*GLenum* face, *GLenum* pname, TYPE param)
  ◇ Sets the material parameters.

face   *GL_FRONT*, *GL_BACK* or
              GL_FRONT_AND_BACK
pname: param:
GL_EMISSION   RGBA values
GL_AMBIENT   RGBA values
GL_DIFFUSE   RGBA values
GL_SPECULAR   RGBA values
GL_AMBIENT_AND_DIFFUSE   RGBA values
GL_SHININESS   specular exponent (1 value)
GL_COLOR_INDEXES   3 values (ambient, diffuse,
                                      specular components)

---

void *glNormal3*<b,i,s,d,f>(TYPE nx, TYPE ny, TYPE nz)
  ◇ Defines a normal vector whose direction is up and
  ◇ perpendicular to the surface of the polygon.
nx, ny, nz   x, y, z magnitudes of the normal vector

void *glNormal3*<b,i,s,d,f>v(**const** TYPE *v)
v   array of three elements where
                         normal vector is stored

A.5 Texture Mapping

Texture mapping is one of the best features that OPENGL offers. If the mapping is done by hardware, one can produce realistic images in a very short time.

void *glTexCoord*<1,2,3,4><dfis>(TYPE s , TYPE t ,
                                      TYPE r , TYPE q);
♦ Specifies the current texture image coordinates (1D-4D)
♦ for the following vertex of a textured polygon.

s,t   x,y coordinates on texture image (0.0 - 1.0)
r   texture image depth coordinate
q   texture image "time" coordinate

void *glTexEnv*<f,i,fv,iv> (*GLenum* target ,
                                 GLenum pname , TYPE);
♦ Sets parameters for texture-mapping environment.

target   must be *GL_TEXTURE_ENV*

pname: param:
GL_TEXTURE_ENV_COLOR   param is a pointer to
                                    an RGBA color value.

GL_TEXTURE_ENV_MODE   to define type of texture mapping
        − *GL_DECAL* texture is directly mapped
        − *GL_BLEND* texture is blended
                          by constant color
        − *GL_MODULATE* texture is shaded

void *glTexGen*<d,f,i,dv,fv,iv> (*GLenum* coord, *GLenum* pname,
                                       TYPE param);
♦ Defines parameters for automatic
♦ texture coordinate generation.

coord	must be GL_S, GL_T, GL_R, or GL_Q

pname:	param:
$GL\_TEXTURE\_GEN\_MODE$	– GL_OBJECT_LINEAR
	– GL_EYE_LINEAR
	– GL_SPHERE_MAP
GL_OBJECT_PLANE	
GL_EYE_PLANE	

---

void *glTexImage2D*(*GLenum* **target**, *GLint* **level**,
          GLint **components**, *GLsizei* **width**,
          GLsizei **height**, *GLint* **border**, *GLenum* **format**,
          GLenum **type**, **const** *GLvoid* ***pixels**);
  ◇ Describes a two-dimensional texture image

target	must be $GL\_TEXTURE\_2D$
level	usually 0 (these are multiple texture resolutions (mip mapping))
width	texture image width (must be a power of 2) + 2*border
height	texture image height (must be a power of 2) + 2*border
border	width of border (0, 1, or 2)
format	usually $GL\_RGB(A)$ or GL_COLOR_INDEX, GL_RED, GL_GREEN, GL_BLUE, GL_ALPHA, $GL\_LUMINANCE$ (grayscale), $GL\_ALPHA\_LUMINANCE$
type	data type of pixel value usually $GL\_UNSIGNED\_BYTE$, GL_BYTE, GL_BITMAP, GL_SHORT, $GL\_UNSIGNED\_SHORT$, GL_INT, $GL\_UNSIGNED\_INT$, GL_FLOAT
pixels	array for pixel data

---

void *glTexImage1D*(*GLenum* **target**, *GLint* **level**, *GLint* **components**,
          GLsizei **width**, *GLint* **border**, *GLenum* **format**,
          GLenum **type**, **const** *GLvoid* ***pixels**);
  ◇ Describes a one-dimensional texture image

target	must be $GL\_TEXTURE\_1D$

see *glTexImage2D*

void *glTexParameter*<f,fv,i,iv>(*GLenum* target, *GLenum* pname,
TYPE param);
◇ Defines how the texture image is mapped onto the polygon.

target   must be *GL_TEXTURE_1D* or *GL_TEXTURE_2D*

pname: param:
mapping parameters
GL_TEXTURE_WRAP_S   *GL_CLAMP*   to clamp texture
GL_TEXTURE_WRAP_T   *GL_REPEAT*   repeat texture until
                                         the end of the polygon

GL_TEXTURE_MAG_FILTER   *GL_NEAREST*   no filtering
GL_TEXTURE_MIN_FILTER   *GL_LINEAR*   filtering

GL_TEXTURE_BORDER_COLOR   RGBA value

for mip mapping use
GL_NEAREST<LINEAR>_MIPMAP_NEAREST_<LINEAR>

---

void *glEnable*(parameter)
◇ This enables texture mapping.
parameter   *GL_TEXTURE_2D* or *GL_TEXTURE_1D*

A.6 Raster Graphics

Raster graphics is a powerful link between pure mathematical calculations and
the actual drawing window. Nevertheless, we tried to avoid it whenever possible,
namely because OPEN GEOMETRY must not rely on the screen resolution; for
example, if we produce a printing of an image, the resolution of the printing
device is usually quite different from the window size.

---

void *glCopyPixels*(*GLint* x, *GLint* y, *GLsizei* width,
GLsizei height, *Glenum* type);
◇ Copies a block of pixels into the frame buffer at
◇ a position defined by glRasterPos.

type	GL_COLOR	to copy color values
	GL_STENCIL	to copy stencil values
	GL_DEPTH	to copy depth values

---

void *glDrawPixels*(*GLsizei* width, *GLsizei* height, *GLenum* format,
     GLenum type, **const** *GLvoid* *pixels) ;
  ⋄ Draws a block of pixels into the frame buffer
  ⋄ at a position defined by glRasterPos.

format	GL_RGBA or GL_RGB, GL_COLOR_INDEX,
	GL_RED, GL_GREEN, GL_BLUE, GL_ALPHA,
	GL_LUMINANCE (grayscale) , GL_ALPHA_LUMINANCE
type	data type of pixel value
	GL_UNSIGNED_BYTE, GL_BYTE, GL_BITMAP,
	GL_SHORT, GL_UNSIGNED_SHORT, GL_INT,
	GL_UNSIGNED_INT, GL_FLOAT

---

void *glPixelMap*<fv,uiv,usv>(*GLenum* map, *GLint* mapsize, TYPE values) ;
  ⋄ Sets a lookup table for *glCopyPixels*, *glDrawPixels*, *glReadPixels*,
  ⋄ *glTexImage2D*, *glTexImage1D*. *GL_MAP_COLOR* or
   GL_MAP_STENCIL
  ⋄ have to be enabled with *glPixelTransfer*.

map:	Define a lookup table for
GL_PIXEL_MAP_I_TO_I	color indices
GL_PIXEL_MAP_S_TO_S	stencil values
GL_PIXEL_MAP_I_TO_R	color indices to red values
GL_PIXEL_MAP_I_TO_G	color indices to green values
GL_PIXEL_MAP_I_TO_B	color indices to blue values
GL_PIXEL_MAP_I_TO_A	color indices to alpha values
GL_PIXEL_MAP_R_TO_R	red values
GL_PIXEL_MAP_G_TO_G	green values
GL_PIXEL_MAP_B_TO_B	blue values
GL_PIXEL_MAP_A_TO_A	alpha values

mapsize	size of lookup table (must be power of 2)
values	pointer to lookup table

void *glPixelStore*<i,f>(*GLenum* pname, TYPE param);
  ◇ Defines how glDrawPixels, glTexImage1D, glTexImage2D,
  ◇ glReadPixels read and store pixel data.

pname:	param:	result:
		bytes are swapped when
GL_PACK_SWAP_BYTES	*GL_TRUE*	stored in memory
GL_UNPACK_SWAP_BYTES	*GL_TRUE*	read from memory
		leftmost pixel of bitmap
GL_PACK_LSB_FIRST	*GL_FALSE*	is stored/read in bit 0
GL_UNPACK_LSB_FIRST	*GL_FALSE*	instead of bit 7
GL_PACK_ROW_LENGTH	integer	
GL_UNPACK_ROW_LENGTH	integer	
GL_PACK_SKIP_PIXELS	integer	
GL_UNPACK_SKIP_PIXELS	integer	
GL_PACK_SKIP_ROWS	integer	
GL_UNPACK_SKIP_ROWS	integer	
GL_PACK_ALIGNMENT	integer	
GL_UNPACK_ALIGNMENT	integer	

void *glPixelTransfer*<i,f>(*GLenum* pname, TYPE param)
  ◇ Sets pixel-transfer modes that affect the operations
  ◇ of *glDrawPixels*( ), *glReadPixels*( ), *glCopyPixels*( ),
  ◇ *glTexImage1D*( ), *glTexImage2D*( ) and glGetTexImage( ).

pname	*GL_MAP_COLOR, GL_MAP_STENCIL,*
	GL_INDEX_SHIFT, GL_INDEX_OFFSET,
	GL_RED_SCALE, GL_GREEN_SCALE,
	GL_BLUE_SCALE, GL_ALPHA_SCALE,
	GL_DEPTH_SCALE, GL_RED_BIAS,
	GL_GREEN_BIAS, GL_BLUE_BIAS,
	GL_ALPHA_BIAS, GL_DEPTH_BIAS;
param	*GLint, GLfloat* parameter value

void *glPixelZoom*(*GLfloat* xfactor, *GLfloat* yfactor)
  ◇ Sets pixel scaling factors for pixel-transfer operations.

xfactor, yfactor	pixel scaling factors along the x,y axes

void *glReadPixels*(*GLint* x, *GLint* y, *GLsizei* width,
  GLsizei height, *GLenum* format,
  GLenum type, *GLvoid* ∗pixels)
  ◇ Reads a block of pixel data from the framebuffer
  ◇ and stores it in the array pointed to by pixels.

format	indicates the kind of pixel data elements that are read *GL_RGBA*, *GL_RGB*, *GL_COLOR_INDEX*, *GL_RED*, *GL_GREEN*, *GL_BLUE*, *GL_ALPHA*, *GL_LUMINANCE* (grayscale) or *GL_ALPHA_LUMINANCE*;
type	indicates the data type of each element *GL_UNSIGNED_BYTE*, *GL_BYTE*, *GL_BITMAP*, *GL_SHORT*, *GL_UNSIGNED_SHORT*, *GL_INT*, *GL_UNSIGNED_INT*, *GL_FLOAT*
pixels	pointer to array

void *glRasterPos*<234><sifd><v>(TYPE x, TYPE y, TYPE z, TYPE w);
  ◇ Sets the raster position at the specified coordinates.

Appendix B

The Programming Package on the CD

B.1 The Contents of the Disk

This book comes with a CD-ROM formatted under WINDOWS NT. You will need a WINDOWS environment to read the CD. If you work in a UNIX environment, you have to transfer the files to your system.

The disk contains both a WINDOWS environment version and a UNIX version of the graphics package directories WINDOWS and UNIX.

An ASCII file read.me contains information about the installation of the disk, the authors, and an e-mail address—in case you have any problems.

The two main directories WINDOWS and UNIX both contain directories with the same names and corresponding contents:

Directory C: It contains part of the system-independent source code of the graphics package (i.e., the *.cpp files and some *.c files).

Directory H: It contains the system-independent header files *.h.

Directory SYS: In this directory, you can find the system-dependent modules and header files.

Directory DATA: In this directory, about a dozen sample data files are stored in ASCII mode (*.asc). Additionally, there are are some *.11x files (CAD3D) and some binary files that are used by the package internally.

Directory BMP: In this directory, several dozens sample bitmap files are stored. Most of these were created by scanning photos of the authors; some are public domain from the Internet.

Directory ANIM: In this directory, some sample animated GIF files are stored.

Directory X: In this directory, most of the sample programs are stored in several subdirectories.

Directory BOOK: In this directory, you can find some residual sample programs that produced parts of the images in this book.

B.2   How to Install the Program Package

- **If you are working in the WINDOWS environment:**

  The WINDOWS version is quite easy to install: just double-click on the icon `install.exe` and follow the instructions.

- **If you are working in a UNIX environment:**

  1. Create a working directory, e.g., OPENGEOM, and change to this directory:

     ```
     mkdir OPENGEOM
     cd OPENGEOM
     ```

  2. Copy the zipped version of the package (**UNIX/opengeom.zip**) and the program **UNIX/unzip** into this directory.

  3. Unzip the package by means of the command line

     ```
     unzip -d -a opengeom.zip
     ```

     (The -d option restores the directory structure. The -a option auto-converts the text files.)

  4. In order to create the executable file x, just type

     ```
     m
     ```

  5. If you work on a SILICON GRAPHICS workstation, everything should be okay now.

     If you do not work on such a workstation, you will have to make minor changes to the makefile.

B.3 How to Use the Program

Once you have managed to install the package, you should start with Chapter 2 ("Getting Started"). When your application is running, you can manipulate the scene. This is very easy in the WINDOWS environment, since there you are provided with toolbars and a menu sytem. On a UNIX workstation, you can use the keyboard in order to manipulate the program.

key	function
H, H, <, >	rotate **h**orizontally (change azimuth)
V, V	rotate **v**ertically (change elevation)
T, T	change **t**wist
Z, Z	**z**oom in and out
N, N	change distance (go **n**earer or move away)
← → ↑ ↓	change target point
1, 2, 3	top view / front view / right side view
4, 5, 6	bottom view / back view / left side view
7	back to former perspective
8	switch between perspective and orthogonal projection
CTRL+N	Draw **n**ext frame
CTRL+F	**f**orce animation
CTRL+R	Force animation + auto **r**otation (only 3D applications)
CTRL+S	Show axes and light direction
CTRL+Q	High **q**uality on/off
CTRL+L	Safe eye and **l**ight
CTRL+← → ↑ ↓	change light direction
CTRL+E	safe image as **e**ps file
CTRL+B	safe image as **b**mp file (24 bit)
CTRL+8	safe image as **b**mp file (8 bit)
ALT+← → ↑ ↓	move background texture
ALT+N, ALT+N	zoom background texture
ESC	**q**uit program

References

[1] R. BANERJEE, J.R. ROSSIGNAC: Topologically exact evaluation of polyhedra defined in CSG with loose primitives. *Computer Graphics Forum* **15**, (4), 205-217 (1996).

[2] E.D. BLOCH: *A First Course in Geometric Topology and Differential Geometry*. Birkhäuser, Boston 1997.

[3] T.A. COOK: *The Curves of Life*. Dover, New York, 1979.

[4] FOLEY J., VAN DAMM, A., ET AL.: *Computer Graphics: Principles and Practice*. Addison-Wesley, 1990.

[5] G. GLAESER: Über die Rotoidenwendelflächen. *Sitz.ber. Öst. Akad. Wiss.* 190, 285-302, Vienna (1981).

[6] G. GLAESER: Über die konoidalen Rotoidenstrahlflächen *Sitz.ber. Öst. Akad. Wiss.* 191, 241-251, Vienna (1982).

[7] G. GLAESER: *Objektorientiertes Graphik-Programmieren mit der Pascal-Unit Supergraph*. B.G.Teubner, Stuttgart (1992).

[8] G. GLAESER: *Von Pascal zu C/C++*. Markt&Technik, München (1993).

[9] G. GLAESER: *Fast Algorithms for 3D-Graphics*. Springer-Verlag, New York (1994).

[10] G. GLAESER, E. GRÖLLER: Efficient volume-generation during the simulation of NC-milling, *Proceedings of VisMath97*, 100-118 (1997).

[11] B. GRÜNBAUM, G.C. SHEPARD: A new look at Euler's theorem for polyhedra. *Amer. Math. Monthly* **101**, 109-128 (1994).

[12] G. HAJÓS: *Einführung in die Geometrie.* Akadémiai Kiadó, Budapest 1970.

[13] H.-C. HEGE, K. POLTHIER (eds.): *Visualization and Mathematics.* Springer-Verlag, Heidelberg, 1997.

[14] J. KRAMES: Dies Striktionslinie der Normalenfläche eines Torus längs eines Loxodromenkreises, *Sb. Akad. Wiss Wien* **127** 1918, 1-22.

[15] FRANZ LESÁK: Ausschnitt02—Hefte zu Themen des plastischen Gestaltens. TU Wien—Abteilung plastisches Gestalten und Modellbau, 1997.

[16] M. MÄNTYLÄ: *An Introduction to Solid Modeling.* Computer Science Press, Rockville, MD, 1988.

[17] A. MEIER, H. LOACKER: *POLY-Computergeometrie für Informatiker und Ingenieure.* McGraw-Hill Book Co., Hamburg, 1987.

[18] H. POTTMANN, B. RAVANI, J. WALLNER, G. GLAESER: Geometric criteria for gouge-free three-axis milling of sculptured surfaces. *Proc. of the 1998 ASME Design Engineering Technical Conferences.*

[19] H. STACHEL: On the identity of polyhedra. *Amer. Math. Monthly* **101**, 162-165 (1994).

[20] H. STACHEL: *Computer Animation—A Tool for the Design of Mechanisms.* Proc. of the 1st Internat. Conf. on Applied Informatics, 127-139 (1995).

[21] H. STACHEL: *Degenerate Intersection in Solid Modeling.* Proc. of the 6th Internat. Conf. on Engineering Computer Graphics and Descriptive Geometry, Tokyo, 1994: Vol. 1, 191-195.

[22] T.F. WIEGAND: Interactive rendering of CSG models. *Computer Graphics Forum* **15** (4), 249-261 (1996).

[23] W. WUNDERLICH: *Darstellende Geometrie II.* Bibliogr. Institut, Mannheim (1967).

Index